city life

SEAMUS O'HANLON is one of Australia's leading urban historians and combines his academic career teaching contemporary and urban history at Monash University with a strong commitment to public outreach and community engagement. He has acted as an advisor on exhibitions on the history of Melbourne for Museum Victoria, the history of shopping for the State Library of Victoria, and the history of clothing manufacturing and the suburb of St Kilda for the Jewish Museum of Australia and Heritage Victoria. Seamus is a regular contributor to ABC local and national radio as well as community radio station 3RRR. His previous books include *Together Apart*, *Go Melbourne*, *Melbourne Remade* and *Federation Square Melbourne: The first ten years*.

city life

THE NEW URBAN AUSTRALIA

SEAMUS O'HANLON

NEWSOUTH

A NewSouth book

Published by
NewSouth Publishing
University of New South Wales Press Ltd
University of New South Wales
Sydney NSW 2052
AUSTRALIA
newsouthpublishing.com

© Seamus O'Hanlon 2018
First published 2018

10 9 8 7 6 5 4 3 2 1

 A catalogue record for this book is available from the National Library of Australia

ISBN 9781742235615 (paperback)
      9781742244266 (ebook)
      9781742248684 (ePDF)

Design Josephine Pajor-Markus
Cover design Luke Causby, Blue Cork
Cover images City silhouette. Adobe Stock/Luke Causby
Printer Griffin Press

All reasonable efforts were taken to obtain permission to use copyright material reproduced in this book, but in some cases copyright could not be traced. The author welcomes information in this regard.

This book is printed on paper using fibre supplied from plantation or sustainably managed forests.

Contents

Introduction:
Globalising the Australian city

On 20 October 1973, millions of Australians – on land, on boats and from the comfort of their own lounge rooms – watched on as Queen Elizabeth II officially opened the Sydney Opera House. This stunning architectural masterpiece, perched on the Harbour at Bennelong Point, became almost overnight both Australia's front door and the standard international visual representation of Sydney as a modern, vibrant cosmopolitan city on the rise. In the four decades since, the Opera House and the adjacent Harbour Bridge have gone on to rival Uluru as the default international image of the Australian nation. While the latter represents antiquity, Indigeneity and an older ideal of Australia as the Outback, these icons of Sydney represent what many Australians like to imagine is its new global incarnation as a successful outward-looking, urban, open, multicultural and diverse society seeking to cement its place in the emerging Asia-Pacific region. As Sydney increasingly became Australia's gateway city in the 1970s and 1980s and beyond – home to the headquarters of the majority of the country's national and international business organisations, most of its big media and cultural outlets, the major entry point for tourists and new immigrants, and of course the Olympic City of 2000 – it also began to market itself as Australia's only global city, able to match it with the likes of New York, London and Paris on the world stage. The opening of the Opera House in 1973 was thus not only symbolic of Sydney's emergence as

1

a major international city, but also the beginning of Australia's entry into the contemporary global era.

For Australia the year 1973 was not just important for the opening of the Opera House. It was also the year in which the last of our troops were withdrawn from Vietnam, the White Australia policy was formally ended and the long-standing doctrine of economic protectionism began to be challenged when the newly elected Whitlam Labor government cut tariffs by 25 per cent across the board. Internationally it was also the year of the Yom Kippur War in the Middle East, which in turn was the prelude to the OPEC oil crisis and the onset of economic stagnation that brought the world rising inflation, high unemployment and the beginning of the end of what historians now refer to as 'the thirty glorious years' of the postwar boom. For Australia, then, 1973 thus marks not only the emergence of Sydney as an international city but also the beginning of the end of an older version of the nation based on racial exclusion, heavily protected manufacturing industries, full employment and the Welfare State, all of which combined into what economists and historians call the 'postwar settlement'. Locally and internationally this economic model and the car-based suburban society it gave rise to is often called 'Fordism', named after the founder of the Ford motor company, Henry Ford, whose cars and production methods helped to radically transform first American cities and metropolitan regions and then those of other nations, including Australia, in the twentieth century.

In the four decades since the end of the long boom, Australia's economy, like that of all western nations, has been restructured to reflect the needs of an international economic system increasingly based on services rather than production, information rather than tangible goods, and the commodification of leisure and culture, the combined phenomena that has come to be known as 'post-Fordism', 'post-industrialism' or more commonly 'globalisation'. Nowhere have the impacts of these processes been more apparent than in the streets and suburbs of the world's major cities, whose economies were once important sites of manufacturing but are now almost totally based on services. As the gateways to nations, cities have been at the forefront of globalisation, the places where new industries have located, where new immigrants have settled, where new ideas have been developed and tested, and where new forms of culture have entered and made their mark on the nation. Globalisation is thus an urban phenomenon, one of the major drivers of which has been new forms of transport and communications technologies – including containerised shipping and cheap airfares, satellite communications, the mobile phone and most importantly the internet – which have essentially erased the tyranny of distance.

So too the economic and cultural rise of Asia – first in Japan and later South Korea, and then the Tiger economies of Singapore, Hong Kong, Taiwan and Malaysia and finally most recently the opening up, industrialisation and urbanisation of China – has had a profound impact on the world's economy, and again most especially on its cities. In the case of China, industrialisation and urbanisation have created unprecedented demand for raw commodities, which are then turned into products for export. Just as when, over two hundred years ago, first Britain and then later the United States and Europe industrialised, the vast wealth the industrialisation of Asia has generated has created an almost unlimited demand for international travel, consumer goods and luxury brands from its burgeoning local middle class. Perhaps more ominously, it has also led literally millions of people to look to invest in overseas real estate markets as a way to protect their new-found wealth from governments that neither respect the rule of law nor private property. More recently the opening up of India and especially its burgeoning high-technology sector has similarly created both a huge demand for luxury goods and also a vast pool of potential migrants looking for a better life in the west. As in the rest of Asia, the rapid rise in incomes and the growth of a middle class population seeking an

3

education abroad has led to the emergence of a vast new industry: the provision of international higher education.

In Australia as elsewhere, Fordism – which was symbolised here not by the Ford but by 'Australia's own car', the Holden – is now virtually gone, replaced by an economy focused on finance, technology, mining, education, tourism, conspicuous consumption, and what a number of economists and politicians like to call 'creativity' and 'innovation'. And, as elsewhere, the greatest impacts of these changes have been felt in the cities, most noticeably in the two biggest, Sydney and Melbourne, which now boast not only some of the world's most expensive residential real estate, partly because of demand from overseas investors, but are also almost totally unrecognisable economically, socially, culturally and perhaps most importantly demographically from their 1970s selves. While in the past four decades Sydney has become Australia's gateway city and Melbourne arguably its most self-consciously cosmopolitan, all the major capital cities have undergone profound change as a result of globalisation, that has seen them turn from essentially inward-looking manufacturing, retail and commercial centres, largely populated by the descendants of long established British and Irish immigrants and more recent arrivals from Continental Europe, to outward-looking, post-industrial service centres with among the highest rates of foreign-born residents of cities anywhere in the world. Sydney and Melbourne take this a step further and are now two of the most ethnically and culturally diverse cities on the planet.

This book documents the globalisation of the Australian city in the period from the early 1970s to the present day, and in so doing shows that while rural and regional Australia has long been integrated into the global economy through the sale of primary products and commodities into world markets, it is in the cities where the major impacts of globalisation – economic, social and cultural – have been most acutely felt and where the challenges of success in the twenty-first century are most likely to be found. While the book looks at all of Australia's major cities and their recent experiences, its particular focus is on the two biggest – Sydney and Melbourne – where the impacts of globalisation have been most profound. In placing the cities at the centre of the national story, the book thus challenges some long-held beliefs about Australia and how it presents itself to the world, and how in turn many Australians perceive and understand themselves. Rather than rehash old stereotypes about mateship, the Bush or Anzac, this book places the globalised city and its residents at the centre of new understandings about twenty-first century Australia and its people.

While the book is mostly about the impacts of globalisation on the people of the cities, it is also about changes in the physical structures in which we live, work and play. Drawing on my expertise as an urban historian, I chart how the transformations associated with globalisation have changed not just the economy, culture and demographics of the city, but also its built form. The 40 years since the 1970s have seen the building of new office towers, new shopping centres and new and refurbished educational and cultural institutions in central business districts (CBDs) and major suburban centres across the major metropolitan areas, but perhaps the biggest change has been in the residential structure of our cities. Though urban historian Graeme Davison's telling aphorism that 'Australia was born urban and quickly grew suburban' still holds true, in the last four decades, and especially since the 1990s, Australian cities have seen profound change in their residential form to the point where, for many, the central city high-rise apartment rather than the brick veneer of architectural and social critic Robin Boyd's suburban ugliness has become the symbol of the Australian Dream. Alongside the emergence of an economy centred on services and lifestyle pursuits, in the last 40 years Australian cities have witnessed a boom in the construction of apartments aimed at both local and international purchasers. Perhaps for the first time ever, the rapid growth in this housing sector has seen the emergence in

Australia of a genuine urban sensibility, most notably in Sydney and to a lesser extent in Melbourne and elsewhere.

To put these changes in some perspective, in 2016, for the first time ever, more apartments than detached houses were built in the three major east coast capitals, most of which were high-rise towers located in the CBDs, inner suburbs and key transport nodes across the suburbs. These towers and their residents are changing understandings of what used to be called 'the Australian way of life'. Central Melbourne, once the dead heart of artist John Brack's grim 5 pm rush to the suburban commuter train, is now one of the fastest growing regions in the country and, at current population growth rates, within 15 years more people will live in the 36 square kilometres of the municipal City of Melbourne than in the whole of the Northern Territory. In the same year the 62 000 people who will by then call Melbourne's CBD home will live at densities rivalling those of Uptown Manhattan. In Sydney the redeveloped area of Waterloo just to the south of the CBD will have population densities similar to those of Hong Kong. By 2030 the 'typical Australian' will as likely be a young female professional of Asian background living in a new high-rise apartment in inner Sydney as a laconic bushman in a blue singlet or soldier in a slouch hat. This book tells the story of their Australia.

The re-emergence of the city as a site of scholarly and popular research in recent years is an international phenomenon. Studies of 'world', 'global' and 'networked' cities and attempts to rank cities according to their status as 'alpha', 'beta' and 'gamma' have spawned a mini-industry of scholars, consultants and spruikers keen to offer quick-fix solutions to civic leaders and business people hoping to get their metropolis a place on the international league tables. Most of these ranking tables look at a city's status as a financial centre and thus put Sydney in the alpha or beta category largely because it is an important regional financial centre that opens just after New York and Chicago close and before Singapore and Tokyo turn on their lights. Melbourne sometimes makes beta status, but most rankings put it in the gamma, or 'locally important' grouping. Other Australian cities rarely warrant a mention on these global financial centre lists but do well in the *Economist* magazine's annual 'most liveable' index, which measures the qualities that most appeal to expatriate business people and their families. Melbourne is the perennial international winner or runner-up on this list, popular for its education and health facilities, cultural ambience, and safety and security. Brisbane, Adelaide and Perth similarly score well in this poll, usually making it into the top ten alongside multiple Canadian and northern European cities. Sydney also invariably ranks in the top 20, whereas because of congestion, cost of living expenses and crime rates most other alpha cities often struggle to do so. These results either mean that Australian cities really are desirable places to live, or that 'most liveable' is not the same as most important, most interesting or most exciting. For obvious reasons, this is a question that Australian civic leaders prefer to avoid asking.

In the late 1970s and early 1980s, as the impacts of economic restructuring, urban decay and what came to be called 'the crisis of the city' became apparent, few would have predicted the re-emergence of cities as the world's economic, social and cultural powerhouses. Deindustrialisation – the closure of factories and the shift of production to the developing world – led to mass unemployment and job shedding in many of the world's older industrial and manufacturing cities and gave rise to the moniker 'rust belt', applied to whole swathes of the northeastern United States and southern Canada. Similar problems afflicted European cities, most notably in the north of England and Scotland, Germany's Ruhr Valley, western France and parts of northern Italy. In the United States urban rioting and escalating crime rates in many of the urban ghettoes of the north-east accelerated a process that had begun in the 1940s and came to be known as 'white flight', the exodus of white and other more prosperous members of the community to suburban fringe locations or to the rapidly growing cities of the southern and western 'sun belt'. Across the world technological changes such as the move towards container shipping and ever-larger freight trucks saw the collapse of former sites of urban employment like London's Covent Garden markets and the city's vast docks region. As these once-thriving areas came to be characterised by desolation and rotting, abandoned buildings, late-1970s London began to be, in historian Joe Kerr's words, marked by pockets of silence, dead zones in a city that seemed to be struck with 'an air of hopelessness'. London was not alone in this; abandoned docks, derelict warehouses and blighted factory districts were features of cities across the western world in the 1970s and 1980s.

Four decades on, the re-emergence of cities, and the increasingly central role they play in driving economic, social, cultural and political change, has captured the imagination of scholars and commentators across the globe. While many are positive about these trends, especially those who remember the grim 1970s, others lament the increasing inequality that has accompanied much of this success. American urban sociologist Saskia Sassen has played a key role in documenting the role of the global finance and services sector in reviving the fortunes of New York, London and Tokyo from the 1980s onwards. Her 1990 book *Global Cities*, which developed some of the earlier 'world city' theories of British geographers John Friedmann, Anthony King and others, has become the standard introduction to the field. More recently Belgian geographer Ben Derudder and others have written of the emergence of 'networked cities', which act as 'nodes' in the global chain of production, with the most important providing direction and finance to those further down the international urban pecking order. Economists too have heralded the re-emergence of the city as a driver of innovation, with former American, now Canadian, Richard Florida becoming something of a guru to city governments seeking to revive their city's fortunes by attracting members of what he calls the 'creative class'

of artists, writers, computer whizz kids, and perhaps most contro-
versially the gay community. Similarly, Harvard University economist Edward Glaeser's *Triumph of the City* argues that by bringing
together individuals and groups from multiple social, cultural and
geographic backgrounds, and encouraging them to co-operate on
new ideas and ways of thinking, the city – 'our greatest invention' –
'makes us richer, smarter, greener, healthier and happier'. Political
theorist Benjamin Barber similarly extolls the virtues of the open,
diverse and welcoming city in his 2013 book *If Mayors Ruled the
World*, arguing that in the global era it is at the city level rather than
the national that real progress towards solving the world's major
problems is being made.

It is not just in economics that cities are at the forefront of
globalisation and economic change. In 2007 the United Nations
officially declared the world 'urban', announcing that for the first
time ever the majority of the world's people lived in cities rather
than in rural areas. While many of these city-dwellers live a precarious existence in makeshift accommodation in the rapidly growing
'megacities' of the developing world, in the developed world demographic change is also primarily an urban phenomenon. Immigration, whether internal or international, has long had an urban focus,
which has been heightened in the global era. In the age of the Industrial Revolution, displaced rural workers flocked to the major cities
of Europe to take up jobs in the new factories and to serve the needs
of the emerging class of factory owners. Later, the industrialisation
of the United States in the decades before and after the Civil War
saw tens of millions of migrants leave their homes in Europe for the
great cities of the American North-East and Midwest. In the twentieth century European cities were transformed by the migration
of millions of people from former colonies, or displaced from their
homelands by Communism or Fascism. In Canada and Australia
the postwar years saw millions of Europeans join the descendants
of earlier immigrants from the British Isles to begin the process of

turning essentially monocultural societies into multicultural, albeit still predominantly European, ones.

Later, beginning in the 1960s in the USA and Canada, and in Australia from the mid-1970s, changes to longstanding restrictions on the immigration of peoples from certain ethnic and racial backgrounds saw the beginnings of the process of creating truly ethnically diverse, multicultural societies. Again, cities were at the forefront of these changes, and scholars have recently begun to document the emergence of 'immigrant gateway cities' in the USA, Canada, Europe, Australia and the Middle East, many noting the increasing ethnic divergences between these cities and the nations in which they sit. Today 'hyperdiverse' cities such as New York, London, Toronto, Melbourne and Sydney each have foreign-born populations two to three times that of the wider host nation. The cosmopolitan citizen of the contemporary globalised world is a city dweller.

Alongside and partly driven by these demographic shifts, contemporary cities are also at the forefront of cultural change. While the decline of manufacturing and reasonably well-paying and secure jobs in the factories of the Fordist city was traumatic for many, especially for older and less well-educated men, the emergence of new forms of leisure and more relaxed attitudes towards social and sexual mores, as well as new ideas about gender and gender roles, has seen the opening up of new opportunities and urban spaces for previously marginalised and oppressed individuals and groups. As tourism and leisure have become central to post-industrial societies, culture and spectacle have emerged as key strengths of the new urban economy. Urban commentators such as Sharon Zukin, Charles Landry and Richard Florida speak of the importance of culture and creativity, alongside banking and finance, as key drivers of success in the contemporary global economic race. Others advocate for the importance of the 'night-time economy' and the need for cities to gain or retain a 'cool' urban edge, albeit one that maintains 'authenticity' in the face of the conformist global challenge. Other urbanists such as Danish architect and planner Jan Gehl speak of the importance of 'place-making' and vibrant streetscapes to urban economic success. Across the world, cities have set out to make themselves 'destinations' by employing the services of international 'starchitects' to design urban landmarks, preferably ones that not only show off the city's style, but also its cultural infrastructure. Following on from the success of French President François Mitterand's 1980s-era *grands projets*, cities as diverse as Bilbao, Los Angeles and most recently Abu Dhabi have sought to market themselves as cultural centres by commissioning iconic architectural showpieces in which to display their newfound wealth and cultural assets.

This book documents how these global processes and changes have played out in Australian cities in the four decades since the end of Fordism in the early 1970s. It explores and develops three themes across time: economics, society and culture. The first theme documents the changing structure of the Australian urban economy since the 1970s, including the decline of manufacturing industries and the emergence of the new economy based on finance, services and creativity. Rather than just a dry account of statistics and job losses, however, this theme sets the scene for the exploration in the rest of the book of the impacts of these changes on individuals and communities, and on different urban regions, as well as the transformations they have had on the physical landscape of the city. What were once sites of manufacturing are now residential apartment towers or skyscraper office blocks; the places where we used to make clothes and food are where we now buy them or consume them in plush, upmarket surroundings. City-based universities and colleges are also central to this story of economic change and have emerged in recent decades as some of the country's largest industries and, alongside hospitals and research institutes, the largest single employers in many urban regions. Whereas higher education was once the privilege of a small elite, today it is an almost universal experience. It is also an international one, with large numbers of students now coming from Asia, and especially China, to study here. Australia's universities are now not only the third largest sources of the country's national export income but are also drivers of the surge in demand for inner city residential dwellings. Remodelled city centre and suburban university campuses – often complete with a signature starchitect-designed landmark building – are, then, alongside the thousands of new apartments and cultural facilities built in recent decades, key features of Australia's revitalised urban economic landscapes.

The second theme explores the demographic changes of the last 40 years. It shows how these changes have overwhelmingly affected the cities; particularly Sydney and Melbourne, which are the major settlement destinations of migrants from non-English-speaking backgrounds. While between them Sydney and Melbourne account for only about 40 per cent of the national population, in recent years they have absorbed between 60 and 70 per cent of all immigrant settlement and up to 95 per cent of immigrants from certain ethnic and religious backgrounds. Given this, it is arguably the case that the two big cities are no longer 'Australian' in the older racially and culturally accepted form of the term. In common with other major gateway cities internationally, parts of Sydney and Melbourne are now international spaces, their residents having far more in common with their urban counterparts overseas than they do with fellow non-urban Australians. Again, as with the economic changes discussed in the first theme, these demographic changes have transformed the geography and morphology of the cities, with individual neighbourhoods and streets increasingly characterised by distinct ethnic, cultural and religious facilities and structures, as well as businesses catering to the needs of a multicultural clientele. Far from the dull conformist caricatures of generations of cultural critics, these ethnically diverse suburbs and neighbourhoods, with their distinctive sounds, smells and structures, are among the most lively, entrepreneurial and culturally rich urban regions in the world.

The third theme builds on these studies of economic and demographic change to show how the people and spaces of the cities have adapted to new forms of social life and culturally based economic pursuits. It examines the emergence of the 'spectacle' economy of major sporting and cultural events; ethnic, sexual and cultural pride; and the development of an economy and society based on leisure and pleasure rather than production. Arguably, in the globalised post-industrial era, culture, fun and spectacle are among the key economic advantages of the city, attractive to locals, those looking for more opportunities and personal support than might be available in rural areas or smaller cities, and perhaps most importantly, international tourists with money to spend. These changes have affected the city physically, not only in the form of the new residential and hotel towers built to accommodate locals and visitors, but also in the building of new or refurbished sporting, cultural and leisure facilities and precincts, especially but not always in the inner city, which as in the case of Sydney's Opera House have now become showplaces of the glittering new global urban Australia.

1

Opening up and closing down

For Australians of a certain age the election of the Whitlam government in 1972 is seen as either the beginning of the end of the long dormancy of a nation stuck in a post-Menzian time warp, or the end of the country's golden age of responsible social and economic management. After winning the election on Saturday 2 December and without even waiting for the full ministry to be confirmed or for parliament to convene, major policy changes were implemented by what came to be known as the 'duumvirate' – a two-person government of Whitlam and his deputy Lance Barnard, who between them held all 27 ministerial positions. By the time the full ministry was sworn in just over a fortnight later, the government had 'ended conscription for national service, released draft resistors from prison, negotiated diplomatic relations with the People's Republic of China, announced a Royal Commission on Aboriginal land rights and re-opened the equal pay case then before the Conciliation and Arbitration Commission', among other initiatives. The flurry of changes on the domestic and international front that followed over the next three years, as well as personal and financial scandals and then the dramatic circumstances of the government's dismissal from office by Governor-General Sir John Kerr on 11 November 1975 have ensured that Whitlam and his government are usually remembered either as a tragedy or a farce. The high inflation and rising unemployment associated with the recession of 1974–75 also means that the government is commonly associated with poor economic management. Defenders of 'the legacy', as it came to be known, note that most of the economic problems were international phenomena, while critics look to increased government spending and high budget deficits as evidence of a government and a party out of its economic depth.

Few beyond a small group of political and economic historians, however, recall that it was the Whitlam government that started the long journey of globalising the Australian economy by opening it up to international competition. In the public imagination, that process began in the early 1980s when the Hawke government, with Paul Keating as Treasurer, floated the Australian dollar, approved the entry of international banks, deregulated much of the economy, and opened up key sectors such as telecommunications and transport to local and international competition. Hawke and Keating are also given much of the credit for internationalising the economy by instituting a series of tariff cuts and removing most industry protection. While there is a lot of truth in this timeline, the process in fact began ten years earlier in the first Whitlam budget, when tariffs on manufactured goods imported from overseas were reduced by 25 per cent across the board. Overnight the cost of electrical and other consumer goods dropped dramatically, although there is ample evidence that many retailers pocketed sizeable chunks of the windfall. The 1973 tariff cuts were just the start of a process of opening up industry to competition, however. In 1974 the Whitlam government introduced the *Trade Practices Act*, which made collusion between companies an offence, and in the same year initiated a major enquiry into the current and future competitiveness of Australia's manufacturing industries.

As the major sites of manufacturing, the cities, and most especially those in the south-east of the country, were hardest hit by changing economic policies from the 1970s to now. My hometown, Adelaide, which was almost totally reliant on the domestic market rather than exports for its industrial production, has arguably never fully recovered from the economic and social problems that arose when changing international patterns of production and the winding back of tariff protection brought an enforced end to its postwar growth strategy of enticing footloose international manufacturers and immigrants to its suburban fringes. As historian Mark Peel has shown, the new town of Elizabeth to the north of the city, with its new houses, new factories and new migrants, went from being a place of work and good times in the 1950s and 1960s to being stigmatised as a welfare ghetto by the late 1970s, a status it largely retains to this day. Similar fates befell other former workers' cities such as Wollongong and Newcastle in NSW and Geelong in Victoria as well as a number of smaller cities and 'government towns' in Victoria's La Trobe Valley. The same problems plagued certain suburbs and regions in metropolitan Sydney and Melbourne but, as we shall see, the sheer size and economic diversity of the two biggest cities cushioned these impacts somewhat, allowing them to emerge in time as successful post-industrial economic powerhouses.

This chapter sketches the broad outlines of policies that, in a period of less than 30 years between the early 1970s and the late 1990s, saw Australia move from being a mostly closed economy with tariffs and other forms of protection to being one of the western world's most open, and where today there are virtually no tariffs or industry protections left in place. While a few key industries such as auto manufacturing retained some protections until their demise in 2017, and some individual industries and companies were supported on an ad hoc basis to deal with short-term crises in the 1990s and again in the early 2000s, the macro policy of embracing free trade, which until the early 1980s was seen as the preserve of a few cranks on the fringes of the neoliberal Right, has essentially been implemented across bipartisan lines in less than a generation. But, as we shall see, within this broad consensus there were debates about how to achieve the desired ends and more importantly how to cushion their effects on different sections of the population and on the communities in which they lived.

The Jackson Report

Barely a week after his government was narrowly re-elected for a second term in May 1974, Prime Minister Whitlam established an enquiry into the state of manufacturing in Australia. Popularly known as the Jackson Committee Enquiry after its chair Gordon Jackson, who was the managing director of the sugar refining and building products conglomerate CSR, the committee also included then ACTU President and future Labor Prime Minister Bob Hawke. Its brief was to advise the government on 'appropriate policies for the development of manufacturing industry' and specifically to investigate and suggest 'the machinery required for integrating such policies with the Government's general economic, social and regional policies', as well as 'the place of exports and imports in the development of manufacturing industry'. In a nod to increasing concerns across the political divide at this time about foreign ownership, the committee was also asked to report on 'the role of firms of overseas origin in manufacturing'.

Commissioned just after the first impacts of the 1973 tariff reductions were beginning to be felt and when the economy was still growing, the committee's report was released in October 1975, just before the government was dismissed and just as the worst of employment and other effects of a deepening recession were beginning to be felt. The committee found that Australia's manufacturing industry was inefficient, uncompetitive, too focused on the small domestic market, and overly reliant on protective tariffs for survival. At a more immediate level, manufacturing industries were facing an 'acute financial crisis' as a result of the recession. Unemployment in the sector was also increasing rapidly (up by more than 100 000 people in a year) and morale among employers and workers was extremely low. But rather than blame these problems on short-term issues related to the recession, the committee suggested that it had simply highlighted and brought to the fore the structural problems of a sector suffering from a 'deep-seated and long-standing malaise'.

Despite these issues, manufacturing was, and was expected to remain, an important component of the Australian economy; while the sector had declined as a share of the national economy from more than 30 per cent in the early 1960s, it still provided 'about a quarter of Gross Domestic Product and employs 1.3 million people – about a quarter of all employment'. The committee noted that manufacturing plants were mostly located in NSW and Victoria, which between them accounted for '75 per cent of value-added and 74 per cent of employment', and further that most of the industry was 'heavily-concentrated in major cities', with three-quarters of NSW's manufacturing jobs located in Sydney and 85 per cent of Victoria's in Melbourne. Certain industries, such as textiles, clothing and footwear (TCF), were particularly concentrated in inner city regions already suffering from overcrowding and what was labelled a 'hostile' urban environment. More than 40 per cent of manufacturing workers were migrants, and roughly 25 per cent were women, a figure that was much higher in the clothing and footwear sector, where it was more than 75 per cent. More than half of these were married women, mostly with children. Manufacturing workers were said to suffer from 'alienation and frustration' in their working lives, which manifested itself in high rates of labour unrest, absenteeism, and indifference to the quality of the products they produced.

Notwithstanding the immediate crisis facing the sector, as well as its deeper structural problems, which would inevitably affect these highly vulnerable individuals and communities, the committee recommended major change, most notably a reduction in protection levels, albeit phased in over a 15- to 20-year period rather than the short, sharp, shock that some more radical elements in the economics and political fringes were by that stage advocating. The committee's major recommendation was to continue with the reductions in tariff protections that had been haltingly underway since the late 1960s but to accelerate these as a means of both opening up the economy to better quality and cheaper imported goods and more importantly as a way of encouraging local manufacturers to export. In a telling pair of sentences, the committee noted that its report was 'not a charter for more protection. We are for lower rather than higher tariffs.' It did, however, recommend that, while a detailed timetable for tariff reductions should be put in place, there should be flexibility to slow the pace of these reductions should economic and employment conditions require it. In language remarkably similar to that which Hawke as Prime Minister was to become famous for in the 1980s, the report called for changes that would aim at 'improving the working of the economy', while also 'improving the quality of worklife' through policies that would promote 'shared aims and ideals', so that change might be achieved while maintaining social cohesion. More broadly it recommended that all new policies for the manufacturing sector should seek to 'increas[e] the involvement of Australians in the systems of decision-making' and thus seek to build 'a capability to adapt to future change, whatever it might be'.

Similar language permeated the official response to the Jackson Report, officially called the 'White Paper on Manufacturing Industry', which was produced by the Fraser Liberal government and released in May 1977. While recognising that there was an argument that 'manufacturing does not need to make as great a contribution to Australian economic and social development as it did in the past', the White Paper cautioned that the 'fact remains that [it] retains its central importance in Australia's economic structure'. The White Paper maintained the emphasis on reducing protection recommended by the Jackson Committee but the language was now much more cautious, perhaps reflecting a recognition that by 1977 world economic conditions had changed and that various sectors of the community, most notably the union movement, were becoming increasingly concerned about the effects of international competition. 'Tariff reductions ... have a role to play in the process of encouraging a more efficient manufacturing industry in Australia', the White Paper noted, but cautioned that the implications of these reductions could be 'so significant in terms of employment effects and industry viability that the ability of the community to absorb change or accommodate the economic and social consequences of these changes within our control needs to be taken into account when formulating protection policy and taking specific decisions'.

Australia at the crossroads

Notwithstanding the recommendations of the Jackson Committee and the Fraser government's response to them, very little happened on tariff policy or in the manufacturing sector until the mid-1980s, largely because the White Paper's insistence that economic and social conditions improve before anything was done never came to pass. Nor, in a time of rising unemployment, were the unions as sanguine about the threat to their members' jobs as had been Bob Hawke when he sat on the Jackson Committee in 1974 and 1975. While the economy did improve somewhat in the late 1970s, the upturn was short-lived and by 1980 things were again looking grim. In 1979 the Iranian Revolution brought the world another oil shock which, like the earlier 1973 OPEC crisis, doubled the price of oil almost overnight, bringing with it a rapid increase in inflation and rising unemployment. Soon after, a major drought gripped rural Australia, meaning that another recession inevitably hit even while the full effects of the earlier one had yet to be fully resolved. And while Australia did not suffer economic devastation at this time in the way that, say, Britain did by having to seek a loan from the International Monetary Fund, nor the USA which saw whole industries and regions labelled rust belts in the late 1970s, nevertheless, unemployment remained persistently high, averaging over 5 per cent between 1975 and 1980 before peaking at over 10 per cent in 1983.

Internationally, the persistently high unemployment of the 1970s combined with high inflation gave rise to the concept of 'stagflation' and the 'misery index', the former referring to the supposedly impossible concept of rising inflation coexisting with economic stagnation, while the latter was the combined number that came from adding together the inflation and unemployment rates. Australia suffered from these problems but was spared the worst of the effects experienced by Europe and North America. Here the misery rate peaked at just over 20 in 1975 (mostly because of an inflation rate of over 15 per cent), before dropping back to the mid-teens through the late 1970s. It then climbed again to 20 at the peak of the 1982–83 recession (split about half and half between unemployment and inflation), before dropping back again to the mid-teens for most of the 1980s. In the USA misery peaked at 21 in 1980, while in the UK it was over 26 in 1975, mainly because the inflation rate there was 22 per cent that year. But it was to remain bad throughout the late 1970s, climbing back to 25 in 1980, largely because inflation was 18 per cent. By 1984 the British index was back to 17, but whereas the inflation component dropped to 5 per cent that year, unemployment rose to almost 12 per cent, or just over three million people.

In Britain and the USA the high misery scores brought about by the second oil shock were exacerbated by policies followed by the emerging doctrine of free market liberalism pursued by the Thatcher government after its election in the UK in May 1979 and Ronald Reagan's Republican administration which took office in the USA in January 1981. In the UK the new government followed a deliberate policy of tight monetary control, a high exchange rate, and a switch from direct to indirect taxation in order to choke inflation out of the economy. The government's policies also sought to expose industries to external competition by refusing to protect them from international market forces. This was the famous short, sharp shock designed to make the economy more competitive that some economists had similarly advocated for Australia, but which had been rejected by both the Whitlam and Fraser governments. That it brought a rapid rise in inflation, most of the effects of which would be borne by the household sector, was seen as a necessary precondition for the economic adjustment that would follow. And that this adjustment would then be followed by the closure of whole industries and mass unemployment – especially across the industrial north, Wales and Scotland – was similarly seen as a necessary price to pay in order to achieve long-term economic success in the emerging post-industrial world. The urban riots that shook British cities in April and June 1981 were portrayed by the Conservative government not as a reaction to the economic despair brought about by these policies but as crimes reflective of the liberal social policies of the 1960s and 1970s that had supposedly undermined thrift and respect for hard work and enterprise. When famously challenged about the harshness of these policies, even by members of her own party in late 1980, Margaret Thatcher refused to countenance a U-turn ('the lady's not for turning'), arguing that 'there [was] no alternative' to her policies, thus earning herself the nickname TINA (There Is No Alternative).

In fact there were alternatives and in Australia in the 1980s and 1990s a number of these were debated and explored in think tank reports, policy documents, election manifestos and Green and White papers produced by parties and governments across the political divide. The first of these was a report by a group of free-market or libertarian economists called *Australia at the Crossroads*, which was released in 1980. Lamenting the Fraser government's timid response to the Jackson Report, as evidenced by its 1977 White Paper, the contributors to this report argued that Australia faced a series of choices about its future direction. The first was to continue down what they described as a 'Mercantilist Trend' scenario 'characterised by risk-averse, inward-looking attitudes and the efforts by established groups to conserve their power positions in an increasingly insecure world', while the second, and preferred, option, was 'a "Libertarian Alternative" scenario which [would] open society up to face the challenges of competition from new technological ideas and concepts, new industrial countries and a new generation of young people'. While the authors agreed that the mercantilist scenario would not 'result in a major economic or social disaster', it would likely lead to stagnation and higher unemployment (and especially high youth unemployment), as well as 'serious failures in meeting non-economic objectives' such as the personal and political freedoms 'to which Western societies aspire'. The libertarian scenario would, on the other hand, allow Australia and Australians to achieve 'full maturity and self-reliance in society and industry', to wean itself off the 'Mother State' and to flourish into 'social and economic adulthood'.

Much like today's digital entrepreneurs who see themselves in revolutionary terms, as outsiders seeking to disrupt cosy monopolies and the establishment, the *Crossroads* authors saw their ideas as promoting freedom and liberty against an established order of both the political Left and the Right. As they saw it, the 'greatest obstacles to the realisation of an alternative to the Mercantilist Trend [were] the Old Establishment (of money, private schools and clubs) and the New Establishment (of unions, media and academics) who will want to conserve their established positions from challenges and new ideas'. The opening up of the economy would instead, they argued, 'give a "fair go" to the unestablished, and especially to our children. It [would] encourage the "battlers" in Australian society and should appeal to the many Australians who are uneasy about our smooth slide into a Mercantilist future'. As this group saw it, the most appropriate policies to break up the alleged establishments and to stop this 'smooth slide' into mediocrity were essentially those long advocated by libertarian and free-market economists such as Friedrich Hayek, Milton Friedman and others associated with what has since come to be called neoliberalism: free trade in goods, services and capital; 'deregulation of many markets and other activities', including wages; and a 'reduction of the government's role as a producer of many basic services, including education, health and welfare'.

The *Crossroads* group was not totally against a role for government spending, provided such spending enhanced the efficiency of the economy and maximised individual economic freedom. For this reason, their report called for an 'expansion of the government's role as a provider of income maintenance and purchasing power for the acquisition by individuals of the basic services they want (through negative income tax, endowment and voucher schemes)'. On manufacturing and tariff protection they were equally strident, calling for the 'acceptance of the structural changes wrought by new technologies and the removal of protection'. Such policies, they argued, would mobilise 'creative forces by facilitating competition, both from overseas and from new, innovative ideas' that would ultimately allow the country to 'catch up with many best practice technologies overseas', and to import products and technologies currently banned or made prohibitively expensive by high tariff barriers. The 'cold shower' of reduced protection and exposure to competition would be 'invigorating' and welcomed 'by most, including many of the most reluctant who had anticipated catching pneumonia', but who would likely find that 'structural change has its rewards and that it can be exhilarating'.

Consensus and reconstruction

Whereas for the emergent neoliberal Right the solution to almost any and every economic problem was to leave things to the market, for many on the social democratic Left there was a strong sense that such policies would invariably cut the jobs of the most vulnerable and lead to the sorts of social problems that were increasingly becoming apparent in parts of Europe and North America. But even in many quarters on the Left there was a growing recognition by the early 1980s that maintaining the status quo was no longer feasible. While some on the hard Left still advocated for socialistic responses to the international economic crisis, others looked to harness the power of market forces and changing patterns of global production and trade to create new jobs while protecting the most vulnerable from the hardships associated with these processes of change. Such ideas recognised that tariffs and protection imposed costs on the economy and that many of these costs were borne by the poor. Whereas protecting jobs for low-paid factory workers was seen as an important and worthy pursuit, saving those jobs through the imposition of tariffs meant that other workers paid more for essential goods than they needed to. The Jackson Report had emphasised this, as have various public and private reports in the years since its release. While tariffs provided tax revenues that governments could then redistribute in the form of social wages and benefits, they were flat regressive taxes that meant that the poor spent a greater proportion of their income on basic necessities than did the rich. Tariff protection also meant that business investment decisions were distorted, with resources going to favoured and inefficient enterprises and industries rather than ones likely to achieve the best longer-term returns.

Throughout the 1980s then, in Australia as elsewhere, a series of intellectual debates raged within the labour movement about how to 'reconstruct' and modernise the economy, with some politicians and unionists arguing for the government to have a strong role in this process and others on the 'rational' Right pushing for more

25

market-based solutions. In hindsight we can see that in the first years of the Hawke Labor government, from about 1983 to 1987, Prime Minister Hawke, his Treasurer Paul Keating and Industry Minister John Button pursued a blended model with market solutions tempered by social policies designed to protect the victims of restructuring, but as the decade wore on more market-based solutions increasingly won out. Even so, as we shall see, the ALP (Australian Labor Party) in government demonstrated that it was possible to modernise the economy and make it more efficient by reducing tariff protection while not inflicting the devastation that free-market policies brought to entire regions of other countries. In doing so they not only followed many of the policies and prescriptions that had been set out in the Jackson Report almost ten years earlier but paved the way for what became known as 'Third Way' politics – the mixing of free-market ideas and social liberalism – which became a hallmark of social democratic governments in Britain, Europe and the USA in the 1990s and beyond.

The main instrument for achieving these aims was the Prices and Incomes Accord, agreed between the ALP and the Australian Council of Trade Unions (ACTU) in late 1982, which committed the two parties to pursuing a policy of full employment in order to improve the lives and prospects of working people while also ensuring that much-needed adjustments were made to modernise the economy. More importantly the Accord sought to ensure that this would occur in a way that shared the burden of adjustment between employers and the employed, rich and poor, and the young and the old. The Accord was based on the assumption that sustained economic growth required inflation and the misery index to be brought down and that the best way to do that was to ensure that both prices and wages growth were kept in check. But in order to ensure that living standards did not decline it was agreed that the ALP in power would pursue what was termed a 'social wage', publicly provided benefits designed to underpin and enhance living conditions for the majority of the population. The most important of these was to be Medicare, a revised version of the Medibank scheme introduced by the Whitlam government in 1975 but progressively dismantled by the Fraser government in stages until 1982. Publicly funded health care would improve the health of the poor and the low-paid by ensuring they had access to quality health services, while at the same time putting downward pressure on inflation by making private health insurance a voluntary rather than a compulsory component of the cost of living. The scheme was to be funded by a small 1 per cent levy on incomes above a certain level. Other elements of the 'social wage' were to include more funds for public housing, public schools, pensions and other social security benefits, and improvements to other elements of the welfare state.

More importantly for our purposes, however, the Accord and the ALP's 1983 election policy platform explicitly recognised that while Australia needed to maintain 'a diversified manufacturing sector (both regionally and industrially) as a means of achieving basic economic objectives' such as full employment, the structure of the sector had to change if the country was to be economically successful into the future. And while both the Accord and the platform argued that there was 'no economic sense in reducing protection levels in the midst of high unemployment' and that 'neither current economic conditions, expected future trends, nor balance of payments constraints justify reduction in protection in the foreseeable future', both recognised that future 'industry policies must address themselves to areas for growth potential, not simply to sustaining declining or weakened industries'. So the parties committed to an industry policy that would seek to 'concentrate increased manufacturing activity' on the producer goods end of the spectrum; that is, in producing higher-value-add goods rather than low-value import-replacement ones.

From its earliest days in government the ALP under Hawke sought to honour this commitment to maintain and enhance the manufacturing sector while ensuring that the burdens of adjustment were shared. These ideas reflected the belief of many in the broader labour movement in the 1980s that the best model for Australia's future was not that of the neoliberal Right or the example of Britain under Thatcher or the USA under Reagan but the social democratic model of northern Europe. As historian Frank Bongiorno has recently argued in his history of the 1980s in Australia, for many on the social democratic Left at this time, the Swedish Model of a dynamic, high employment, low inflation, export oriented, free-market economy was an 'attractive exemplar' for Australia's future, in contrast to that of the 'free-wheeling English-speaking' model. Industry Minister Senator John Button, who 'had visited Europe early in 1984', was at the forefront of these ideas, having been impressed by the Swedish system which he saw as a potential 'source of ideas and inspiration for Australian manufacturing'. Best known for the car and steel 'plans' which sought to rationalise those industries by cutting subsidies, an insistence on mergers and of makers sharing production platforms as well as encouragement to pursue export markets, almost immediately after being elected to government Button set about cutting tariffs and protection in order to make Australian industry internationally competitive.

In doing so, however, he faced formidable opponents both internally within the labour movement and more broadly in the electorate. His biggest problem was reforming the TCF industries, whose work practices and facilities were, as we have seen, recognised as outdated even at the time of the Jackson enquiry almost ten years earlier. Then Treasurer Paul Keating has claimed that Australia resembled an 'industrial museum', so out of date and backward were many of its factories, especially in the TCF sector, by the 1980s. Button backs this claim, writing in his memoirs of a 1988 visit to his office by the head of the Italian Benetton fashion label, who informed him that a textile mill he had recently visited in Australia had machinery that was 'ancient', and looked like something that had not been seen 'in Italy for fifty or sixty years'. Change was in the air, however, and by the time of Benetton's visit Button had been working on plans for the TCF industry for several years. Beginning in 1984 he had set up enquiries into future rates of protection for the sector, the most recent of which was a 1986 Industries Assistance Commission report that had recommended a phase-down in tariffs to 50 per cent and the abolition of all local supply quotas by 1996. As Button tells it, he was lobbied by employers, employees, unionists, politicians and community representatives to keep tariffs as they were, but from 1986 and then more rapidly from 1988 tariffs were reduced, until by the early 2000s they were essentially gone.

In arguing for tariff cuts and the phasing out of industry protection, members of the Hawke government saw themselves as advocates for a new type of Australia, one that was outward looking, competitive and, above all, efficient. As such, it would raise the living standards of all its people rather than protect those of the select few. As Bongiorno notes, on his return from Sweden in 1984 Button had specifically written to Hawke about these things, arguing that, 'the Swedes believe in the free market' and 'do not believe in bailing out weak industries' or indeed individual firms. Rather, 'their industry policy is based on deciding in broad terms what part of the market they want to be in' and directing resources to that. Others within the broader labour movement, even those who had traditionally been associated with the hard Left, were coming to similar conclusions. A report written by members of a union and government delegation to northern Europe in 1986, led by trade unionist and former communist Laurie Carmichael, provides further evidence of this new thinking. Released in 1987, *Australia Reconstructed* has been labelled 'the most comprehensive policy manifesto ever published by the mainstream left in Australia' by labour historian Andrew Scott, who sees it as 'an important reference point for an alternative and more interventionist Labor political and economic approach that came to dominate the period 1983–96'.

So what did *Australia Reconstructed* recommend and why were these ideas so attractive to people on the Left at this time? Its most important recommendations were that 'Australia should develop a central national economic and social objective', with the aims 'to achieve full employment, low inflation and rising living standards which are equitably distributed'. In order to achieve this, the country needed 'an innovative, positive and consensual approach to the management of change and to the removal of all impediments to achieving these objectives'. Such ideas appealed to the unions, as they would have a key role in national decision making and economic planning, much as the Jackson Report had recommended in 1975 and the Accord in 1982. Peak national economic planning bodies would include representatives of government, industry and the unions, working together to formulate future directions for both the national economy, key industry sectors and, in certain instances, specific enterprises. As Bongiorno argues, Button's ideas and more importantly those advocated in *Australia Reconstructed* were landmarks in Australia, especially for 'the union movement not least because it redirected attention from tariff protection and state ownership to markets, productivity, skills and competitiveness – a shift entirely in tune with the government's own, and one that blunted opposition to tariff cuts'.

But their timing was terrible and the release of this report coincided with a sharp downturn in Australia's economic fortunes, mostly related to a significant drop in the country's terms of trade – the prices received for exports, which in Australia's case, then as now, were mostly commodities such as agricultural goods and minerals. As these prices went down the difference between what the nation earned and what it spent – the current account deficit – began to balloon. The initial response to this problem was a rapid devaluation of the Australian dollar, which fell from 90 cents to the US dollar when floated in late 1983 to under 60 cents US by the middle of 1986. The better known response is Treasurer Keating's declaration to Sydney radio shock jock John Laws and his audience that Australia's economy was facing a crisis and the country risked becoming a banana republic if something was not done soon to fix it. The government's response to this crisis was much closer to that advocated by the authors of *Australia at the Crossroads* rather than that of its own *Australia Reconstructed* allies. Government spending was cut sharply, wage fixing was made flexible and some government assets and services were privatised or outsourced to the private sector.

An agenda for change

In pursuing privatisation at the national level, federal Labor paved the way for their ideological opponents at the state level to undo one of the most important features of the Fordist city: the idea that governments – national, state and local – should be central players in the urban economy. Across the western world for much of the twentieth century it was generally agreed that governments had a key role to play in not only stabilising the urban economy, but also in regulating how cities operated. This was especially true for Australia, where the ideal of the detached suburban home meant that the cities covered vast geographical areas and thus urban services could never be provided cheaply as there were simply not enough people in any given area to cover costs. Every city and state in Australia was thus home to major government or semi-government organisations that were responsible for the provision of water, electricity, gas, transport, roads, ports, housing and myriad other things essential for the efficient running of the city. The names, acronyms (e.g. Melbourne's Metropolitan Board of Works or MMBW) and the tasks performed by these organisations were, until the 1990s, familiar elements of daily life for Australian city dwellers, many of whom were also employees of what were significant players in the urban economy. As responsible authorities for the administration of urban markets, ports, transport and communications, these organisations were also significant holders of urban property portfolios, with much of their land in high profile locations adjacent to the CBDs of the major cities.

As we shall see in chapter 7, what to do with these increasingly economically redundant landholdings became a major issue in urban renewal debates in the 1980s and 1990s, as did debates about the role of these organisations and specifically about whether governments should own and operate businesses and provide urban and other services that could be performed by the private sector. Although there is no real evidence to prove the point either way, throughout the 1980s and early 1990s there were endless assertions by advocates from the Right that the private sector is always the more efficient, that only in extreme cases of market failure should government involve itself in the market and that most, if not all, urban services should be provided by the private sector. Representatives of the unions and the Left responded with the equally unprovable argument that only government owned and run organisations could be trusted to put citizens' interests before profits and that privatisation would always lead to higher prices and worse outcomes. The Right view was behind the *Crossroads* group's call for a 'reduction of the government's role as a producer of many basic services, including, education, health and welfare', while the Left's could be seen in *Australia Reconstructed*.

Again, as with the *Australia at the Crossroads* initiative, it was libertarian economists and thinkers who provided the intellectual backing for these policies, in this case a group associated with Monash University's Centre of Policy Studies. One of the strongest advocates of this thinking was Michael G Porter who was to become a highly influential figure in free-market circles in Australia in the 1980s, especially so in his home state of Victoria where his privately funded think tank, the Tasman Institute, was to become a major driver of the political and policy agenda under the Kennett Liberal government in the 1990s. At the height of the 1990–91 recession the Tasman Institute released a report, *Victoria: An agenda for change*, commissioned and funded by employer groups, which argued that 'government failure is more not less than a problem of market failure' and called for a vast reduction in 'the role of government in running businesses', such as the provision of electricity, gas, public transport, and the ports, most of which it recommended should be corporatised and privatised in order to make them more efficient and more responsive to entrepreneurial management initiatives.

These ideas about reforming and privatising urban services were experimented with by the Greiner Liberal government, elected to power in NSW in 1988, and then followed meticulously by the Kennett government, elected to power in Victoria at the height of the early 1990s recession. They have since essentially become bipartisan policy for federal and other state governments across the country, both Labor and Liberal. The theory behind the changes was that as older establishment blockages to innovation were removed, more 'nimble' and 'responsive' organisations would flourish in their place, and to a certain extent this has been the case, with a range of new businesses and indeed whole industries having emerged in recent decades to do the tasks that used to be performed in-house by these government and semi-government organisations. But the reality is that much of Australia's urban service provision has essentially been rebranded and sold off, often as monopolies or oligopolies, to businesses owned by private global corporations or by overseas governments.

While service levels have largely stayed the same or declined, prices, especially for electricity, have skyrocketed, as have the pay packets of managers. But the major outcome of these policies has been a massive drop in employment in former government service provision sectors like electricity generation, transportation and the provision of water and sewerage services. To be clear, these organisations were often grossly overstaffed in the 1970s and 1980s but in seeking to make them more efficient, thousands of jobs, especially those of young people, many of whom were apprenticed to these organisations to learn a trade straight from school, have been lost. And, as with the various plans to reduce protection in the TCF and other manufacturing industries, the impact of these job losses has often been highly localised, affecting specific, mostly urban, regions and communities, such as the northern suburbs of Adelaide and Victoria's La Trobe Valley, which were simultaneously grappling with economic restructuring in the manufacturing sector. In the case of Victoria, employment in the 'electricity, gas, water and waste services' sector declined from more than 40 000 people in 1988 – almost all of whom were full time – to a low of 15 100, 1000 of whom were part time, in 1997. The number climbed back to about 30 000 in November 2016, but 10 per cent of these were part time, and the state's population was by then 50 per cent larger than it had been 30 years earlier.

At the same time, the once numerous apprenticeships offered by these organisations, which used to provide on-the-job training and a secure career trajectory for young people in fields as diverse as plumbing and electrical engineering, have been replaced by an ad-hoc training system, often run by large international private sector organisations more interested in short-term profit and government subsidies than long-term skills development. As a 2017 Australia Institute report found, more staff in the privatised electricity industry are now involved in sales and management than in direct service provision. So neither the promised savings for governments nor the reduced prices and improved services for consumers have occurred. Privatisation and outsourcing have brought extensive rewards, but most of these appear to have gone to managers and shareholders (including foreign governments) rather than to the general public.

Conclusion

While some of the ideas from the Accord and *Australia Reconstructed*, about the role of partnerships and planning in economic restructuring and protecting the poor from the worst ravages of economic restructuring, were implemented by the Hawke and Keating governments, for the most part it has been the economic ideas first set out by the *Crossroads* group and subsequently their free-market followers that have dominated economic policy in Australia since the 1980s. Tariffs have been reduced to virtually zero, government spending and taxes have been cut, unions have been emasculated and wage fixing has been made more flexible, government assets and services have been privatised or outsourced, and the private sector has been allowed to take an ever larger role in the economy. And while Australia has been spared the devastation and hardship that afflicted and continues to afflict many parts of the northern hemisphere, for the most part commitments to sharing the burden of economic restructuring have been a one-way street with most of the burden of change falling on those who could least afford it.

While it is true that all of this has coincided with an economic expansion that has now lasted for more than 26 years, over that time the gap between the rich and the poor in Australia has grown markedly. Arguably, while the policy of opening up the economy to international competition has worked for the majority of us, there remains a question about how we judge success; we now have access to tariff-free goods and services sourced from almost anywhere on the globe which, although still more expensive than in most other comparable nations, are comparatively cheaper than they were a generation ago, but fewer of us have the full-time jobs which would allow us to afford them. Clothes that were fashionable in the 1980s and are again so today, such as a pair of Levi's 501s or a pair of Doc Martens boots, cost about the same in dollar terms as they did in the 1980s, at about $100 and $200 respectively. Average full-time weekly incomes, on the other hand, have almost quadrupled in that time from $409 per week to $1575 before tax, meaning that clothes and shoes are now about one-quarter of their former price. Cars are also cheaper, with entry-level vehicles essentially the same price in dollar terms today as they were in the early 1990s, while including many of the luxury and safety features – such as driver air bags – that back then were only available in top of the range models. Thus, cars, like clothes and other manufactured goods, now cost between a quarter and a third of what they did before tariffs were reduced. But again, because fewer of us work full time, we have less ability to pay for them out of our diminishing pay packets.

All of this means that access to cheaper clothes, shoes and cars has, for many, come at a significant personal price. In the process of becoming more open, Australia has lost almost all of its manufacturing capacity, seen unemployment and underemployment rise sharply, and seen the country build up a huge foreign debt. Whereas we used to pay extra for things that were either made here or imported, we now borrow to fund 'lifestyle' goods that are almost all made elsewhere. We have also become a more unequal society and have incurred massive personal and corporate debts, which have been used to fund investment in unproductive real estate speculation rather than in the promised creation of new high skilled and high value-added industries of the twenty-first century. While employment across all manufacturing sectors has shrunk by 40 per cent from the 1.3 million identified by the Jackson Committee in 1975 to around 680 000 now, in TCF it has declined by 75 per cent from 149 000 in 1971 to under 40 000 today; this at a time when the national population has nearly doubled from under 13 million to over 24 million. Manufacturing employment has declined from almost 25 per cent of all jobs in 1975 to less than 10 per cent today, while services have gone from 66 per cent to more than 80 per cent. Under both Labor and the Liberals a number of government subsidised restructuring schemes have been created to help businesses reorient their focus to exports, but the emergence of China as the world's factory since the 1990s has meant that hardly any Australian manufacturing businesses, and certainly no TCF ones, can compete in any form other than as niche, artisanal providers.

The effects of these changes have not been shared equally across the nation, or indeed across different regions of the cities. In the next chapter we look at how the impacts of the new economic policies have played out on the ground in different city regions and communities. In chapter 3 we move on to look at the new jobs and industries that have emerged in the decades since the 1980s, and specifically at how these have created not just a nation divided along class and socioeconomic lines but also geographical ones, between urban, rural and regional Australia, inner urban and suburban Australia and, increasingly, between Sydney and Melbourne, and the rest of urban Australia.

2

The twilight of the Fordist city

Decisions made have costs, but so too do those not made. It is possible that Australia could have kept its manufacturing sector and gone on making things as it had done for more than a century, but had we done so our clothes, shoes, cars and household appliances would today likely be very expensive and of a quality below what we have come to expect. But on the other hand tens and possibly hundreds of thousands of manufacturing jobs might have been saved. While free-market critiques of the quality and the prices of products made in Australia until the 1980s are somewhat overblown, there is no question that much of what we wore and drove at that time was both technologically lacking and distinctly overpriced. It is possible that as a society we could have decided that this expense and technical mediocrity was a price worth paying in order to protect our most vulnerable citizens and to ensure that their communities could maintain their reasonably well-paid jobs. Had we done so, our economy and society would be very different today.

So too would be our cities. Our streets and neighbourhoods might still hum with the sounds of machinery and production, the sound of the factory whistle might still demarcate the beginning and end of the working day and our other senses might still be assaulted by the sights, smells and sounds of the industrial city: the noise made by racks of half-made clothes as they are wheeled from workroom to warehouse in Flinders Lane or Surry Hills; the smell of cooking yeast on brewing day in Carlton, East Melbourne or Chippendale; the clang of printing machines covered in black ink in newspaper rooms and book binderies in West Melbourne and Adelaide's Light Square; or the sight of thousands of newly-built Fords and Holdens waiting to be delivered to car dealerships in factory holding pens in Broadmeadows and Elizabeth. We might also still smell the smoke of the steel and coke furnaces of Newcastle and Whyalla, and possibly breathe the sickly goo that for decades emanated from tyre plants in Somerton and Salisbury. Our cities might also still reek of the smell of sheep and cattle waiting to be sold in urban livestock markets like the one in Gepps Cross in northern Adelaide where I started work as a 16-year-old auctioneer's clerk in 1980, or that used to dominate my now gentrified neighbourhood of Kensington in inner Melbourne. So too might the days of the week be marked by the distinct smells of the by-products of the abattoirs that used to be such a distinguishing feature of similar neighbourhoods across the country when I was young.

All of these things are possible but unlikely, given the changes in the world economy since the onset of globalisation in the 1970s. To have maintained these industries would have required either an unprecedented scaling up of capital investment and workplace productivity, ever-higher levels of tariff protection, or a massive reduction in the wages and conditions of working Australians. The industrialisation of first South-East Asia in the 1970s and 1980s and then China from the 1990s onwards has meant that most of the things we used to make can now be produced at a fraction of the cost that we would need to pay an Australian for the same task. What economists call our 'comparative advantage', the things that we do best at a price that we and the world are prepared to pay, is no longer in goods but in natural resources and services. Everything else is available through trade. The transport, technological and communications revolutions of the post-industrial era have meant that we not only have access to these things that are made more

cheaply elsewhere but we also have almost instantaneous knowledge about them. The tyranny of distance no longer protects inefficient producers and no longer ensures that consumers are ignorant
about what is available out there and at what price.

So perhaps Margaret Thatcher was right and there really was no
alternative to the free-market global economy? Possibly, but as we
saw in the last chapter there were varieties of globalisation on offer
and under Labor in the early 1980s, and to a lesser extent the Liberals in the 1990s and the early 2000s, at least some effort was made
to spread the pain of restructuring. Governments of all persuasions
made decisions at the national level to abandon tariffs and protection and to embrace the opportunities and costs of the free-market, global era, but the effects of these decisions were often highly
localised. Almost all of the factories of the industrial era and their
associated sights, sounds and smells are now gone from the Australian city but only some of the communities they once served have
prospered and only some of the jobs these people used to do have
been replaced. Some people and localities have seen their former
dirty jobs replaced by newer, cleaner jobs and industries but many
others have only seen once-productive spaces replaced by nothing
but abandoned buildings and empty blocks of land.

Historian, political advisor and former resident of Doveton in
Melbourne's southeastern suburbs, Dennis Glover, has written of
his disgust when returning to his former neighbourhood (home of
Holden, International Harvester and Heinz foods) in 2015: 'The
vast flat stretches of tarmac, which thousands of gleaming new
vehicles once covered, are now empty, weeds growing through the
cracks'. Stripped of equipment, the remaining buildings of a once
huge landscape of production in which whole families (including
his own) worked are now 'places of almost infinite emptiness. I
walked through its cavernous remains like visitors through the
sacked ruins of Rome' he wrote in his searing indictment of what
had been done to communities such as his over the 40 years of what

self-congratulatory chroniclers of recent Australian economic history are increasingly calling the period of heroic economic reform. Historian Mark Peel has similarly written of the contemporaneous abandonment of Elizabeth in South Australia, Broadmeadows in northern Melbourne and Green Valley in western Sydney in the name of economic reform, while Erick Eklund has documented the slow, seemingly inexorable decline of Port Kembla from Steel Town in the postwar years to somewhere without much of a future now. Internationally, scholars such as Steven High and David Lewis, Michael Frisch and others have similarly documented the stories and haunting images of the deindustrialised and abandoned corporate wastelands of the northeastern states of North America and elsewhere.

The various futures available to former industrial and manufacturing places were both highly location specific but also historically contingent. The abandoned knitting mills and warehouses and rundown nineteenth century streetscapes of the economically redundant inner city rag trade districts of 1970s and 1980s Sydney and Melbourne were reasonably easily adapted and reinvented as shabby-genteel 'creative' spaces in the 1980s and beyond, while the newer and vastly bigger factories of the postwar Fordist economy of Doveton and Elizabeth had and have few alternative uses other than as storage spaces or logistics hubs. And while the creative spaces of the inner city generate far fewer jobs than did their manufacturing predecessors, their reuse as offices, restaurants and hotels, and more recently as chic dwelling spaces, has at least brought life and buzz to neighbourhoods and streets that had an eerie sense of abandonment throughout much of the 1980s and early 1990s. Not so the cavernous spaces of the outer suburban factories which closed in the 1990s and beyond, which in their new guise provide jobs in the dozens rather than the thousands of their former lives.

In this chapter I document the local impacts of the national political decision to embrace globalisation and free-market economics, made in the 1970s and 1980s. I do so by first charting the changing demographics and geographies of employment in the major economic zones of Sydney, Melbourne and Adelaide – the inner suburbs and the geographically vast Fordist regions of what are now the middle suburbs developed after the Second World War, 15–25 kilometres from the city centre – from the early 1970s through to today. While the former were the primary locations of the TCF industries and small-scale manufacturing workshops, the latter were home to major manufacturers such as the car industry, appliance manufacturing and, in Sydney, heavy engineering works. Each of these regions has seen major change since the 1970s, with most of their manufacturing facilities radically shrunk or closed. But as follow-up detailed case studies of Fitzroy in inner Melbourne and Broadmeadows in its outer north will show, while the inner cities have been reinvented as sites of consumption in recent decades, outer regions have never been given the opportunities or resources to fully adapt to change and have essentially been abandoned to their fate by governments and the private sector.

Demographic and economic change in Sydney, Melbourne and Adelaide, 1971–2016

Some sense of the major economic changes seen in Australia's cities in recent decades can be gained by using census data to track changes in employment of the resident population of the broader metropolitan areas (Statistical Divisions) across the 45 years between the censuses of 1971 and 2016. In Greater Sydney in 1971 about 28 per cent of the labour force was employed in manufacturing. More than 70 per cent were men, although, as we have seen, women were an important group in certain sectors, most notably TCF. In Melbourne manufacturing represented just over 30 per cent of employment, with males again being by far the majority at nearly 70 per cent of these employees. In Adelaide manufacturing accounted for 27 per cent of all employees, but the male to female ratio there was much higher, at 78.5 per cent male to 21.5 per cent female. There were reasons for this discrepancy between female employment numbers in Adelaide and the other manufacturing cities, which we will come back to later.

As the Jackson Report had noted, manufacturing employment was not evenly spread across the metropolitan areas of the cities, and nor was female employment evenly distributed within it. In 1976 inner Melbourne, the heartland of the national TCF sector, 28 per cent of the resident workforce was employed in manufacturing: 30 per cent of the men and 26 per cent of the women. But even there, manufacturing workers were not evenly spread out and ranged from a low of 22 per cent of the population of the City of Melbourne – which included the already gentrifying Parkville and East Melbourne and traditionally upmarket South Yarra, as well as then working-class Carlton, North Melbourne and Kensington – to fully 47.5 per cent in then solidly working-class Collingwood. As elsewhere across the metropolis, Collingwood's manufacturing workforce was predominantly male but the preponderance of shoe factories, knitting mills and machine shops still in existence there meant the male to female ratio was 60:40 rather than the general 70:30. In inner Sydney 40 per cent of the workers of the then municipality of South Sydney (covering Redfern, Newtown, Alexandria and Darlington) were employed in manufacturing, with only about a third of these women. In Adelaide the inner western municipalities of Hindmarsh and Thebarton had much higher levels of manufacturing employment than did the wider metropolitan area, with about 40 per cent of the admittedly small workforce of about 9000 across the two immigrant and working-class areas employed in manufacturing. In both cases, the male to female split was about 70:30.

In the three major southeastern cities, the inner areas were not only home to manufacturing workers but also the site of their work. In Melbourne figures compiled by the then metropolitan planning authority, the MMBW, in the mid-1970s, show that in 1971 the central core region of the city (encompassing a roughly 5 kilometre arc around the CBD) hosted just over 430 000 jobs, which was about 42 per cent of all jobs in the metropolitan area. The largest employment sector, with 170 000 jobs (40 per cent), was in what were deemed to be blue-collar industries, that is in businesses that made things. But equally many of these jobs could be designated 'blue apron' as they were undertaken by women, especially migrant women. Another 30 per cent of jobs were designated white-collar jobs, that is in offices and services such as retail, hospitality, catering and such. Again, many of these could be deemed 'pink collar' or 'pink apron' as they were undertaken by women, especially young women. And finally the other 30 per cent were in mixed industries, that is organisations or enterprises that both produced things and stored them in the vast warehouses that used to be a feature of the city centre and inner suburbs, and then distributed them across the metropolis, the state and the nation, although rarely overseas. These figures represented respectively 56, 34 and 45 per cent of all such jobs in the metropolitan area.

Until the 1970s such 'mixed' industries and workplaces were a common feature of the Australian inner city. Beginning in the late nineteenth century and consolidating into the twentieth, inner city suburbs began to be characterised by streets and sometimes whole blocks of multistorey industrial structures and warehouses where production, distribution and administrative functions of a single business or sometimes a whole industry would be located within either one building or an integrated complex. In many instances one of these buildings would be the administrative headquarters of the firm or organisation while the others would each have a designated function which was often embedded into the design of the building as one of its architectural features. The vast complex of more than ten five- to eight-storey buildings that made up Foy and Gibson's Gibsonia facility in Melbourne's Collingwood, which served as the production, distribution, administrative and retail hub of the national retail chain, is an example of this phenomenon. At its height in the 1930s it provided employment to more than 2500 people, most of them locals and most of them female. So too the nearby 'White City' complex developed by chocolate entrepreneurs Macpherson Robertson (later famous as MacRobertson's) from the 1890s to the 1930s and the vast Bryant and May and Rosella foods complexes in Richmond, developed from the early twentieth century onwards as inner Melbourne began to industrialise. Similar facilities could be found in inner city neighbourhoods in Sydney and on a smaller scale in Adelaide.

However, while certain types of manufacturing – such as textiles, clothing, footwear and food production, as well as printing and small-scale engineering – remained important places of employment for residents of the inner city into the 1970s, for the most part the manufacturing heartland of the nation was no longer the inner city but the outer suburbs, which had expanded rapidly in the decades after the war. So while Melbourne's Collingwood, Fitzroy and Richmond and Sydney's Redfern and Surry Hills remained iconic working-class suburbs famous for their history of deprivation and political resistance, technological change and their dwindling populations meant that by the 1960s they were no longer major centres of manufacturing employment or particularly important sites of working-class politics. While the headquarters of the major unions and the various city and state trades halls may have remained centrally located, manufacturing workers and the factories in which they worked had long moved out.

As an example, by 1971 Collingwood's population of 21 000 was less than two-thirds of its prewar peak and, while it remained a centre of clothing and especially footwear production, it was a bit-player population-wise and on the city and national manufacturing employment stage. By then Melbourne's manufacturing heartland

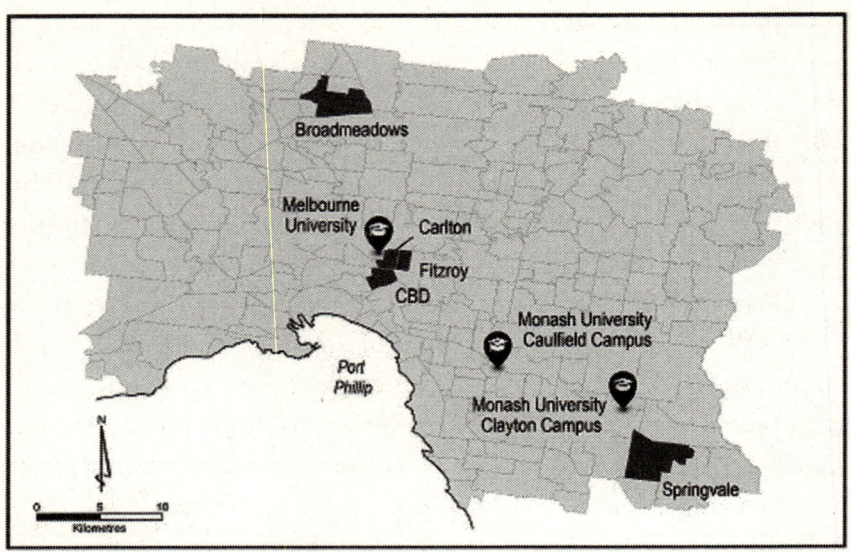

**Melbourne, showing the locations of Fitzroy and the CBD
and the suburbs of Broadmeadows and Springvale**
Map created by Kara Rasmanis

had moved north and south-east to the point where, by the 1970s, Broadmeadows, the home of the vast Ford factory complex, had nearly four times the population of Collingwood and four times as many manufacturing workers. Indeed its manufacturing workforce of just over 16 000 was nearly four-fifths of the size of the Colling-wood's entire population, while its total population of just over 100 000 dwarfed Collingwood in economic and political importance. In outer south-east Melbourne, Dandenong (the home of Holden) and Dennis Glover's Doveton – where many former Collingwood residents were moved by the Housing Commission of Victoria as part of its postwar slum clearance policies – just under 40 per cent of the workforce, or nearly 7000 people out of a total population of 41 000, were employed in the manufacturing sector in 1971.

In Sydney manufacturing moved west and south-west in the postwar years to Parramatta, Bankstown and Fairfield among other

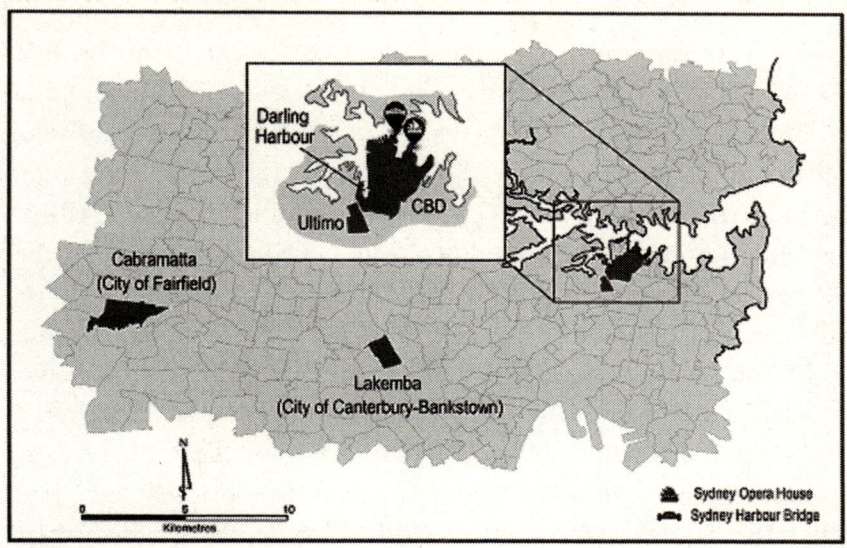

Sydney, showing the locations of Darling Harbour, Ultimo and the CBD, and the municipalities of Cabramatta and Canterbury-Bankstown
Map created by Kara Rasmanis

places. In 1971, 34 per cent of Parramatta's nearly 50 000-strong workforce was employed in manufacturing, while in Fairfield it was more than 38 per cent. In giant-sized neighbouring Bankstown, with its population of more than 160 000, 36 per cent of the workforce of over 75 000 were manufacturing workers. In the other manufacturing capital, Adelaide, similar trends occurred in the postwar years, with manufacturing moving from its former home in the inner western suburbs to Elizabeth in the north where 36 per cent of a workforce of just over 13 000 were employed in manufacturing in 1971.

As with the inner cities, in many outer suburban areas manufacturing was particularly male dominated and, while there were substantial numbers of women who worked within the giant car and other plants of the suburban fringe, these were a minority and seem to have been confined to a limited number of roles, perhaps working in the upholstery shops of the major car plants or, like Dennis Glover's mother, as cooks, cleaners and cashiers in the in-house canteens that were a feature of these workplaces until the 1980s. In Broadmeadows and Dandenong, for example, women accounted for over 30 per cent of the manufacturing workforce in 1971, similar to the ratios of the inner city, but less than the 42 per cent found in Bankstown. Elizabeth was the outlier here, with only 21 per cent of its manufacturing workforce female and, unlike in outer suburban regions of the bigger cities, Elizabeth's women were more likely to be employed in wholesale and retail trade than in manufacturing, perhaps because the high proportion of English migrants there meant they would likely have had the necessary language skills to work in these fields, which their Continental-born sisters in Sydney and Melbourne possibly lacked.

The inner cities not only lost jobs in the 1970s and 1980s, they also lost population, both numerically and proportionately to the rest of the city. In 1971 the population of Melbourne's 'core area', defined by the MMBW as the City of Melbourne and its seven immediate municipal neighbours, was just under 310 000, which was about 12 per cent of the total metropolitan population. Five years later it had dropped by nearly 50 000 to just under 260 000, and by 1981 it was just 245 000. Melbourne's inner city thus lost more than 20 per cent of its population in the single decade of the 1970s, with most of these leaving in the five years to 1976. The decline continued into the 1980s, admittedly at a slower rate. By the time of the 1986 census another 14 000 had left, leaving a population of about 231 000, before it stabilised in the 1990s and then recovered to just under 373 000 in 2016. Perhaps more tellingly, by the mid-1980s, the inner core had become a tiny fraction of the metropolitan population, home to less than 10 per cent of the city's more than three million people. As we shall see in chapter 7, concerns about the ongoing economic viability of inner Melbourne became a real topic of concern in business and government

hit the appliance manufacturing industries far harder than TCF. Almost half of the manufacturing establishments in the municipality (154 of 346) made clothes in 1968–69, with the sector employing almost 80 per cent of the suburb's female manufacturing workforce. Thus, slightly more women than men were employed in manufacturing in Fitzroy (4975 to 4745); however, given that, as we saw above, more men who *lived* in Fitzroy were manufacturing workers than were the local women, this suggests that women worked locally, perhaps for family reasons, while men travelled to their jobs. That said, the clothing industry was not totally female dominated as it was also the largest single employer of men in Fitzroy, accounting for about one-third of jobs. Job losses through the period 1968–69 to 1975–76 across the manufacturing sector were about equally spread between men and women; however, the vast majority of losses occurred in the clothing sector which lost over 2000 jobs, most of which had been held by women. Male jobs were mostly lost in food, beverages and tobacco, paper and paper products manufacturing and in the clothing industry.

The effects of these changes were particularly noticeable in suburbs like Fitzroy where single industries and sometimes single employers had been the mainstay of the local economy for years, sometimes decades, and whose factories, warehouses and administrative offices were important local landmarks, dominating streetscapes, or indeed entire suburban blocks. One such local urban landscape was Victoria Street, a wide, east–west thoroughfare that runs between Brunswick and Nicholson streets just south of Johnston Street in Fitzroy's central area. As my colleague Simone Sharpe and I have argued elsewhere, the story of Victoria Street and its major employers – the corset maker La Mode Industries and grocer Moran and Cato – is emblematic of the rise and fall of manufacturing in Australia in the twentieth century. Rebuilt from its mid-nineteenth century residential origins as a series of three- to six-storey clothing and food factories and distribution facilities in the last decades of the nineteenth century and the first decades of the twentieth, until the late 1980s Victoria Street was a major site of industry, overwhelmingly dominated not only by the buildings of its two historically great employers but also by their economic demands and social and cultural ethos, and in the case of Moran and Cato by the smells of their various food products.

A local Fitzroy success story, the rise and fall of Moran and Cato is particularly apposite to the broader story being told in this book, as it covers both the growth and decline of manufacturing and industry in the inner regions of Melbourne in the twentieth century, and later the emergence of new forms of industry and employment in a suburb that is now almost totally deindustrialised. Founded in the late nineteenth century by Thomas Moran and Fred Cato, but largely under the strong Wesleyan influence of Cato – Moran died aged 39 in 1890 – Moran and Cato grew from one small grocery store in North Melbourne to a national chain by the 1920s. Like MacRobertson's nearby White City complex, where the Freddo Frog was invented in 1930, Moran and Cato was an integrated administrative, production and distribution hub consisting of a series of three-, four- and five-storey buildings located at the corner of Victoria and Brunswick streets and constructed from the early 1880s through to the late 1920s. Until the late 1960s the company's administrative headquarters and national distribution centre were also housed here, meaning it was an important employment centre for both men and women, mostly working-class people, but also sizeable numbers of white- and pink-collar workers, responsible for keeping the books, paying the staff and organising the business.

In many ways Moran and Cato was much more an early twentieth century company than a modern one, with Cato typical of old-style authoritarian and paternalistic owner/managers who saw their businesses as extensions of their personal life and moral values. Unlike the practices of some of the newer department stores that came into existence in the 1920s and 1930s and the traditional 'tick' system used by corner store proprietors, Cato insisted on cash payments from retail customers as credit was bad for both business and the character of working-class people. Nor was alcohol sold in any Moran and Cato store, again reflecting Cato's personal and religious beliefs. Staff were expected to conform to these personal, religious and moral standards, with most recruited from local church-going Methodist families. As with many Protestant-run businesses in Australia, Catholics knew they 'need not apply' for jobs with Moran and Cato as they had no chance of being employed. That said, for many locals in Fitzroy and elsewhere the company was a sought-after employer for the 'right sort', offering generous staff bonuses, one week annual paid leave, and a half day off on Wednesdays to compensate for working on Saturday afternoons and evenings. Staff were also offered financial incentives to invest in the company, earning 10 per cent interest on any loans they might make to it.

Moran and Cato not only brought a certain type of attitude and culture to Victoria Street, and Fitzroy more generally, but also the sounds and smells of industry and production. As many of the company's products were home-brand labels manufactured or blended onsite, Victoria Street was a hive of sound and activity for most of the year. Coffee beans from Arabia, India, Ceylon and Java were roasted and ground onsite before being packed and distributed to stores nationally, while tea was imported directly from India and Ceylon. At any time, up to 100 tons of tea would be stored in a Victoria Street warehouse where male employees would blend and taste it in one room while next door women were employed to weigh and pack it in specially marked bags and boxes. Similarly, jelly crystals, baking powder, self-raising flour, dried fruits, pepper, curry and other spices and condiments were packed in company-labelled bags in the Victoria Street factories before being distributed to stores across the city and the nation. From the early 1900s the company also made its own butter from cream brought to Fitzroy by train from the country, with the butter factory at 14–22 Victoria Street (opposite the main buildings) having its own steam plant and refrigeration engine.

Given all this, it is no surprise that Moran and Cato prospered and expanded in the first decades of the twentieth century and indeed into the early postwar years. But like other older, inner city–based businesses documented in the Jackson Report, the second third of the century was not kind to the company. Management was slow to adapt to the new realities of the rapid expansion of suburbia and suburban shopping centres and to the changes in the demographics and tastes of its core inner city clientele base. As with many older businesses locally and nationally, the 1961 credit squeeze and subsequent recession seemed to have caused cash flow problems, with board minute books from the 1960s expressing concerns about the economic situation, especially in NSW. Internal company correspondence from this time shows increasing concerns regarding the reduction in profits, with the state of the NSW branch of the business being of special concern. Notwithstanding these issues the company continued to actively invest in its stores and factories throughout the 1960s. But change was in the air. In 1966 its Perfection Tea label was sold to a former employee, Robert Timms, whose eponymous label is another inner Melbourne local success story, granted that it is owned today by Fresh Food Holdings, a Western Australia–based multinational food company. Three years after the sale of its coffee business, the board of Moran and Cato agreed to a takeover offer for the whole firm from rival grocer Permewan Wright, a longstanding wholesale and retail business with roots stretching back to the Victorian gold rush era, and which at that stage was undergoing rapid expansion nationally. Moran and Cato ceased to exist as a separate company in September 1969.

We do not have figures for the number of people employed by Moran and Cato in 1969, but we do know that its Victoria Street buildings ceased to have a manufacturing, distribution or administrative function for the takeover company after 1970. The buildings and Victoria Street remained major sites of manufacturing employment into the early 1990s, however. Sold to a company associated with the immigrant Jewish Rothstein family in 1970, some of buildings were repurposed as the Rotson Knitting Mills in the 1970s, a role they maintained until the demise of the TCF sector in the face of tariff cuts and the recession of the early 1990s. Other parts of the Moran and Cato complex were put to different uses, more reflective of the changing structure of Fitzroy's economy and demographics. My first recollection of Victoria Street when I came to live in Melbourne in the mid-1980s is of the former ground floor Moran and Cato corner store as a giant Brotherhood of St Laurence opportunity shop. Upstairs was the long-running pool hall, The Cue, while next door was an equally long-running Indian restaurant, and around the corner on Victoria Street, one of the buildings retained its links with the food sector, being used as storage and distribution facility for a Brunswick Street organic vegetable shop.

BROADMEADOWS

Whereas Fitzroy's major businesses were founded by locals and were locally owned and managed for most of their existence, in the 'new town' of Broadmeadows, developed by the Housing Commission of Victoria in the 1950s on the then northern fringes of the metropolitan area, nearly all the major employers were local subsidiaries of major international corporations. Fitzroy's manufacturing and distribution economy was born Australian but died when it was unable to adapt to the more internationalised economic environment of the late twentieth century, while Broadmeadows, which was born global – though protected behind the high Australian tariff wall – was equally unable to thrive in the new competitive world of the more open, post-1980s economy. As we have seen, at the time of the

1971 Census, Broadmeadows' population was 101 000, with 40 per cent of its workforce of about 42 000 employed in the manufacturing sector. Ford was the largest single employer in the municipality, with over 6000 employees in the early 1970s, although the area was also home to a range of other businesses related to the car industry, including Goodyear Tyres, which opened in 1960. Broadmeadows also had important TCF businesses, including one of its few local success stories, the work clothes manufacturer Yakka, which moved from its original premises in Brunswick to a purpose-built facility in the suburb in 1960.

As a manufacturing centre, Broadmeadows was affected by the recessions of the mid-1970s and early 1980s as well as the broader processes of economic restructuring we saw in the last chapter, but likely because its factories were newer and bigger than those of Fitzroy and other inner city suburbs, the threats posed by the globalising economy did not become so apparent there until later. Population continued to grow in the area during the 1970s to reach 103 000 in 1981 but it then abruptly stopped, remaining essentially static for the next ten years. A municipality that had seen rapid population growth on the back of manufacturing employment and state intervention in the Fordist years thus stagnated in the emerging post-Fordist ones. However, unlike Fitzroy, at least its population didn't shrink, largely because it became an important site of immigration, especially family reunion immigration in the 1980s and beyond. Also, unlike in Fitzroy, Broadmeadows' manufacturing sector and workforce remained roughly steady throughout the 1970s and into the early 1980s, albeit subject to periodic bouts of mass labour shedding during recessions.

Data from Australian Bureau of Statistics (ABS) annual economic censuses show that in 1971, nearing the end of the long postwar boom period, there were 119 manufacturing establishments in Broadmeadows employing just under 13 000 workers, nearly 70 per cent of whom were men. Four years later, when the same survey was undertaken during the 1975 recession, the number of establishments had declined slightly to 116 but in line with the growth of the suburb's population the number of employees had climbed by roughly one-quarter to nearly 15 500. The largest single manufacturing employment field at that time was 'transport equipment', but likely for reasons which we would now call 'commercial in confidence', the ABS did not list the exact number of employees in the 11 establishments involved in this sector, no doubt at the request of the area's largest employer, Ford. But the figures we do have, as well as other sources that document the sheer size and importance of Ford to the local economy, suggest that the majority of these were likely employed by the Ford plant and by its suppliers.

Like Fitzroy, Broadmeadows became a major TCF employment node in the 1960s and early 1970s and was therefore also an important centre of female employment. In 1975, 13 clothing and footwear establishments employed about 900 people in the suburb, 700 of whom were women. It was also home to 11 food, beverage and tobacco factories, employing more than 2000 staff, 60 per cent of whom were men. The economic restructuring that began nationally and internationally in the late 1970s and into the 1980s did affect Broadmeadows, but nowhere near as hard or as swiftly as Fitzroy. However, the signs of future problems were beginning to become apparent. One of these was a rapid slowing of new investment and the creation of new manufacturing businesses. So while the population of Broadmeadows kept growing – although slowly – during the 1970s, the local manufacturing workforce remained essentially static to the point where, by 1982, the 120 establishments then still in existence employed pretty much the same number of people as they had in 1975. We do have figures for 'transport equipment' in that year, which show that the 22 factories now involved in this industry employed nearly 7000 staff, 86 per cent of whom were men. TCF remained an important industry, with 12 establishments employing just over 900 people, 80 per cent of whom were women, while the 14 food, beverage and tobacco factories employed just under 2500 people, 60 per cent of them men.

Dramatic change came to Broadmeadows' manufacturing economy in the 1980s and 1990s rather than in the 1970s as it had in Fitzroy. While the ABS stopped doing small-area studies of manufacturing in the late 1980s, we can continue to get a sense from census counts of the impacts of the tariff cuts and the multiple recessions of the final decades of the twentieth century on places like Broadmeadows. Historian of poverty Mark Peel calls these a 'triple whammy', with each recession 'more grinding than the last', and each taking longer to 'loosen its grip'. As he demonstrates, unemployment in Broadmeadows rose from 1 per cent for men in 1971 to 11 per cent in 1996. For women the corresponding figures were 0.7 per cent to 7 per cent. Awful as these figures are, however, they actually hide the extent of the problems visited on the suburb, especially in the 1990s, when local men (and to a lesser extent, women) of working age were forced from the employment market:

> Of the men aged between 20 and 64 in Broadmeadows in 1971 … six per cent did not participate in the labour force; by 1991 that proportion had increased to 16 per cent and in 1996 it had reached 23 per cent. In all, therefore, more than one-third of the working-age men in Broadmeadows in 1996 were unemployed or were no longer even looking for work, and fewer than half worked in a full-time job.

The 1996 Census, from which these figures are drawn, shows that the largest employment sector in Broadmeadows remained manufacturing, but by then it only accounted for just over 6500 employees, most of them men aged 25–54. The restructuring of the economy in the 1980s combined with the recession of the early 1990s essentially turned this former working-class suburb into a welfare ghetto in which men aged over 54 had either voluntarily left the workforce or more commonly were forced from it by redundancy, injury or ill health. Of a local population of 2647 men aged between 55 and 64 in 1996, only 1227 (46 per cent) were still in the workforce, with only 413 of these employed in manufacturing. Twenty years later at the census of 2016, in the state electorate of Broadmeadows (which covers most of the same area as the former municipality), of a total population of just under 50 000 aged between 15 and 64 only 53.5 per cent were in the labour force, with only 50 per cent of these in full-time work. Of these, just over 2200 were employed in manufacturing, more than two-thirds of them men. For men aged between 55 and 64, more were either outside the labour force or unemployed than were in full- or part-time work. All of this even before the Ford factory closed down later that year.

When Ford finally ceased production in early October 2016, the day was marked in Broadmeadows (and Geelong) with both a celebration of what had been achieved there and a sombre foreboding mood among the workers who had lost their jobs. Media organisations, unionists, politicians and Ford enthusiasts gathered with the workers and their families to mark the passing of what was both a major local employer and a way of life. 'A sad day for Australia. A sad day for manufacturing', said Ford worker Bill Lozanovski, who had been at the Broadmeadows plant for 12 years, reported the *Age*, while diesel mechanic Nick Doria, who had worked at Ford for 22 years, 'began crying as he walked out from the sprawling factory for the last time'. As a skilled tradesman, Nick was relatively optimistic about his future options but was not so sanguine about many of his former workmates: 'a lot of the guys here can't read or write or use computers... They're going to struggle'. The evidence of what had happened to automakers in the wake of the shutdown of Mitsubishi's Lonsdale plant in southern Adelaide in 2004 meant he had cause to worry; a study of these workers by a Flinders University research team found that '12 months post-redundancy only 34 per cent of displaced workers were in full-time employment ...

over 20 per cent of respondents were in casual or part-time employment, with some 69 per cent of those in casual employment reporting that they would rather be working full-time'. More recently, the lead researcher on that team, Andrew Beer, has suggested that up to 20 per cent of workers made redundant from the industry would never work again.

Conclusion

The decline of manufacturing means that in both Fitzroy and Broadmeadows today it is unusual to hear the sound of any machinery other than that associated with building and construction. In Fitzroy's case, that sound usually involves the building of new apartment blocks or the conversion of old factories and warehouses for residential use. That has been the fate of almost the entire Mac-Robertson's White City complex although not (yet) the Moran and Cato buildings, which remain predominantly commercial. Today, most of those buildings, which were until the 1960s food production and packaging facilities and where in the 1970s and 1980s knitting machines used to rattle, have become the Rotson Studios, 'co-working spaces' described by its head-lessee the Australian Graphic Design Association on its website as 'light, bright and airy with incredible views of the city' with features such as 'polished wood floors, big windows and metal pressed ceilings'. 'Surrounded by some of the best pubs, cafes and bars Melbourne has to offer' the Rotson Studios are full of 'great people who work and collaborate together on a regular basis'. Higher up, the top floor of the corner building and the rooftop is home to a fashionable restaurant and bar called Naked for Satan. Abstemious Methodist Mr Cato would not be amused!

As the example of the Rotson Studios demonstrates, things are still made in Fitzroy, though at a much smaller, artisanal scale than they were in the industrial era. Such co-working spaces are becoming a common feature of the contemporary inner city, where artists and designers make one-off and small-run items that are sold at high prices to the newer, richer residents of these former working-class neighbourhoods, or where freelancers sell their labour online to local, national and international employers. The economic model here is closer to that of the pre-industrial era rather than the industrial one and stresses low-output but high-value production runs as opposed to the low-value, high-output model of the industrial era. So too the freelancers are contractors rather than employees and thus have few of the protections afforded to unionised labour in the Fordist era. The internet and low-cost transport and distribution networks also mean that unlike in the pre-industrial and industrial eras, some of these artisanal products are sold internationally to consumers in cities across the globe whose values, tastes and incomes have much in common with those of inner-city Australia. Artisan workers in Fitzroy and similar inner-city suburbs across the country also create or rejuvenate furniture and other household items from the days of Australian mass production, which, like the new products of the co-workers, are sold at high prices to discerning connoisseurs of mid-twentieth century design.

Twenty kilometres north in Broadmeadows the story is very different. There, while there is some evidence of cranes and other construction equipment on the horizon, as yet these are mostly associated with destruction of the old economy rather than creation of a new one. The closure of South Pacific Tyres in 2008, then Yakka a few years later, and then most recently Ford, has left behind a number of gigantic, redundant former industrial spaces alongside the major holes in the employment prospects of unskilled locals. As was the case in Dennis Glover's Doveton in the early 2010s, the once productive factory spaces of Broadmeadows now lie empty, waiting to be repurposed for consumption, housing or some other facet of the post-industrial economy. In the next chapter we investigate these 'something elses' by documenting the major employment fields of the contemporary Australian city.

3

Working and not working
in the post-industrial city

In 1988, at height of an office building boom that was transforming Melbourne's CBD, Victorian Premier John Cain bolstered his
claim for re-election in that year's state poll on the number of cranes
on the city's skyline, which he said was evidence of the economic
strength of the city and the state under his government's leadership.
From one crane when the ALP was elected at the height of the 1982
recession – the then tallest building in Australia, the Rialto Towers
being constructed at the west end of Collins Street – after six years
of a Labor government there were 57 cranes dotted across the CBD.
Most of these were constructing office towers but the largest site
was the massive Melbourne Central development by Japanese construction giant Kumagai Gumi. A mixed-use office and shopping
complex whose anchor tenant was to be another major Japanese
company, the department store Daimaru, Melbourne Central – the
new 'life of the city' according to the developers – was designed to
shift the corporate and shopping axis of the CBD from its traditional east–west orientation to a north–south one.

Sydney's CBD and inner suburbs were similarly undergoing a
building boom at this time, even more so than Melbourne and even
more influenced by Japanese foreign investment. Further north, on
Queensland's Gold Coast, Japanese-funded tourism developments
were also transforming the skyline with new hotels, apartment

towers and shopping centres built to cater for what was until then the largest influx of tourists ever witnessed in the country. At around the same time Federal Treasurer Paul Keating, echoing John Cain, extolled the virtues of a massive building boom as evidence of a national economy doing well and adapting to the challenges of a globalising world. In his inimitable style, he recommended that any Australian who doubted the strength of the economy, and by extension his policies, should look out of the window in any capital city at the number of cranes on the skyline. In Cain and Keating's view, and that of many others at the time, the late 1980s building boom showed that in reaching skywards Australia's cities were visibly joining the global free-market economy.

In hindsight the construction boom and the Japanese stock market bubble that funded it looks like a folly that was always destined to end in tears. And so it did. The Japanese stock market crashed in 1990, signalling a decline that saw it fall by nearly 60 per cent between late 1989 and mid-1992 and never really recover (28 years later, it is still nearly 50 per cent down on its peak). The stock market crash was soon followed by a property collapse, which saw central Tokyo real estate prices follow share prices down until they too settled at less than 40 per cent of their peak. These twin crashes meant that many of the major Japanese companies that had funded and built developments in Australia needed to repatriate cash quickly in order to repair balance sheets. This reversal of cash flow meant that all the hotels built to cater for the Japanese tourists – and the restaurants, department stores and souvenir shops built to cater to their wants and needs – found themselves in trouble, which in turn meant that what in the late 1980s seemed like a new paradigm of Japanese-inspired and funded investment and development in Australia proved to be a short-term speculative bubble, which in the case of the Gold Coast was quite literally built on sand.

Thirty years on there are again multiple cranes on the skylines of Australian cities, especially in Sydney and Melbourne. Some of these are constructing new office buildings and hotels but most are related to a massive surge in apartment building which, like that of the 1980s, is mostly funded by overseas investors, but this time from South-East Asia and China rather than Japan. The cranes and the types of buildings they are creating are symbolic of the new urban services-based economy that has arisen in the wake of the decline of manufacturing since the 1970s. As we have seen in the first two chapters of this book, we hardly make anything in factories in Australia anymore but the major capital cities are now growing rapidly and remain the economic powerhouses of the nation – increasingly more so than they were in the industrial era when smaller regional cities and indeed some small towns in NSW and Victoria were also important employment hubs. Hundreds of thousands of manufacturing jobs have disappeared from our cities since the 1970s but many more jobs have been created in other fields, some of which – such as banking and finance, and indeed construction – have always been around, while others – such as computing and app/software development – were only invented in recent decades. Still others are employed in what is now called 'logistics', the movement of goods from the farm or the docks and on to the shops, which are also major sources of jobs, especially for women and young people. Other employment growth areas are in education, health and personal services, as well as tourism and hospitality. And as we saw in the last chapter, design and artisanal production are niche employers in certain parts of the city, especially the fashionable inner suburbs of the major capitals.

In this chapter we continue the story of economic change in Australia's cities by updating the nation's urban employment profile to take account of the figures found in the most recent census, taken in June 2016. Whereas until the 1970s residents of the cities worked in factory jobs (or increasingly lost their jobs from factories), today we find them on building sites, working in offices and education institutions, in co-work spaces like Rotson, or perhaps more worryingly as freelancers or self-employed members of what is now sometimes called the 'precariat', casualised or part-time workers juggling multiple jobs and contracts as they try to make ends meet in the increasingly expensive cities. And as we saw at the end of the last chapter, in places like Broadmeadows and other formerly working-class manufacturing suburbs, many have found themselves outside the workforce altogether, their talents and skills surplus to the needs of the globalised twenty-first century economy.

Census 2016: Deindustrialisation, globalisation and the innovative city

The census of 2016 paints a very different picture of the Australian city, its economy and the national and local labour market from that which existed in 1971 at the tail end of the Fordist years. Like the national population, the workforce is now much larger and, at about 10.6 million people, is just on twice its former size. It is also much more female, with women accounting for 47.5 per cent of the labour force as opposed to 32 per cent in 1971. It is also overwhelmingly service- rather than manufacturing-oriented, meaning that manufacturing employment has declined from about 23 per cent of all jobs in Australia at that time to about 6.5 per cent now. Numerically, the number of manufacturing workers had declined from 1.3 million in 1971 to under 700 000 in 2016, or about half of the earlier total, but it remains the eighth biggest industry sector, just behind 'public administration and safety', and still well above its nearest rival, 'transport, postal and warehousing', whose numbers were just shy of 500 000.

The largest single manufacturing occupation in 2016 was 'food production', which accounted for more than 167 000 employees or nearly a quarter of all manufacturing jobs. Very few people in Australia still worked in the TCF sector, which, with just under

22 000 employees had become a niche, artisanal occupation. Men still dominate manufacturing, accounting for about 72 per cent of all employees but, as would be expected, women still dominate TCF, where they make up just under 60 per cent of all employees. The men who remain in manufacturing are an increasingly aging demographic; almost half are aged over 45, with less than 3 per cent under 20, the group that used to be apprentices. The 190 000 women still employed in the sector are more evenly spread across the age pyramid, with nearly 70 per cent aged between 25 and 54, but as with the males there are very few aged under 20. Oddly, the number of males and females in this age group is roughly similar, at about 10 000, again perhaps suggesting that in Australia manufacturing is now an artisanal pursuit, increasingly carried out by both young men and women in brightly lit co-working spaces rather than the gender-segregated, cold and dark factories of yesteryear. Not only have the nation and its major cities been deindustrialised as a result of global economic changes and national policy decisions, so too have city regions. As a result, their social and economic status has altered markedly. Gentrification has added to this and what were once inner urban working-class manufacturing heartlands are now highly valued centres of the new post-industrial, creative economy, while the postwar Fordist frontier suburbs are either places of casualised service work, or sometimes no work at all.

As the above employment figures suggest, it is a mistake to think that we no longer make anything in our cities. We do, but just not cheap clothes, textiles and shoes, or indeed cars. In Melbourne, once the centre of Australian manufacturing, fewer than 165 000 people – or less than 8 per cent of the workforce – are now employed in the sector, with the once mighty TCF sector now a shadow of its former self, with less than 7000 employees, 56 per cent of them women. At a more local level, the former heartland of this industry in inner Melbourne now has fewer than 13 000 people – or under 5 per cent of the local population – working in manufacturing, with just over

600 of these being machine operators or drivers. TCF now only accounts for 1289 employees, while in Fitzroy that number drops to double figures, with only nine of these being machine operators or drivers. In neighbouring Collingwood the number is 13.

As is obvious from these figures, Melbourne's manufacturing sector is no longer based in the inner city. Rather, the largest employment group in the sector is now 'technicians and trades workers', who account for nearly one-quarter of all employees. What this suggests is that while job losses in manufacturing have been catastrophic since the removal of tariffs, there has been, as promised, some movement up the value-chain, and rather than produce expensive and bad-quality products, Australia's few surviving manufacturers now compete on quality rather than price and seek to compete globally rather just locally. The employment structure of the broader manufacturing sector has also changed to now be more administrative and technical than unskilled. After tradespeople, the largest groups of employees in manufacturing today are not the people who actually make things but those who design, sell, or manage those who do the making. Of the nearly 700 000 people who work in the sector, fully 42 per cent are managers, professionals, administrators or sales people. Only a third are machine operators and drivers or labourers.

As would be expected, manufacturing work is neither evenly spread across the country, nor indeed across the suburbs of the cities. In the former heartlands of manufacturing – Melbourne, Sydney and Adelaide – the sector now accounts for 7.5, 5.7 and 7.6 per cent of employment respectively. But again, these are not necessarily people working on the production line. In Melbourne, perhaps reflecting its emergence as a design and logistics rather than a manufacturing centre in recent decades, while there remains a large trade-trained manufacturing workforce (20 per cent of employees), in the overall workforce there are more managers (18 per cent) than labourers (16 per cent) and nearly as many professionals (12 per cent) as there are machine operators (13.5 per cent). The same is not true for Adelaide, which, as in the Fordist years, retains its branch office rather than headquarters status. There, nearly half the workforce are tradespeople, machine operators or labourers, with less than 16 per cent being managers and less than 10 per cent professionals, suggesting that while production still occurs there, planning and design does not.

Such manufacturing industry as remains in Australia is increasingly found in the far outer suburbs, close to the airports, major freeways and what are sometimes called inland ports: major truck and railway freight hubs where goods are transhipped along what are now recognised as local and global supply chains. Nor in Melbourne is manufacturing still centred on the big factory landscapes of Broadmeadows, Dandenong or Doveton. Instead, it is to be found in a wide arc of suburbs in the city's middle-suburban southeast, especially around my university, Monash; a region which the Victorian state government has recently designated one of five suburban 'National Employment and Innovation Clusters'. But again, the focus here is not on the traditional tariff-protected industries of the past but increasingly hi-tech niche providers whose employee numbers are small but whose value-added output is high. A local employer, municipal and state government body established in the region in 2010, the Southeast Melbourne Innovation Precinct (SEMIP), which includes Monash among its members, claims that the area is 'home to 40 per cent of Victoria's manufacturing activities and over 56,000 registered businesses. Industry sectors encompass manufacturing, retail, property and business services (including scientific and engineering services)', with a particular focus 'on the high end and growth sectors, such as chemicals, polymers, machinery and equipment, applications in transport, health, construction and the environment'.

As we shall see in chapter 6, while Monash is a substantial generator of export income through the provision of international education, it is still a public institution largely funded by the tax-payer rather than a private business. With more than 16 400 staff based at its Melbourne campuses, the university dwarfs even the largest of these private SEMIP companies and is far bigger than any of even the largest of the manufacturing companies at the height of the Fordist era. And while almost half of its employees are pro-fessional and administrative staff and many of the academic ones are on exploitative sessional teaching contracts, most of these jobs pay far higher salaries than did the manufacturing jobs of the past. As this example shows, education and related industries have not only emerged as major sources of export income for the country in the post-industrial era but are substantial employers too. In fact, 'education and training' is now the third largest single sector of the national economy, employing more than 925 000 people. If 'profes-sional, scientific and technical services' are added to this figure, it jumps to over 1.7 million people, or nearly 16 per cent of the national workforce. Further, if we add the related 'health care and social assistance' category – which includes the university teaching hospi-tals – to these figures, we can see that over three million people, or more than 28 per cent of the national workforce, are employed in these three sectors, which is why these fields are now more impor-tant to the national economy than was manufacturing at the start of our period. And given that many of these jobs are high paying, they are arguably much more important.

They are also female-dominated, with more than 70 per cent of the employees in education female, as are more than 75 per cent of those in health care. The professional, scientific and technical services sector is, however, more male-dominated with only 45 per cent of employees being female. None of this is to suggest that women are either achieving equal status or pay in these fields, how-ever, as we know that women make up the bulk of the lower-paid members of these professions, such as teachers, nurses, carers and administrators. We also know on the other hand that the rise of these new jobs has allowed women to join or remain in the work-force at far higher rates than they could before both the rise of the post-industrial economy and the concomitant emergence of the women's liberation and feminist movements. Women now make up nearly half of the labour force, and not only have their numbers grown since 1971, so too has their age profile changed as more women with children have joined or remained in the workforce. While in 1971, more than a third of the female workforce was aged under 24, today that figure is less than 10 per cent. Instead, the biggest single female age group today is 25–34 year olds, whose numbers are roughly equal to their male counterparts. In 1971 men of this age group outnumbered women by more than two to one.

The location of the universities and indeed of the major public and private hospitals in the cities means that these institutions are not only important national industries but also largely urban ones. Of the more than 900 000 education jobs in Australia, almost two-thirds are located in the six major state capitals, with Sydney and Melbourne each accounting for about 20 per cent, roughly equal to their shares of the national population. This makes sense, as most of these employees are school teachers and thus their job location reflects population distributions across the states and the nation. The same is not true in the more specialised scientific and profes-sional research sector of the economy, however, where the major cities dominate. Of the 775 000 jobs in this field nationally, Sydney accounts for 29 per cent and Melbourne 25 per cent. At a state level, the urban bias of this sector is even more stark, with Sydney accounting for 82 per cent of the employees in these fields in NSW, whereas it only represents 65 per cent of the state's population. In Melbourne the corresponding figures are 88 per cent versus 76 per cent. The differences become even more pronounced when we look at where the most senior staff, and hence the highest-paying jobs, are based. Of the 519 000 'management and professional' jobs in this sector nationally, 57 per cent are based in Sydney or Melbourne, while 130000 (85 per cent) of NSW's 162000 managers and professionals are to be found in Sydney. In Melbourne the figure is 90 per cent.

It is not only the jobs that these people perform that are based within the cities, the places where they live are also geographically narrow. While the epithets latte-land and chardonnay-belt thrown at academics and the Left by conservatives and cultural warriors are overblown, certain neighbourhoods and electorates within the big cities are home to disproportionately high numbers of academics and workers in the public and community sector. Needless to say, many of these are located in the inner city and often adjacent to university campuses. In the state electorate of Newtown in Sydney, which covers a number of suburbs in the city's gentrifying inner west and which has been represented by the Greens since its creation in 2013, more than half of the workforce are managers or professionals. More than 10000 of these work in the fields of 'professional, technical and scientific services' and 'education and training' alone, while another 2250 are managers or professionals in the 'information, media and telecommunications' sectors. Nearly 3000 have the same roles in 'health care and social assistance'. In contrast, in what was until the 1970s a working-class area, fewer than 2700 people (6 per cent) are now machinery operators and drivers or labourers.

The occupational profile of the new working-class heartland of Sydney to the south and west of the CBD is markedly different. In the state electorate of Liverpool, which has been held by Labor since its creation in 1950, managers and professionals represent less than 15 per cent of the workforce, with health care and assistance workers the single largest professional group. Just over 25 per cent of the locals are machine operators, drivers or labourers. But perhaps the biggest difference between the two electorates is in educational attainment. In Newtown high proportions have degrees and indeed postgraduate qualifications, whereas in Liverpool most people only have a high school education. Although 44 per cent of Newtown's adults have degrees, only 11 per cent of Liverpool's do, and perhaps more tellingly, while 53 per cent of Newtown's under-44s – the age groups that have had access to the massively expanded and democratised higher education system of the post-industrial era, which we will come back to in chapter 6 – have degrees (and 15.5 per cent postgraduate qualifications), in Liverpool the comparable figures are 20 per cent and 5 per cent. Newtown is not only very different to other parts of Sydney in its educational profile, however. So too are both it and Sydney more generally different from the national norm; across Greater Sydney 30 per cent of the adult population and 38 per cent of the under-44 population has a degree, while in Australia more generally the figures are 24 per cent and 30 per cent. Melbourne's numbers are almost exactly the same as Sydney's, being 30 per cent and 38 per cent, which in turn means that of Australia's nearly 4.2 million degree-qualified adults, more than 50 per cent live in the two major cities that between them only account for 40 per cent of the national population.

It is not just in degree qualifications that the two biggest cities stand apart from the nation, however. Globalisation and the increasing importance of the financial sector has also seen the two major cities', and indeed parts of the cities', economies diverge from the national norm in recent decades. In this case, however, there is a divergence between Sydney and Melbourne and the rest, but also between Sydney and Melbourne, with Sydney way out in front. While until the 1970s Melbourne was the nation's business capital, home to the major banks and other finance houses as well as the major resources and manufacturing companies, beginning in the late 1970s Sydney began to take on that role and in the 1980s became by far the dominant city for finance, business services, the media and tourism. It is these industries that give Sydney its global feel. Of the almost 385 000 financial and insurance services jobs in Australia in 2016, 145 000 (38 per cent) were located in Sydney, while its nearest rival Melbourne had less than 95 000 (25 per cent). And here again, as with the scientific and research jobs discussed above, Sydney also has an outsized share of the more senior and hence high-paying jobs in this field, with more than 40 per cent of the nation's financial services, managers and professionals based there. Again, Melbourne comes in a very poor second, with 26 per cent. The rest of the nation – urban, rural and regional – makes up the remaining 32 per cent.

Jobs in the information, media and telecommunications fields are also disproportionately based in Sydney and to a lesser extent Melbourne, with the former home to about 35 per cent of the national jobs and the latter about 25 per cent. As the headquarters of nearly all of the nation's major media outlets, Sydney not surprisingly has about 37 per cent of the jobs in publishing, 46 per cent of those in broadcasting, and is by far the dominant force in the emerging field of internet publishing, with 64 per cent of the jobs in what is admittedly still a very small field (only 2122 jobs nationally) based there. Motion picture and sound recording activities are more evenly shared between the two big cities, with Sydney amounting for 32 per cent of these jobs and Melbourne 26 per cent. But again, in all these fields it is less about raw numbers and more about power. It is no surprise then that the managers and professional employees in these industries overwhelmingly live in Sydney – 40 per cent of the managers and 42 per cent of the professionals. Melbourne comes in a distant second with 29 per cent and 27 per cent respectively. But again these figures mean that the rest of the country, with 60 per cent of the national population, has less than one-third of the managers or professionals in these industry sectors.

Not only are disproportionate numbers of these well-paid finance jobs located in Sydney and Melbourne, the people who do them are increasingly residentially segregated from non-urban Australians and also from their fellow city dwellers. In Sydney the senior echelons of the banking and financial industries disproportionately live in a few suburbs east and north of the Harbour, while in Melbourne they are to be found in the inner east and south-east. In

Mosman on Sydney's lower north shore, for example, 10 per cent of the workforce of 14 000 people are managers or professionals in the financial services field, while 16 per cent perform the same roles in professional, scientific and research services. Between them, then, managers and professionals in these fields represent 26 per cent of the local workforce, whereas nationally they represent less than 0.6 per cent. So too in the electorate of Kew in Melbourne's inner east, a wealthy blue-ribbon electorate held by the Liberal Party and its predecessors since 1927, these people represent 15 per cent of the labour force, 25 times the national average. Across town in the formerly industrial electorate of Broadmeadows the figure is 0.35 per cent. Such disparities might mean it is debatable which of these places should more rightly be labelled ghettoes.

Hundreds of thousands of other Australians work in what anthropologist and critic David Graeber calls 'bullshit jobs', the seemingly ever-growing ranks of managers, marketers and others who Graeber alleges 'spend their entire working lives performing tasks they secretly believe do not really need to be performed'. Many of these jobs, such as human resources professional, simply did not exist in the industrial era when most of us worked in factories and got paid in cash at the end of each week, and when administration was a function of production rather than an end in itself. Finance managers and professionals, media analysts and computer nerds (and indeed academics, including historians) may or may not perform these bullshit jobs, but business, human resource and marketing professionals arguably do. Such workers, who for many of us are the bane of our daily existence and whose job tasks and titles seem to be understood by no-one but themselves, now account for nearly 600 000 people, or 5 per cent of the national workforce. Needless to say, most of these are resident in the two major capitals, most notably Sydney, which accounts for over 30 per cent of the national total. Melbourne has 25 per cent. And again, like their peers in finance, the media and education, they tend to settle near each other in select neighbourhoods of the city, especially in Sydney's north and Melbourne's east. Nearly 11 per cent of the of the 211 000-strong workforce of North Sydney and Hornsby statistical district perform these possibly unnecessary tasks, as do 8 per cent of the 144 000 workers of Melbourne's inner east, which includes the suburbs of Hawthorn, Kew and Balwyn among others.

As in the industrialising nineteenth century when, as a number of economic and urban historians pointed out years ago, building the city was one of the key drivers of economic growth, so too in the post-industrial period building, construction and property development is one of the major economic activities of revitalised cities across the world. Building the workplaces that house all these white-collar workers, teachers, academics, doctors and nurses, as well as the hotels, apartments and leisure facilities that characterise the modern leisure- and tourism-based economy, is not only an important employment sector in the post-industrial era but also one of the few high-paying occupations left in the city for unskilled, mostly male labourers. Census figures bear out this out and show that just over 900 000 people – about the same number as those in education – work within this industry sector. But unlike that sector, most of these are men (87 per cent) rather than women. Tradies and technicians dominate, accounting for almost 50 per cent of workers in the sector, but unlike manufacturing, which has upskilled in recent decades, large numbers of construction workers remain labourers, who number nearly 140 000 or 15 per cent of the national construction workforce. As such this is one of few industries left in the nation that is both dominated by blue-collar workers and, especially in the commercial and high-rise residential field, is still heavily unionised. And like education and research, this sector of the construction industry is also distinctly urban, with a strong bias in favour of the two major cities, which are currently witnessing major building booms. This is especially the case in Sydney, which has for several years now resembled a giant building site.

Working and not working in the post-industrial city

While some current politicians still like to extol the virtues of cranes on the horizons of their capital cities as a reflection of economic vitality, others are a little more coy about claiming responsibility for the good times, worried perhaps that given that the 1980s boom ended in tears and double-digit unemployment, they, like Cain and Keating before them, might also get the blame if and when it all goes bad. Other players are not so reticent about the linking construction activity and economic good times, with various organisations here and abroad now extolling 'crane counts' as a symbol of a city's economic power. One such international organisation is Rider Levett Bucknall (RLB) Oceania Research & Development and Communication, which in 2012 'created the RLB Crane Index' which, it argues, offers 'a simple insight into the construction sector's health'. Conducted biennially, its July 2017 count certainly showed the extent of the recent Sydney residential construction boom. The city's 334 cranes represented 50 per cent of the national total, while Melbourne – which came in second place – could only muster 146 (22 per cent). Brisbane came in third with 81 (12 per cent), while Perth's dismal 24 clearly demonstrates the impact of the collapse of the post-2010 building boom funded off the back of the mining sector; its count was 50 per cent lower than it had been the previous year.

Of Sydney's 334 cranes, more than 87 per cent (292) were building apartment blocks, with only 13 constructing offices. Unlike in other cities, where the building boom is quite localised and mostly centred on the gentrifying inner suburbs, in Sydney cranes were to be found across the metropolitan area with the city's 'second CBD', Parramatta, alone having 12, almost as many as the whole of metropolitan Adelaide (15). In Melbourne the residential figure was roughly similar at 84 per cent, but most of these were in the CBD and inner suburbs. In the southern capital there were nine office project cranes while ten were being used to build and rebuild the city's health, education and civic facilities. In Sydney this figure was

13 with five in the health sector, while a series of massive infrastructure projects, needed to catch up with let alone get in front of the pressures of rapid population growth in the city, saw seven cranes working on civil projects.

The wide geographic spread of Sydney's current construction boom means that many of the city's tradies and labourers are likely to live in some proximity to their work. Not so in Melbourne where the construction sites are in the city centre and the inner north and eastern suburbs while the workers live in the outer regions. As with finance and research services, the contrast between the residential profiles of the electorates of Broadmeadows and Kew is stark here. In the former, nearly 80 per cent of the nearly 2000 residents who work in the construction sector (which accounts for just under 9 per cent of the local workforce, and thus about the same as the national average) are tradespeople or labourers, while in Kew the managers and professionals proliferate. There, more than 580 (44 per cent) of the 1334 people in the electorate who work in this industry sector (less than 5 per cent of the local workforce) are mangers or professionals. Kew is not all white collar though, as nearly 500 construction tradespeople and technicians also live there. Not labourers, however, with only 108 resident there in 2016, significantly less than the 166 clerks and administrators from this industry who also reside in the electorate.

While the vast majority of the cranes on the national skyline are building apartment blocks, just 30 are for new office buildings. Nor is it a surprise that RLB found no cranes anywhere in Australia devoted to the construction of new factories. It did, however, find 11 on the sites of new hotel developments and six more constructing or extending shopping centres – all of which, as in the 1980s, are symbolic of the needs of the post-industrial consumption-based economy rather than the old productive industrial one. These hotels and shopping centres represent the final major sectors of the new Australian economy: hospitality and retail; which between them account for nearly 1.8 million jobs, or just under 17 per cent of the national workforce. At just over one million employees, retail is the largest employment category in the country after health care and social assistance. And as with both the education and the health sectors, retail and hospitality are not only industries that have grown massively in the post-industrial era but are also dominated by women. And like education and health, they both also have distinctly bifurcated employment profiles, with a small number of high-paying and secure jobs at one end and a large majority of precarious low-paying ones at the other.

Retail now accounts for about 10 per cent of all jobs nationally, up slightly from 1971 when it was 8.5 per cent But unlike back then, it is now predominantly female, with about 60 per cent female employees today compared to 48 per cent in 1971. It is also dominated by part-time workers – that is, people who work for less than 35 hours per week – who account for 63 per cent of employees. Nearly 40 per cent work less than 24 hours per week and 25 per cent less than 15 hours. While many of these part-timers are likely women with children who juggle part-time work with family responsibilities, many others are likely the tens of thousands of local and international students who now combine their studies with part-time work, both of which are groups and employment opportunities that hardly existed before the restructuring of the economy in the 1980s when employment was mostly full-time, there were very few university students and virtually no international ones. The fact that nearly as many young men work part-time in retail as do young women seems to confirm this.

The growth in part-time jobs not only reflects the restructuring of the economy and thus what sorts of jobs we do, or indeed just the spectacular growth in student numbers since the 1980s, but also the profound changes in the way we shop and socialise and what we spend our money on today. Until the mid-1980s shopping was something you did in a hurry as most shops closed at 5.30 or

6.00 pm on weekdays and at 11.00 am or midday on Saturdays. That said, most states permitted late trading till 9.00 pm or so on one designated night of the week, usually Thursday or Friday, sometimes one night for suburban centres and the other for the city centre. Other than in designated tourist areas, few shops – apart from milk bars, bakeries and what were then called mixed businesses (essentially large milk bars or delis) – opened on Sundays. This meant that city suburban streets and shopping centres were dead zones most evenings and on Saturday afternoons and Sundays, and given that there were no customers around, by definition there was also no need for staff – especially part-time ones.

This all changed in the 1980s and 1990s when shopping hours were extended in most cities to Saturday afternoons and well into the evenings on most other days, and then later to Sundays as well. In Victoria under the Kennett government, trading hours were deregulated entirely in the 1990s, allowing shopkeepers (or more often their landlords) to choose their own hours, meaning that many supermarkets now trade 24 hours per day, seven days per week, although most other businesses – including department stores – tend to close in the early evening. Similar ideas and deregulatory impulses have seen hotel and liquor trading hours relaxed in recent decades. While until the 1970s hotels mostly closed at 10.00 pm after trading hours were extended from 6.00 pm in most states in the 1950s and 1960s, many states now allow bars, pubs and clubs to trade well into the night, and in some places 24 hours a day, seven days a week. 'Dry' evenings and Sundays are now a distant memory. So too are restrictions on gambling and poker machines, which in all states bar Western Australia are now a ubiquitous feature of urban, suburban and regional landscapes.

While these relaxations on restrictions on shopping, drinking and gambling reflect changing social and cultural attitudes as well as new ideas about freedom of choice and the free market, they are also a reaction to the emergence of mass tourism, and especially mass international tourism since the 1970s. By definition, the tourist industry requires accommodation to be available, shops and restaurants to be open and rooms and beds cleaned and made at whatever hours customers demand. It also requires airports and other tourist facilities to be open 24 hours a day, seven days per week, to handle international time zones. In 1971 when the shops were mostly closed and the pubs barely open and international tourism was virtually non-existent, what were called service, sport and recreation workers – which back then included, alongside workers in the hospitality and tourism sector, police, ambulance drivers and fire fighters – were a minor component of the national workforce, employing fewer than 400 000 people or less than a quarter of those employed in manufacturing. Even in 1981, as tourism and the leisure industry began to blossom but before the Japanese-led tourism boom got underway, there were still twice as many manufacturing workers as workers in the hospitality fields, whereas today that figure has essentially reversed. And while the Fordist factory economy also ran 24 hours per day and often seven days per week, at least those workers had regular full-time hours and overtime pay if they did extra shifts. Today's hospitality workers are part-timers or casuals who work irregular hours, albeit usually on penalty rates for night-time and weekend work; more than half of them are employed for less than 24 hours per week, nearly one-third of them less than 15.

Conclusion

In the wake of the Tokyo share- and residential property-market crash, the major 1980s Japanese property development companies vacated the Australian market. Their former trophy developments, which for a short time in the late 1980s had seemed like such good investments, were soon seen as expensive follies, evidence of a boom that was based on inflated land and share values and speculation rather than solid investments in the then-emerging post-industrial services economy. Because of this, liquidating these assets or converting them to new uses became one of the growth areas of the mid-1990s Australian economy, helping to jump-start it from the deep recession of the early years of the decade. The massive Hotel Nikko, built on the site of the former Chevron Hotel in Sydney's Potts Point, in 1988 was sold to Australian developer Mirvac and in 1997 converted to apartments, less than ten years after it was built; while its sister hotel in Darling Harbour became a Four Points by Sheraton in the early 2000s and more recently has been extensively refurbished to become a Hyatt Regency. Closer to the Harbour Bridge, another extravagant late-1980s Japanese-funded hotel, the ANA, was bought by a company associated with the Singapore government in 2003 and became part of the Hong Kong-based Shangri-La group. It is now controlled by the Malaysian Kuok family. On the Gold Coast, the group's second Australian hotel became a Holiday Inn in the early 2000s and is now managed by the Australian-owned Mantra Group.

In 2001 Daimaru finally pulled out of Australia after sustaining years of losses on its Melbourne and Gold Coast stores, while its former landlord Kumagai Gumi had bailed out of its Melbourne Central investment in 1994, selling the complex to Australia's General Property Trust for about one-third of its construction cost of $1.2 billion. What had been a symbol of Premier John Cain's post-industrial Melbourne success story in 1988 was by the mid-1990s seen as evidence of all that was wrong with basing the new economy on speculative foreign property-based capital rather than genuine long-term sustainable growth options. Whether the 300-plus cranes currently building the largely foreign-funded apartment blocks that are such a feature of Sydney's contemporary skyline will in future be similarly regarded is of course as yet unknown. Certainly as I walked the city's streets and rode its trains while researching this book in October 2017, I was eerily reminded of Melbourne in 1989 and indeed of Dublin in 2007 just before its property bubble burst. But for now Sydney is booming, its current unemployment rate below 5 per cent which, while high by the standards of the Fordist era, is around the lowest it has been since the early 2000s, partly because the industrialisation of China is both sending billions of dollars of apartment investment its way but also because that same industrialisation is feeding the city's population growth and tourism sectors.

In Melbourne a rapidly expanding international education sector and an economy increasingly based on consumption and leisure rather than production has led to massive population growth in recent years, most of it through international immigration. In each of these areas – immigration, education and the built fabric of the cities, as with the new structure of their economies we have discussed in this section – Sydney and Melbourne are increasingly different from the rest of the country. As we shall see in chapters 4–6, both are the major destinations and settlement nodes of immigrants – Sydney previously more so than Melbourne, but the latter is catching up fast – and the main destinations for international students who now number almost 600 000 and who have since the 1990s become the third largest source of foreign income for the nation, which no longer rides on the sheep's back nor indeed in the hull of a bulk carrier. The big cities are also where new forms of urbanism are being experimented with, in city-centre and inner-urban apartment living and new leisure and pleasure precincts, often built on the sites of the factories and docks that have closed in the wake of the economic restructuring we have documented in this and the preceding chapters. It is to these aspects of the new Australian city that we now turn.

4

Cosmopolis: Urban multiculturalism

It is not only the number of cranes on Sydney and Melbourne sky-lines, nor the jobs that the residents of each of these cities do that sets them apart from the rest of Australia. So too do their roles as the nation's immigrant gateways, and thus their demographic pro-files. Sydney and Melbourne are now essentially ethnically detached from not only the hinterlands of their own states but also most of the other state capitals too. While immigration statistics are counted at the national level, even the most cursory glance at figures for birthplace at the city level demonstrates that immigration and its impacts – for better or worse – is almost entirely an urban phenom-enon and becoming increasingly so. Commentator Tim Colebatch's recent analysis of the 2016 Census figures demonstrates that, while the two biggest cities maintain their national share of population at about 40 per cent, between them they are the preferred destina-tion of more than 70 per cent of new immigrants to Australia, and virtually all new migrants from certain countries, especially China and the Middle East. His figures also show that not only are the two major cities home to the vast bulk of immigrants from these source countries but also that almost all immigrants from these countries are city dwellers, with virtually none choosing to reside in rural or regional areas.

This is not a new phenomenon, however. As Rachel Stevens and I have recently shown, the urban bias in Australian immigrant settlement patterns has been evident since the beginnings of the mass immigration program that got underway in the 1940s and has widened since the end of the White Australia policy in the early 1970s. The outcome of this, we suggest, is that rather than Australia being a multicultural nation it should more rightly be classified as a nation of multicultural cities; with two – Melbourne and Sydney – more appropriately called hyperdiverse, such is their level of their ethnic diversity. As we shall see in this chapter, the cities became more ethnically diverse than the regions in the 1950s and 1960s but since the 1970s this divergence and the increasing separation of Sydney and to a lesser degree Melbourne from the national ethnic profile has become ever more pronounced. That these changes have coincided with the emergence of globalisation and the post-industrial economy is no coincidence.

Nor is it a coincidence that these differences are increasing, and that they are breeding some of the resentments we are seeing in national political debates, such as the rise of political parties committed to slowing immigration and ending multiculturalism; and indeed the increasingly harsh treatment of refugees and asylum seekers, very few of whom settle in the regions where supporters of these policies tend to live. Opposition to immigration is thus likely to represent a fear of 'the other' and a sense of potentially becoming a stranger in one's own country rather than a rational reaction to new neighbours with possibly exotic values and customs. This is not simply a local phenomenon, of course. Across the world we are seeing not only increasing numbers of immigrants and asylum seekers but also electoral backlashes against them. We are also seeing growing resentment against cities and their residents who, as in Australia, are increasingly ethnically and culturally different from their other countrymen and women.

In this and the following two chapters, then, we move on from documenting the economic changes seen in the last four decades to look at the social and demographic changes. In doing so, we again see that major changes in government policy implemented at the national level have had a disproportionate effect at the city level, and especially so on Sydney and Melbourne. And arguably, as with the economic and employment changes documented in the previous chapter, more so on Sydney than Melbourne. In this chapter we look at national and urban demographic changes across time to trace the impact of migration on the major cities, especially in the four decades since the 1970s. Before that, however, we go back another generation to look at immigration since the end of the Second World War and the beginnings of the postwar immigration program to see how the increasing ethnic divergence of the cities from the regions goes back to the early days of that policy but stepped up after the 1970s.

As with the phasing out of tariff-based industry protection and the integration of Australia into both the Asian economy and the wider globalising world economy, so too did the ending of racially based immigration policies affect different regions of the country, and indeed regions of the cities, in different ways. This chapter also demonstrates that while policy and economic changes have seen the two major cities diverge not only from national norms and the experiences of the smaller state capitals, but also from each other. Beginning in the late 1970s, Sydney's ethnic profile began to move away from Melbourne's and to develop firstly a strong Middle Eastern flavour and then, especially after the deregulation of the financial sector in the mid-1980s and into the 1990s when Sydney became the nation's immigrant gateway and financial centre, a much stronger Asian one. Finally, however, we shall see that in more recent years this difference has narrowed somewhat, with Melbourne first catching up with Sydney as an immigrant gateway in the 1990s and then in the 2000s beginning to overtake it as the fastest growing and likely to become into the future the most ethnically diverse city in the country.

Becoming multicultural

When Australia embarked on its mass immigration program after the Second World War, the assumption was that most of the new arrivals would come from traditional sources: essentially England, Ireland, Scotland and Wales, with only small numbers coming from continental Europe. It was therefore assumed that the country would change only slightly and that its existing ethnic make-up would remain largely intact. To the modern city-dweller's eyes that ethnic make-up is almost impossible to imagine; in 1947, at the time of the first postwar census, less than 10 per cent of the national population was overseas-born, with the vast majority of these hailing from the United Kingdom and Ireland. At that time less than 2 per cent of the population were from a non-English-speaking country, with many of these having been born in colonies of the former British Empire and thus almost certainly ethnically European. While these numbers are striking enough in themselves (the national figure for the overseas-born at the 2016 Census was 32.3 per cent), more surprising to contemporary observers is that those overseas-born numbers were essentially the same for both urban and rural areas. Whereas today 10 per cent overseas-born would be considered a high figure in many country towns, in the major capitals the number climbs from a low of 20 per cent in Hobart to 43 per cent (nearly 2.5 million people) in Sydney. Of these, less than 200 000 were born in the United Kingdom or Ireland, with far more contemporary Sydneysiders born in China than in England.

Differences between the ethnic make-up of the major cities and rural and regional Australia (and indeed the smaller capitals) happened very quickly and were already quite pronounced only 20 years after the war in 1966, when the fourth postwar census was taken. That census showed that in less than a generation the ethnic profile of the Australian population had been transformed by immigration. While the national population had grown by more than one-third to 11.5 million in those 19 years, the overseas-born portion nearly doubled to 18.5 per cent with fully 10 per cent of the population from non-English-speaking countries. More than 267 000 Italians, 140 000 Greeks, 108 000 Germans, 100 000 Dutch and more than 60 000 Poles settled in Australia in the early postwar years, as did a sizeable non-European-born population, including more than 100 000 who had been born in Asia. But given this was still the period when non-European immigration was strictly controlled by the White Australia policy, it is likely that most of those born in Asia were members of European expatriate communities, especially from India and Indonesia, who settled here rather than return to their European homelands after decolonisation. The same is true for the more than 22 000 settlers from the United Arab Republic and a further 10 000 from Lebanon, who were likely members of diasporic Jewish, Italian, Greek and Armenian populations who were either expelled from these countries at that time or decided to leave their long-established homes there in the face of rising nationalist and religious tensions.

For our purposes, the major change seen in the years between 1947 and 1966 was not only that the country had changed, but also that the major cities, and most especially Sydney and Melbourne, had begun to diverge demographically from the rest of the nation. Whereas in 1947 the two big cities had ethnic profiles that essentially matched the national norm, by 1966 Sydney's population was 22 per cent overseas-born and Melbourne's 26 per cent. Perhaps not surprisingly, given its high concentration of manufacturing industry, Melbourne's overseas-born population grew rapidly in the postwar years when these jobs were plentiful; by 1966 Melbourne's overseas-born population was larger percentage-wise than Sydney's but also numerically too, even though Melbourne's total urban population was 300 000 less than that of its northern counterpart. The two big cities were not only magnets for immigrants generally, but for non-English-speaking settlers in particular. Whereas between them Melbourne and Sydney accounted for approximately

40 per cent of the national population in 1966, together they housed nearly 47 per cent of all immigrants and 57 per cent of those born in non-English-speaking countries. Melbourne was exceptional in that nearly two-thirds of its overseas-born population came from such countries, and it had especially high numbers of Southern Europeans. Home to less than 20 per cent of the national population, Melbourne accounted for more than 30 per cent of the country's Italians and more than 40 per cent of its Greeks. More than one-third of Australia's Polish-born population also lived in Melbourne, many of them Jews, especially Holocaust survivors, who we know from other sources overwhelmingly settled in Melbourne. Sydney on the other hand had a disproportionately high number of Jewish settlers from Hungary and other Central European countries. More than one-third of Australia's Hungarian-born population lived there in 1966, as did a similar percentage of the Austrian-born. The Chinese-born were also over-represented in Sydney, with more than 60 per cent of what was then still a very small national population total based there.

At a local level, by the 1960s distinct areas of ethnic concentration had begun to develop in the cities and arguably for the first time Australian cities began to take on some of the features of the famous concentric city model of Robert Parks and Ernest Burgess of the Chicago School of Sociology, first applied to their home city in the 1920s. In inner Adelaide, 30 per cent of the populations of the municipalities of Hindmarsh, Kensington and Norwood were European-born (in both cases more than 10 per cent from Italy alone), while in inner Melbourne, Carlton, which had had been home to small Italian and Jewish populations before the war, took on a distinctly European feel afterwards. As novelist Arnold Zable, among others, has documented, in the postwar years Carlton became a refuge for Holocaust survivors granted entry under the Displaced Persons humanitarian program, grudgingly instituted when the full horrors of what had happened in Europe began to become clear. The suburb was also an important site of residence and business for the small Italian community in the 1930s but fully came into its own in the postwar period. As sociologist Frank Lancaster Jones observed in the mid-1960s, this area accounted for 'one in seven Italian born persons in the Commonwealth of Australia'. Just to the north of Carlton, Brunswick was similarly an important centre of primary and secondary immigrant settlement in the postwar years, so much so that by 1966 40 per cent of its 52 000 residents were overseas-born, more than 10 000 from Italy alone.

By the mid-1960s immigrants formed an arc of settlement across Melbourne's inner city, with more than 40 per cent of the populations of the municipalities of Fitzroy and Collingwood being European born. If the Australian-born children of these immigrants are included in these totals, possibly as many as two-thirds of the residents of these suburbs were immigrants or their children. Two decades earlier, less than 1800 of Collingwood's 30 000 residents had been born in Europe, with fewer than 300 born outside of the British Isles. South of the city centre, in the formerly salubrious but now declining seaside resort of St Kilda, the European-born immigrants became a notable feature of the demography, culture and business community in this period. In 1966 just over 10 per cent of St Kilda's population were Polish-born, many of whom were recent Jewish immigrants – many Holocaust Survivors and their families. The Jewish community went on to become a highly visible cultural and commercial presence in St Kilda after the war, with their business activities in the retail and property sector having a profound impact on the residential and morphological structure of this region in the 1960s and 1970s.

In Sydney most Central and Eastern Europeans lived in the inner eastern suburbs, particularly in the municipality of Waverley, which was home to nearly 16 per cent of the city's Hungarian community. As in Melbourne, Italians lived in inner city neighbourhoods, with the core City of Sydney municipal area home to 7 per

Opening of the Sydney Opera House, October 1973.

National Archives of Australia

Street Life, Cabramatta, Sydney 1991.

National Archives of Australia

Burundian dancers, Little Africa, Footscray, Melbourne 2018.

Seamus O'Hanlon

Above Melbourne, the Yarra and Southbank looking east from the Rialto Tower, 1983.

State Library Victoria, photograph by Laurie Thomas

Right A model of the proposed South Yarra Development, Melbourne, early 1980s.

Image courtesy of DCM Architects, Melbourne

Above Darling Harbour, Sydney 1984.

City of Sydney Archives, photograph by Graeme Andrews

Top right The Boys Next Door, Melbourne 1978.

Gallery and National Library of Australia, photograph by Peter Milne

Below right Rundown housing, Gertrude Street, Fitzroy 1979.

Image courtesy of Graeme Butler

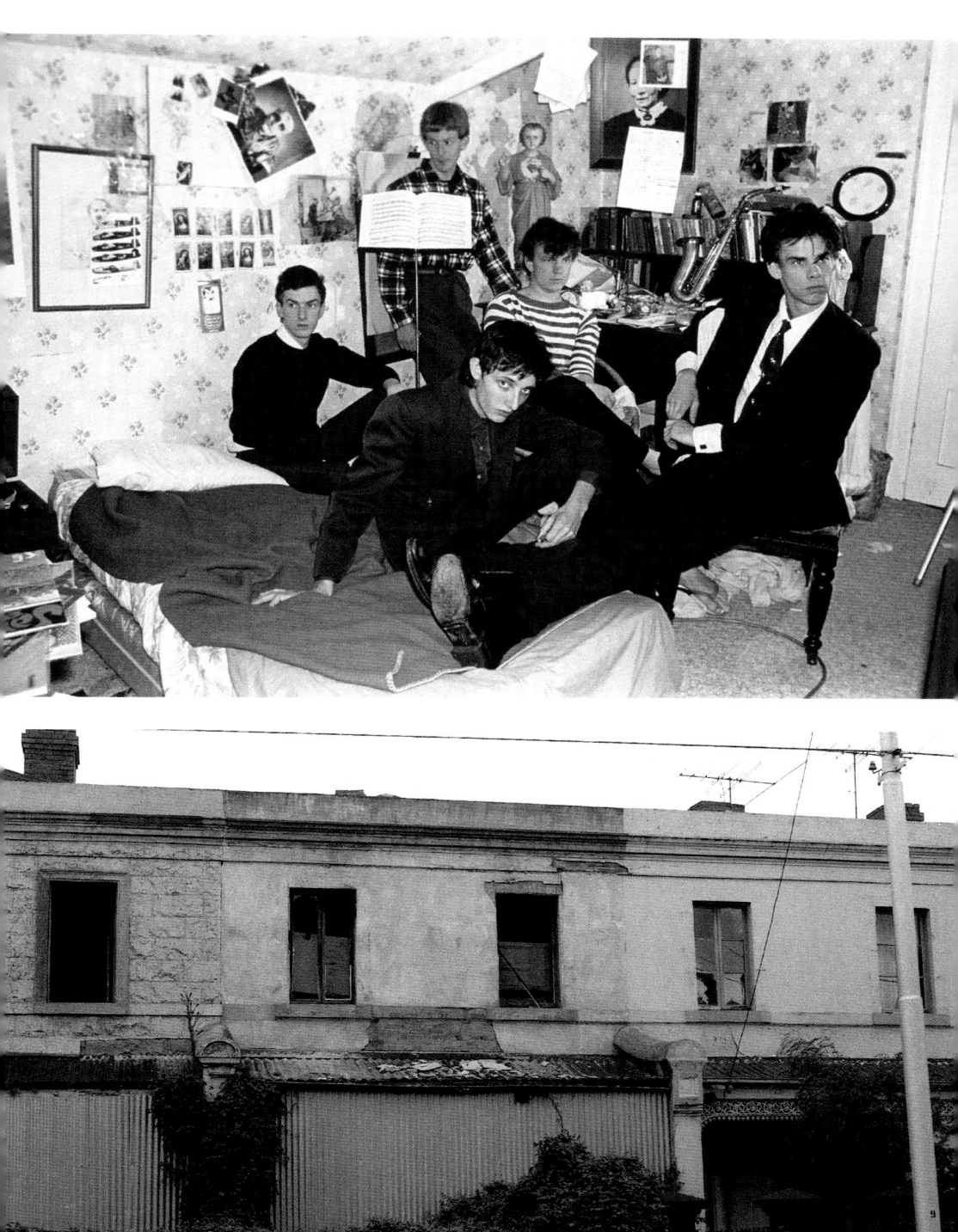

9

Australia's front door: Sydney Harbour 2015.

iStock, Getty Images, photo by courtneyk

Urban grunge, AC/DC Lane, Melbourne 2018.

Image courtesy of Catherine Strong

cent of the city's more than 56 000 Italians. Neighbouring Leich-hardt accounted for a further 10 per cent. The City of Sydney was also home to by far the largest municipal concentration of Greeks in the country, with its 12 500 Greeks accounting for more than one person in five of the area's population. This geographically small area housed almost 30 per cent of Sydney's metropolitan Greek-born population and almost 10 per cent of the national population at this time.

While the majority of European immigrants settled in inner city areas in Sydney, Melbourne and Adelaide, there was emerg-ing evidence of the growth of outer suburban ethnic enclaves by the 1960s. In the new outer urban satellite town of Elizabeth on the fringes of Adelaide (home of General Motors Holden – GMH), 45 per cent of the population was British- or Irish-born at the time of the 1966 Census; while in Melbourne, large numbers of English immigrants, such as Dennis Glover's family (see chapter 2), settled in Dandenong and similarly took up work in the automotive and other factories there. On the other side of the city in the outer west-ern suburbs, large numbers of Eastern Europeans settled in places like Sunshine, St Albans and Ardeer; while in Sydney future shop-ping centre moguls Frank Lowy and John Saunders started the Westfield chain from a small shop in Blacktown selling continental foods to the increasing numbers of Central and Eastern Europeans then settling in the city's outer western suburbs. South of Black-town, the semi-rural municipality of Fairfield, with its market gardens and other food production industries, was home to almost 10 per cent of Sydney's Italian-born population and to large con-centrations of Yugoslavian and Maltese immigrants. Werribee, in Melbourne's outer south-west, was similarly home to large numbers of European-born market gardeners.

It is no accident that the largest concentrations of immigrants were in the three south-eastern cities that were, as we have seen, the centres of the Australian manufacturing sector. In each of these cities, both skilled jobs that required formal training and thus English-language skills, and unskilled jobs that did not, were in plentiful supply as manufacturing expanded, especially on the sub-urban fringe. As manufacturing expanded so too did metropolitan populations. But when it stopped, problems began to set in, especially in Adelaide which even more so than Melbourne was overly reliant on protected industries for its prosperity. While today Adelaide is often portrayed as the poster-child of all that was wrong with relying on protected manufacturing industries for prosperity, until the early 1970s it had the opposite reputation. Like Sydney and Melbourne, in the 25 or so years after the war Adelaide was a magnet for immigrants like my Irish-born, working-class parents and their then six children, and like its big eastern states cousins was seen as a dynamic go-ahead city, strongly contrasted with the sleepy small-town vibe of Brisbane and Perth. In the first 20 years after the war Adelaide's population more than doubled and by 1966 27 per cent of its residents were overseas-born, higher than Sydney and Melbourne. More than 13 per cent were, like my family, from the UK or Ireland, but the city was also home to sizeable Italian, Greek, German, Polish and Dutch communities, which by 1966 between them accounted for nearly 10 per cent of the population.

Some of Adelaide's go-ahead reputation came from its youth-fulness, and especially the reputation of its music scene, which was heavily influenced by young people recently arrived in the city from the thriving music centres of London, Liverpool and Manchester. Nearly 40 per cent of Adelaide's population was aged under 21 in 1966, with about 10 per cent teenagers aged between 15 and 19. Outer suburban Elizabeth's population was heavily immigrant, with nearly half of its population of just under 33 000 born over-seas, almost all of them in the UK and Ireland. More than 50 per cent of Elizabeth's population was aged under 21, with just under 10 per cent aged 15–19 and a further 12 per cent aged 10–14. All these figures show us that in the postwar years both Adelaide generally and Elizabeth especially were major centres of immigration and the baby boom.

For this reason, for most of the early postwar period, Adelaide was Australia's third city, usually spoken of in combination with Sydney and Melbourne as one of the nation's three major metropolises. It was only in the late 1970s that it began to slip down that list and became, somewhat unfairly, the butt of jokes about its lack of excitement. As manufacturing declined nationally, Adelaide's population growth began to slow markedly before essentially grinding to a halt in the 1980s and beyond as the effects of deindustrialisation took effect. As a child growing up in the northern suburbs of Adelaide in the 1960s and 1970s, I knew many migrant kids whose fathers (and a few mothers) worked in the factories of Kilburn and Gepps Cross, Enfield and Salisbury. I also knew many who worked on the assembly line at GMH in Elizabeth. And while most of us were aware that Elizabeth had a reputation as a tough place — whose skinhead gangs were to be feared — at that time it, and Adelaide more generally, was still growing and was still a place where jobs were plentiful. That was no longer the case from the late 1970s when, while the population did continue to grow, it did so at a much slower rate: less than half the rate it had achieved in the period 1947 to 1966. The city also began to lose its young people to Sydney and Melbourne and ceased to be attractive to immigrants, even those from the UK and Ireland, who increasingly opted for Perth as their preferred Australian destination. Brisbane and the Gold Coast were also growing at this time, becoming increasingly popular permanent homes (rather than short-term tourist destinations) for people fleeing rising unemployment and the cold of the southern states, as well as attractive destinations for retirees and other immigrants from New Zealand. Adelaide was therefore overtaken by Brisbane as Australia's third largest city by the time of the 1971 Census and then in 1986 by Perth, relegating it to the position of the fifth largest urban centre in the country, a status it maintains to this day.

Becoming hyperdiverse

While Adelaide was stagnating and Brisbane and Perth were grow-ing on the back of internal migration and settlers from the UK and Ireland, Sydney and Melbourne were being rapidly transformed in the 1970s and 1980s by immigrants from an increasingly broad range of source countries. While the White Australia policy was slowly unwound from 1966 it was only formally abandoned in 1973, after which small numbers of immigrants from Asia began to settle in various places around the country. However, it was the end of the Vietnam War in 1975 and the subsequent arrival of refugees from there that really heralded the end of Australia's racially exclu-sive immigration policies. Again, it was the two major cities which were central to the resettlement process and which were to emerge as important international immigrant gateway cities from the late 1970s onwards. In becoming gateway cities, they were to further distance themselves from the ethnic make-up of not only rural and regional Australia but from the smaller capitals too.

The impacts of these changes and of the globalisation of Aus-tralian cities in the 1980s were to become very apparent at the 1991 Census, which showed that while nationally the number of overseas-born had increased to 4.125 million (or 24.5 per cent of the population), the number born in non-English-speaking countries had doubled to almost 2.2 million. The same census also showed that, for the first time, the majority of recent arrivals to Australia had come from non-European rather than European countries. Those born in continental Europe had stagnated at around 1.1 mil-lion, with some groups having actually declined in number: both the Italian- and Greek-born populations had shrunk from their late 1960s highs, mainly as a result of death and return migration. At the same time, and as a direct result of the end of the White Aus-tralia policy and the refugee flows caused by the end of the Vietnam War, Australia was increasingly sourcing its immigrants from Asia, especially East Asia. By 1991 the number of Australians born in

North and South-East Asia had grown to more than half a million, with the majority of all new immigrant arrivals (51.5 per cent) now coming from Asia rather than Europe. The vast majority of these were now ethnically Asian rather than European expatriates, with more than 250 000 Australians now speaking a Chinese language at home. The largest single national group was the 122 000 Vietnamese, but the combined Chinese and Hong Kong total exceeded them by nearly 18 000. When these are added to the large numbers of Malaysian-Chinese settlers, it is likely that by 1991 the ethnic Chinese already accounted for the largest proportion of Asian-Australians.

As had been the case since the 1940s, ethnic diversity was much more pronounced in the two big cities – and increasingly so in Sydney – than it was elsewhere. Whereas in 1991 the overseas-born represented 24.5 per cent of the national population, in Sydney they made up 33 per cent of the population and for the first time ever an Australian city had more than one million overseas-born residents. As a marker of Sydney's growing diversity, nearly 75 per cent of its overseas-born residents came from non-English-speaking backgrounds. A major spike in immigration nationally, and especially into Sydney in the late 1980s, also meant that by 1991 more than 275 000 people – nearly 9 per cent of the city's population – had been living in Australia for less than five years and nearly 7 per cent of Sydney's population was now Asian-born, up from only 2.6 per cent a decade earlier.

With 30 per cent overseas-born, Melbourne also received a disproportionate number of immigrants in the 1980s but at a slower rate than Sydney. Its ethnic profile was also increasingly characterised by more different national and cultural groups than that of its northern rival. Although by 1991 Melbourne had a large and growing Asian community, these people represented less than 4 per cent of the population and less than 12 per cent of those born in non-English-speaking countries. Most were from South-East Asia rather than Hong Kong or mainland China as in Sydney, with the largest group being the 44 000 Vietnamese, whose population had risen four-fold in a decade. Due to the surge in immigration in the late 1980s, large numbers of immigrants were recent arrivals, with more than 20 per cent of the city's overseas-born population having been in the country less than five years; but as Melbourne's manufacturing economy came under strain so too did its attraction for the unskilled, who could no longer be guaranteed work in the car factories or the TCF sector. Indeed as these unskilled jobs declined so too did the numbers of Greek- and Italian-born Melburnians, some of whom decided to spend their early retirement payouts and later, pensions, back in the cheaper home country.

Through the 1990s and early 2000s and then even more so with the surge in immigration from 2006, the major cities have further separated themselves from national demographic norms. Recently released census figures for 2016 bear this out, with both Sydney and Melbourne now having more than 40 per cent of their populations foreign-born. The number of Australians born in China now exceeds 500 000, most of whom are new arrivals, their numbers having swelled from just over 200 000 ten years earlier and by nearly 200 000 since 2011. Almost 44 per cent live in Sydney, with Melbourne accounting for another 30 per cent. Between them, then, the nation's other cities and regions (which account for four-fifths of the national population) are home to just a quarter of the national Chinese-born population. If the Hong Kong-born are added to these figures (never mind the Malaysian- and the Singaporean-born, who are predominantly ethnic Chinese), the two major capitals' popularity with Chinese-Australians is further strengthened. Nearly 50 per cent of the Hong Kong-born persons counted in Australia on Census night 2016 lived in Sydney and almost 25 per cent in Melbourne. Similar rates of dominance are found for the Vietnamese-born (75 per cent Sydney or Melbourne), the Iraqi-born (57.5 per cent Sydney, 26 per cent Melbourne), and most especially the Lebanese-born who are overwhelmingly (71 per cent) concentrated in Sydney.

The second fastest growing group, the Indian-born, are more evenly spread across the nation's cities but there is a distinct Melbourne bias, with over 35 per cent of the national population residing there, and Sydney accounting for another 28.5 per cent.

To fully understand a city's ethnic diversity, however, we need to look at more than simply place of birth. Numbers for recent arrivals give us a very clear sense of 'foreignness' as, by definition, these people are immigrants and were thus born overseas. But diversity must also account for the local-born offspring of immigrants who, while Australian born and raised, may be visibly ethnic and may maintain and cultivate cultural traditions. To ascertain the numbers and cultural impacts of more established ethnic communities, such as the descendants of those who arrived in the early postwar years, then, we need to look first at how many people have one or more overseas-born parents and second at how many self-identify as belonging to a particular ancestry group. Doing so again shows a disproportionate urban skew in Australia's ethnic profile. In drawing on census material for these figures, however, we need to be careful, as they are both optional and self-selected categories. It is also of course possible (indeed it is encouraged by the census collectors) to choose more than one ancestry, which means the totals add up to many times the national population. For example, a grandchild of a postwar European immigrant whose grandmother was born in Italy to a Maltese father and a Sicilian mother and whose father was born in England to an Irish mother and a Polish father could choose any or all of these ancestries as well as Australian, should they choose to. Such a scenario is possibly far-fetched but, given the extraordinary ethnic diversity of parts of contemporary Australia, not beyond the bounds of possibility. The success of Christos Tsiolkas' 2012 novel *The Slap*, with its myriad couplings and hence the multiple ethnic and cultural identities of its characters, suggests that this might be the experience of many families in the twenty-first century, who saw versions of themselves and their family stories in the book. Certainly, within my own extended family and friend-ship groups, such combinations are increasingly becoming the norm rather than the exception.

So while birthplace counts tell us that in 2016, 32 per cent of Australians were born overseas, less than 50 per cent of us are the children of two Australian-born parents. Perhaps not surprisingly, given recent immigration patterns, Sydney and Melbourne both score very highly on these counts. In Sydney less than one in three people have two Australian-born parents while nearly 50 per cent are the children of two immigrant parents. Another 11 per cent have an immigrant mother or father. In Melbourne the percentages are roughly similar, with 36 per cent having two Australian-born parents, 46 per cent having two immigrant parents and another 11 per cent having at least one. But as we noted above, it is not just the numbers of overseas-born that give us a sense of a city's ethnic profile and diversity. So too does where the immigrants come from. And here again the two big cities stand apart from the rest of the nation. Across the country, other than Australia the most common birthplace nationally was England, with New Zealand, China, India and the Philippines rounding out the top five. But here again Sydney and Melbourne are different. In Sydney the Chinese-born outnumber the English-born (225 000 to 150 000), with the latter about to be overtaken by the Indian-born who now total 130 000, up from just 53 000 ten years ago. They are then followed by New Zealand- and Vietnamese-born. In Melbourne the top five were India (up by 300 per cent in ten years), China, England, Vietnam and New Zealand.

As these figures suggest, raw numbers of overseas-born do not necessarily equate to ethnic diversity. While there is no ques-tion that Sydney's very high proportion of overseas-born reflects its extraordinary ethnic mix, Perth — which has the second highest per-centage of overseas-born after Sydney — although multicultural, is dominated by a very large number of immigrants from one place:

the United Kingdom. With nearly 43 per cent of its population born overseas and 66 per cent having at least one overseas-born parent, Perth has a higher percentage of immigrants than Melbourne, but unlike Melbourne it remains overwhelmingly white and ethnically European. Nearly 10 per cent of Perth's population were born in England, Scotland or Wales, while another 5 per cent were born in New Zealand or South Africa. A further 2 per cent were born in Ireland, meaning that nearly 40 per cent of the city's immigrant population is from white English-speaking countries. In Melbourne the corresponding figure is 15 per cent. To be fair though, Perth does have sizeable and growing population of residents from Asian nations such as India, Malaysia and the Philippines.

Perth's unusual situation of high levels of overseas-born combined with low rates of ethnic diversity shows us that ancestry can be used as a better indicator of a city's ethnic profile than the number of overseas-born. As we saw above, in Australia the census makes this a self-designation and allows for multiple descriptors, which means that it is a wholly unscientific measure of race and ethnicity (as it should be, given the historical misuse of such categories both in Australia and elsewhere), but even so these counts do give us a sense of the diversity of the nation and of the individual cities. Nationally at the time of the 2016 Census, other than Australian, the five most commonly cited ancestries were English (at 7.8 million, higher than Australian), Irish (2.4 million), Scottish (2 million), Chinese (1.2 million) and Italian (1 million). These rankings were broadly similar in Sydney, although there the Irish and the Scots were outranked by the Chinese, whose numbers, as we have seen, are rising rapidly, although it is unlikely they will ever challenge the English who still outnumber them 2.5 to 1. In Melbourne the Irish (410 000) are still a long way behind the English (1.2 million) and still outnumber the Chinese (356 000), although the latter are catching up fast. The Scots (329 000) come in third, just ahead of the Italians (300 000). Behind them, the Indians have challenged Melbourne's long-held status as an important Greek city, overtaking them to come in sixth (198 000 to 162 000 and rising fast).

Another measure of diversity is language spoken at home. And again, the stories of the cities differ from each other and from the nation. Whereas nationally nearly 75 per cent of us claim to only speak English at home, in Melbourne that figure drops to 60 per cent and in Sydney to 58 per cent. Across the country the most common language other than English is Mandarin, followed by Arabic, Cantonese, Vietnamese and Italian. Again, not surprisingly, these figures are heavily distorted by the sheer numbers of settlers from these groups in Sydney and Melbourne. Of the nearly 600 000 Mandarin speakers nationally, 38 per cent live in Sydney, as do 50 per cent of the Cantonese speakers. Sydney is also home to 60 per cent of the nation's Arabic speakers. Melbourne, the prime destination for European migrants in the 1950s and 1960s has, on the other hand, more speakers of European languages. Just over 37 per cent of the nation's Italian speakers live there, as do 45 per cent of those who speak Greek. The other big destination for postwar European migrants, Adelaide, also has large numbers of Greek and Italian speakers; while the city is home to only 5 per cent of the national population, nearly 10 per cent of the nation's Italian speakers live there, as do just under 10 per cent of the Greek speakers. Perth too has a reasonably large Italian-speaking population, about 10 per cent of the national total; but very few Greeks – less than 5000 – in a city approaching two million people.

Brisbane is the most 'Australian' of the big mainland capitals. With 32 per cent of its population born overseas it almost exactly matches the national profile of local versus overseas-born but, like Perth, most of these immigrants come from English-speaking countries, with New Zealanders disproportionately represented, accounting for almost 5 per cent of the population. South Africans also seem to like Brisbane's warm climate. Their numbers have nearly doubled since 2006. The most numerous ancestries for

Brisbane (after Australian) are English, Irish, Scottish, German and Chinese, with the latter having doubled in the last ten years, suggesting that they too like the sun. Other than English, Brisbane's major language is Mandarin, spoken by just over 50 000 people. Another 19 600 speak Cantonese. The growth in Chinese-speaking immigrants suggests that Brisbane may in future join the other big mainland cities as an important immigrant settlement destination, but if so it still has a long way to go to catch up with Melbourne and Sydney in its ethnic and language diversity. Based on its current language profile it remains a place that has little attraction for European immigrants or their children and grandchildren. Just 10 000 people out of Brisbane's population of more than 2.2 million speak Italian and only 7500 speak Greek.

The urban–rural divide

While Brisbane's overseas-born numbers and its growing Chinese-born population might parallel the national story, its ethnic profile is, like that of all the other major cities, way out of sync with non-urban Australia. The high numbers of immigrants in the cities increasingly artificially inflates the national average for the percentage of overseas-born, meaning that many city-dwellers have a very distorted view of Australia's contemporary ethnic make-up. While people in Sydney can easily be forgiven for assuming that about one in ten of us is of Asian background, or Melburnians that Italians and Greeks are 'typically' Australian, in reality the vast majority of us remain white and Anglo-Saxon (or Celtic). When an advertisement entitled 'Build Australia First', about providing jobs to locals rather than visa holders, was put out by the ALP in 2017 it caused uproar because only one of the 12 actors depicted was of Asian appearance. The ensuing outcry saw the advertisement described as 'a throwback' and 'a shocker' by politicians and commentators before it was hurriedly withdrawn. And indeed the advertisement did represent a throwback to an older, less diverse nation for most residents of urban Australia. But it did actually depict the reality of non-urban Australia, where very few people are immigrants, and the overwhelming majority of those who were born overseas are of a European background.

As Tim Colebatch argues in his recent *Inside Story* article, the 2016 Census proved that there are now multiple Australias, with geography and ethnicity one of the significant cleavages between these. His analysis featured three federal electorates in Victoria: the first, Melbourne, an inner urban seat held by the Greens; the second, Aston, an outer suburban seat held by the Liberals; and the third the rural seat of Wannon, which was once the seat of former Prime Minister Malcolm Fraser and based on Hamilton in western Victoria. While I do have some concerns with some aspects of Colebatch's analysis, it is worth looking at some of the differences between these seats to see just how different are the ethnic profiles of urban and non-urban Australia. As Colebatch shows, Melbourne, centred on the city's CBD and inner northern and north-western suburbs, has an overseas-born population of nearly 50 per cent. More than 10 per cent of these are from China, with similar numbers from Malaysia and other 'ASEAN countries'. Many are international students, who, as we shall see in a later chapter, are now a significant component of the inner city economy and society. Fewer of Aston's residents are immigrants although large numbers are likely the children and grandchildren of postwar arrivals from Europe. Even so, fully one-third are immigrants from 'a wide range of countries, including an outsize share from Sri Lanka. In fact, one in forty of Aston's residents comes from that island, part of a large community that started settling in Melbourne in the 1960s and is now 54 000 strong.'

In comparison, Wannon, 300 kilometres to the west, has barely been touched by postwar immigration from Europe, let alone the more recent arrivals from Asia:

The census found only 8.7 per cent of its residents were born overseas, and most were from Britain, New Zealand and other Anglo countries. The biggest contingent among the non-English-speaking countries were the 597 residents who had migrated from the Netherlands, most of them at least fifty years ago.

Malcolm Fraser opened Australia to Vietnamese refugees, yet forty years later, only sixty-nine Vietnamese-born people live in his old electorate, compared with 5098 in the electorate of Melbourne. Wannon has just 261 residents born in China; the electorate of Melbourne has 20,739.

This in an electorate of nearly 134 000 people. A political advertisement looking to be statistically representative of Wannon, then, might – like the 2017 ALP one – have a single Asian face, but more likely would have none.

Conclusion

Wannon is not alone in its ethnic homogeneity and, like any number of electorates in regional and rural Australia, maintains an ethnic profile that is not dissimilar to what it was 70 years ago, before the onset of mass immigration. A walk down the main street of many of the major regional towns and cities of Australia is for many of us from Melbourne and Sydney in some ways like a visit to another country, one that we have read about in books or seen in movies or television rather than the one we currently live in. The residents of these towns look like Australians used to look and perhaps reflect the way many would still like us to be today. Certainly they look similar to the Australians a number of people in politics and the advertising industries still like to project to the world as 'typically'

Australian. As with urban Australia, however, certain places in regional Australia have experienced major changes in their ethnic profiles in recent years. Just across the border from Wannon in the neighbouring electorate of Mallee in the little town of Nhill (population 2144) live 83 people born in Myanmar and another 44 from Thailand. Of Karen ancestry, these people are part of a community that now numbers more than 200, who have settled in the town since 2009. The original group was co-sponsored by immigration agency AMES to work in the local Luv-A-Duck abattoir, which was finding it difficult to attract and keep workers. A recent report on the group notes that while the abattoir is still a major source of employment for the group, many have now moved into other occupations or started their own businesses in the town.

Across the country such communities are beginning to make their presence felt in towns and cities that were until recently starkly white. Australian multiculturalism is thus spreading its wings, but for the most part it remains a distinctly urban phenomenon. Hyperdiversity is even further geographically specific and remains a feature of Sydney and Melbourne, not the other state capitals. But before the residents of inner Sydney and Melbourne get too smug about their cosmopolitanism and worldliness, it is worth our while to take a step back and examine how the changes in the economic profiles of the inner areas of the two big cities over the last few decades have intersected with property prices to skew immigrant settlement patterns. These changes have also altered the social and cultural structure of the cities in ways that have undermined old ideas about the ethnically diverse and cosmopolitan centre versus the homogenous and conformist suburbs. In the next chapter we test whether this characterisation of the Australian city is still accurate when many of the gentrified suburbs at the heart of the major cities are now rich, white and monocultural, while the outer suburbs are, like Aston, increasingly ethnically diverse. As we shall see, unlike in the 1950s, 1960s and 1970s when Carlton and Fitzroy, Kings Cross and Leichhardt became bywords for cosmopolitanism and later urban sophistication, today in order to find the places of real ethnic and cultural diversity we need to travel outwards from the centre to the fringe rather than inwards from the allegedly bland suburbs to the supposed cosmopolitan core.

5

Global migrations, local impacts

In the concentric model of the city developed by Park and Burgess in Chicago in the 1920s, the inner city was considered to be the zone of transition through which newly arrived immigrants passed on their way to assimilation and economic success in the new country. Famously depicted in photographs by Lewis Hine and documented by anti-slum crusaders such as Jacob Riis and Upton Sinclair as a place where hope for a better life mixed with despair at the current one, the zone of transition was dirty, congested and home to all manner of vices. But in theory at least it was a place of temporary abode, where – once economic success and the American Dream had been achieved – the immigrants would join the mainstream and settle down in the ever-expanding suburbs of the outward growing metropolitan area. In the contemporary gentrified post-industrial city, however, this process of transition has been reversed and immigrants now mostly settle in the outer regions of cities where housing is cheaper and unskilled service-sector jobs more plentiful.

Scholars of immigrant gateway cities in the USA, Canada, Britain and elsewhere nowadays talk of 'ethnoburbs', in which the most multicultural zones of the city are increasingly found in suburban rather than urban areas. In the quintessential immigrant city, New York, for example, the most recent census showed that the most ethnically diverse region of the city is no longer the Lower East Side of Manhattan, nor Brooklyn or the Bronx, but semi-suburban

Queens. The unusual case of the electorate of Melbourne notwithstanding, this increasing suburbanisation of ethnic diversity is now true of Australia too. As the inner areas of Australia's two major cities became more fashionable and the location of higher-skilled jobs in the post-industrial era, newer immigrant groups began to concentrate in the cheaper outer suburbs rather than the increasingly expensive inner city. And so, as Sydney and Melbourne became home to newer and more visibly different immigrant groups in the 1980s, 1990s and beyond, their growing ethnic diversity paradoxically became more hidden from view, especially after hours when the immigrant workers who increasingly make up the service class retreat from the expensive inner city to their homes in the outer suburbs.

Beginning in the 1970s newer immigrants have tended to settle in middle and outer suburbs rather than the cramped terraces and cottages of the old inner city. Some of these middle and outer suburbs became popular because of their proximity to the government-sponsored immigrant reception hostels which were the primary settlement points for several generations of immigrants – especially refugees – until their closure in the early 1990s, while others were popular because that was where the bulk of public housing was located. In this, Melbourne's story is slightly different to Sydney's, largely as a legacy of the activities of the former Housing Commission of Victoria which spent most of the 1960s demolishing old housing in the inner city and replacing it with publicly-owned high-rise blocks, many of which became important first-step housing for new immigrants in the 1970s, again especially refugees. Thus, unlike Sydney where public housing is much more suburban, Melbourne retained and retains a sizeable portion of poorer and immigrant households at its core. One outcome of this is that inner Melbourne looks and feels more genuinely multicultural than does inner Sydney, which – to this outsider at least – seems increasingly monocultural. Not quite the 'world's biggest gated community' as geographer David Harvey has labelled contemporary Manhattan, but certainly inner Sydney is more and more a region dominated by wealthy, white people whose lifestyles might be cosmopolitan, but whose ethnicity is not.

In this chapter we continue our exploration of the demographic transformation of the Australian city since the 1970s, but rather than concentrate on the macro story as we did in the last chapter, here we go more local and explore the impact of recent migration on particular neighbourhoods and suburbs, especially in the outer regions of Sydney and Melbourne. We also examine how rapid were some of these transformations, especially in the late 1970s and early 1980s. While obviously one way of doing this is to again use census records to see who moved in and when, another is to look at the ethnic make-up of the major shopping streets in these suburbs to see how new residents' tastes and demands have changed them. In doing so, we go back to the ideas we began to explore in the first three chapters, about how in seeking to understand changes in cities, we need to draw on a range of our human senses rather than simply relying on statistics. In this case we will use our eyes to see new sights and shop signs, our ears to hear new voices, our noses to smell the new and exotic foods on sale in these places, and perhaps most temptingly our mouths to taste them.

The 1970s and 1980s

As we saw in chapter 2, inner Melbourne lost population in the 1970s and 1980s, in the same way it had for much of the twentieth century. From what was already a postwar low of just under 310 000 in 1971 it fell by another quarter to 230 000 in 1986 before it began a slow climb back to its near postwar high of just over 370 000 today. The inner city was already gentrifying in the 1970s with first East Melbourne and then, more famously, Carlton becoming places of refuge for what were then called 'trendies' looking for a more cosmopolitan lifestyle than seemed to be available in the suburbs. The trendies brought with them new ways of living and new cafes, restaurants and venues, but they also helped to empty the place. This was not immediately obvious when the first groups, mostly students, arrived, as they tended to share houses and thus maintain the residential densities established by extended immigrant households in the 1950s and 1960s, but when they were replaced by well-to-do professionals who might or might not have children, the two, three or four people who now lived in houses that had until recently accommodated twice that number saw local population numbers decline sharply. The rapid growth in private flats and more importantly the huge towers built by the Housing Commission staved off this decline for a while but by the late 1970s the inner suburbs were clearly in trouble. As a 1977 MMBW report to the Victorian state government put it, Melbourne's inner area was facing a crisis as jobs, population and resources fled the region.

While Carlton was losing its population and its distinctly European and Italian flavour, other inner suburbs remained heavily dominated by migrants until well into the 1980s. Nearby Richmond's population, like that of the rest of the inner city, had declined in the 1960s and early 1970s to only 26 000 people by 1976 but unlike Carlton it was yet to gentrify and still retained both a strong traditional Australian working-class and large European-immigrant population. In 1976 just over 40 per cent of Richmond's residents were immigrants, with the largest single group being the Greeks, whose cafes, restaurants and other businesses gave the three main shopping streets – Swan, Bridge and Victoria – a distinctly Hellenic feel. Swan Street's Greek restaurants (known widely as Little Athens) become a staple of Melbourne dining in the 1970s and were to remain so until the 1990s. Richmond was also home to sizeable communities of immigrants from the UK and Ireland, Italy, Turkey and Lebanon (whose numbers were curiously combined for census count purposes). So mid-1970s Richmond was multicultural, but it was European, with less than 650 residents categorised as 'Other Asian'-born.

Similar trends were beginning to appear in Sydney where, by the mid-1970s, the trendies had begun to spread out from their initial beachheads in Paddington, Balmain and Glebe to form an arc of settlement that was increasingly circling the southern end of the CBD. As this region became progressively wealthier and more monocultural in the 1980s, the ethnic heartland of the city began to move west. Whereas in 1976 the City of Sydney and its immediate neighbours were still characterised by the Italians of East Sydney and Leichhardt and the Central European Jews of Woollahra and Bondi, many other established European communities had moved on to Burwood and Canterbury, among other places. The newer post–White Australia policy immigrant communities, on the other hand, began their lives in these places, with some having never moved on. These changes in the geography of the city's ethnic heartland can be seen in two censuses taken just ten years apart, in 1976 and 1986. In the former, the municipal City of Sydney was an important site of immigrant settlement with about one-third of its population overseas-born, with the UK and Eire-born the largest single group, accounting for just under 10 per cent of the local population. They were followed by the Greeks, the Yugoslavs and the Italians, although if counted as one group, those classified as 'Other Asian' would have outnumbered each of these three. Ten years later, the number of overseas-born in the redrawn City of Sydney had grown to over 44 per cent, with most of the immigrants still European, mostly from the United Kingdom and Ireland (7 per cent) and Southern and Eastern Europe (11 per cent). The same was true of neighbouring (and rapidly gentrifying) Leichhardt, where 90 per cent of the population was either Australian-born or from Europe. Less than 5 per cent of the population of either municipality was born in Asia or the Middle East. In contrast, figures for the more westerly municipality of Canterbury across this period demonstrate that in the late 1970s and early 1980s, Sydney's ethnic profile was changing rapidly and at the same time suburbanising. While in 1976 the percentage of Canterbury's population was, at 30 per cent overseas-born, slightly lower than for the City of Sydney, its ethnic profile was already beginning to diverge from urban and national norms. Already by then the municipality had a strong Middle Eastern flavour, with nearly 6000 residents, or just under 5 per cent of the population (and 15 per cent of the overseas-born) classified as Turkish or Lebanese. Ten years later, while the percentage of overseas-born in Canterbury was marginally lower than in the City of Sydney, at 42 per cent, as a much bigger municipality population-wise this number represented nearly 70 per cent of the former's total population. And unlike in the City of Sydney, only 17 per cent of these were European-born. Instead, Canterbury had emerged as an important site of settlement for people from the Middle East, whose numbers had doubled within ten years. South-East Asians were also becoming an important local presence, with a population of just over 7000. But of course these immigrant groups were not evenly distributed across the municipality. The Middle Eastern migrants (with most of the more recent ones from Lebanon rather than Turkey) were heavily concentrated in the suburb of Lakemba where, as we shall see, their presence was to have a major impact on the character of the suburb in the 1980s and beyond.

Further south and west, in Fairfield, which — as we saw in the last chapter — began to develop a migrant presence in the 1960s when Yugoslav and Italian market gardeners moved there, the arrival of Vietnamese refugees was to have an even more profound impact in the late 1970s and early 1980s. Largely influenced by the location of two migrant hostels, Fairfield, and within it the suburb of Cabramatta, was to emerge as the best-known and probably most important Vietnamese-Australian suburb in the country in the 1980s and 1990s. In 1976, just after the end of the Vietnam War and just at the beginning of the Vietnamese refugee crisis and migration process, there were less than 2500 Asian-born people in Fairfield; just over 2 per cent of the municipal population. Ten years later the total was nearly 20 000 and, as in Canterbury where the Lebanese were concentrated in Lakemba and its surroundings suburbs, so too were Fairfield's overseas-born (and especially the Vietnamese) heavily over-represented in one suburb: Cabramatta. By the time of the 1991 Census, almost three-quarters of that suburb's residents were overseas-born, nearly a third of them from Vietnam alone. This meant that more than 12 per cent of Australia's Vietnamese-born population lived in Fairfield, which, alongside Lakemba, was on track to become the archetype of Australian immigrant suburbia.

Similar trends were beginning to appear in Melbourne but because of its high concentration of public housing the inner city remained far more ethnically diverse into the 1990s and beyond than was the case in inner Sydney. Melbourne's post-1970s and post–White Australia policy immigrants, most especially the Vietnamese community and their businesses, were far more widespread than they were in Sydney, with inner urban Collingwood, Fitzroy, Flemington, Kensington and Richmond, each adjacent to major public housing estates, all developing highly visible clusters of Vietnamese residents and businesses in the late 1970s and early 1980s. Victoria Street in Richmond quickly became famous for its Vietnamese restaurants in the early 1980s, as did Footscray in the inner west. But as in Sydney, Melbourne also developed clusters of Vietnamese settlement in the suburbs, with Box Hill in the east and Sunshine and St Albans in the west gaining sizeable Vietnamese populations in the 1980s and 1990s. To the south-east, the suburb of Springvale became the place in Melbourne that most closely resembled Cabramatta. As in Sydney, these suburban settlement zones each included a mix of public and affordable private housing, including thousands of low-rise 'six-pack' flats built in the 1960s, but more importantly, they were all adjacent to major migrant hostels.

There were very few Asian and virtually no Vietnamese-born people in Melbourne in 1976, yet within a decade they were a major presence in numerous suburbs across the metropolitan area. Richmond had hardly any Asian-born residents in 1976 but ten years later 16 per cent of the population was Asian-born, most of them Vietnamese. Similarly, in Footscray, a strongly immigrant but overwhelmingly Southern European-born postwar population was joined by just over 4000 South-East Asians in the early 1980s, almost all of whom had arrived within the previous ten years. In the outer south-east, Springvale, home to the Enterprise migrant hostel since 1970, rapidly developed a strong Asian flavour in the late 1970s as mostly Vietnamese-run businesses became the dominant feature of the suburb's main shopping strip. From a suburb with less than 650 Asian-born residents in 1976, within a decade Springvale and its surrounds had become part of a major arc of suburban ethnic diversity that was quickly usurping the inner city as the heartland of multicultural Melbourne. By the mid-1980s a rapidly growing Asian-born population lived side by side with nearly 7500 Southern Europeans, more than 3500 Eastern Europeans, 2500 South Asians, 1700 Africans, 1100 South Americans and 1000 people of Middle Eastern background.

While today inner Sydney and Melbourne remain visibly multicultural, their overseas-born numbers are dwarfed by those in the middle and outer suburbs, most of whom have arrived since the 1980s. In the City of Greater Dandenong, which swallowed Springvale in 1994, for instance, only 34 per cent of the current population of more than 152 000 are Australian-born, and only 12 per cent are the children of two Australian-born parents. After the Australian-born, the largest communities are the Vietnamese and the Indians, which between them account for over 20 per cent of the population, followed by the Cambodians and the Sri Lankans.

Another rapidly growing group are the Afghanis, many of whom arrived by boat (and offshore detention) in the last decade or so, and whose businesses are beginning to make a strong impression on central Dandenong. However, as with a number of these outer suburbs now, it would be a mistake to allocate them to any particular ethnic group as they are simply so diverse that they are beyond single labels. In Greater Dandenong for instance, no single ancestry group is claimed by more than 10 per cent of the population and the third largest birthplace group, accounting for almost 10000 people, is 'not stated'. Fourth on the list is the 'born elsewhere', who number 7750 and likely include many recent settlers from Sudan.

The same is true for Fairfield in Sydney, where over 60 per cent of the population of just under 200000 are immigrants and only 10 per cent are the children of two Australian-born parents. Almost 80 per cent have two overseas-born parents and less than 15 per cent nominate Australian or English as their ancestry. Nearly 17 per cent claim to be Vietnamese, 11 per cent Chinese and 6 per cent Assyrian. But even these numbers are likely to understate the ethnic diversity of the municipality, as nearly 31000 people (16 per cent) were actually born in Vietnam, which likely means their Australian-born children (and grandchildren) have not been properly counted among the Vietnamese ancestry group. This is not the case for the Assyrians, most of whom are recent arrivals, and whose Australian-born children would be vastly outnumbered by those born in the home country. So, like Greater Dandenong, Fairfield has large numbers people from multiple different ethnic groups but it too is now so ethnically diverse that it is not dominated by any one particular group. But within the broader municipal region certain individual suburbs do have a particular ethnic and cultural character. One-quarter of Fairfield's Vietnamese-born live within the suburb of Cabramatta, outnumbering the Australian-born there by more than 20 per cent (and, as we have seen, many of the Australian-born may also be of

Vietnamese ancestry). The Vietnamese live alongside nearly 2000 Cambodians and 1000 Chinese but again this numerical dominance by a small number of ethnic groups hides the sheer diversity of the suburb, more than 10 per cent of whose birthplaces are either not stated or 'other'. Fairfield municipality is also home to Australia's largest Iraqi-born population, with nearly 19 000 residents, 20 per cent of whom live in the suburb of Fairfield itself and account for more than 22 per cent of the local population and nearly 10 per cent of that of the municipality.

Eating, shopping and festivals

The arrival of diverse immigrant groups has left an indelible cultural mark on local neighbourhoods, and at the street level ethnic diversity is evident in a number of ways. From the 1950s onwards, ethnic fairs dotted the calendars of the major cities and a few of the larger regional centres as newly arrived immigrant groups celebrated national or saints' days, although usually in the semi-private surrounds of a church or community centre rather than in the streets. It was only the more long-standing communities such as the Irish Catholics and some of the more militant Protestants who took their respective St Patrick's Day parades and those recalling the Battle of the Boyne on July 12 public. But that began to change in the early 1970s when the promotion of multiculturalism began to not only encourage but also increasingly insist on the open celebration of difference. Thus, from the mid-1970s onwards, inner city and then later outer suburban ethnic festivals became an important component of urban life. Usually centred on a visibly ethnic shopping strip or neighbourhood, these celebrations would see the main shopping street closed to traffic to make way for food stalls, cultural activities, music, dancing and the inevitable speeches of politicians and other notables.

An early example of such a public celebration of multicultural-ism was the Festival of All Nations, first held in inner Melbourne's Fitzroy Town Hall in November 1973 before becoming an annual event held in nearby Victoria Street, the former home of Moran and Cato (see chapter 2), from 1975. In a 1979 speech recalling the early years of the festival, the chair of the organising committee and later Mayor of Fitzroy, Greek-born Mike Zafiropoulos, attributed the idea for the event to Anita Joubert, a social worker employed by the Fitzroy City Council, who believed that as a locality 'with more than 50 per cent of its population being of ethnic background' Fitzroy was the 'ideal place for an ethnic festival'. The first festi-val in 1973 was small and 'involved seven ethnic groups and was held over a period of three days in the Fitzroy Town Hall with a range of activities including a folkloric concert, sporting events, an art exhibition and ball attended by the then Immigration Minister, Mr Al Grassby'. A year later it went public with a parade through the streets and a pop concert and fair in the grounds of the recently completed Atherton Gardens public housing estate in Brunswick Street, before in 1975 moving to Victoria Street, which the organ-isers promised would 'undergo a transformation so dramatic that someone finding themselves unwittingly in the middle of this street could be pardoned for imagining it was London's Petticoat Lane or Portobello Road, a Florentine Market or a Turkish Bazaar, all com-bined'. Such was the increasing ethnic diversity of Melbourne by the mid-1970s that on offer that day were Murano-style glassware 'with its multi-coloured textures, beaten copperware, handcrafted soft Spanish leatherware, Russian ikons, Aboriginal artefacts, Fili-pino woodwork, Sri Lankan clothing, Peruvian mountain clothing, pottery from many nations ... the list is almost endless'.

Recalling these early days in his 1979 speech, Zafiropoulos stated that festivals such as All Nations reflected a growing appreci-ation by communities of the importance of 'retaining and fostering ethnic culture'. He saw ethnic festivals such as his own as helping to enrich 'our social and cultural life', creating a 'better understanding between people from very diverse origins'. Zafiropoulos also noted that the success of the Festival of All Nations had acted as an example to other regions and communities which were increasingly staging their own events. He was right, and through the late 1970s and especially into the 1980s such ethnic festivals became commonplace across the country. In nearby Carlton, the Lygon Street Festa began as a celebration of Italian culture in 1980, while Melbourne's Greek community began its street festival Glendi (now Antipodes) in the community's traditional commercial strip, Lonsdale Street in the CBD, in 1987.

While Zafiropoulos was correct in noting that the timing and popularity of these festivals was a grassroots response to pride in and a determination to celebrate cultural diversity, it is no accident that their emergence also coincided with the decline of manufacturing in these regions and the beginnings of a new economy based on consumption and spectacle. For this reason, while the Festival of All Nations and similar street festivals nationally began as celebrations of local diversity, in reality they were harbingers of the changes in the economies and demographics of the inner city that we have discussed throughout this book that would see these neighbourhoods become increasingly wealthy and monocultural in the decades to come. As inner city neighbourhoods lost their manufacturing base and their ethnic diversity, the remnants of that cultural diversity became a commodity to be marketed and sold to locals and visitors alike. Thus, today it is not only at festival time that such diversity is celebrated, and while inner city eat streets are still lauded for the ethnic colour and food, many are now Italian or Greek in name only and retain their ethnic attachment for historical reasons rather than because of their contemporary residential patterns. Carlton's Italians are very few in number, while Greeks have never really lived in Melbourne's CBD. Similarly, today's Leichhardt residents are more likely to be highly educated professionals rather than semi-literate

Italian peasants (although they may be the children or grandchildren of these earlier immigrants). In both Sydney and Melbourne, the areas around central CBD Chinatowns do have increasingly high concentrations of the Chinese-born, but as we shall see in the next chapter many of these are now international students rather than long-term residents.

Even Melbourne's North Richmond public housing estate, which gave the nearby Victoria Street its Little Saigon reputation in the 1980s, is slowly losing its Vietnamese population as the original community becomes more established and moves out to be replaced by newcomers, notably from Africa. So while Victoria Street's businesses remain overwhelmingly Vietnamese, many of the newer bars and restaurants established in recent years reflect the wider area's gentrified hipster sensibility more than its older immigrant one. Richmond is thus becoming more like Carlton and Leichhardt than another inner city suburb, Footscray in Melbourne's inner west which, while currently under major development pressure, has retained both its Vietnamese-born population and Vietnamese businesses. But it too is undergoing gentrification and demographic change and is increasingly known as much for its African restaurants and bars as it is for its Vietnamese ones. Distinct micro-neighbourhoods are emerging in Footscray, each reflecting an income and/or ethnic characteristic. Thus, the streets around the railway station are rapidly gentrifying and subject to high-density development pressures, while Hopkins Street and Leeds Street at the entrance to the suburb are now Vietnamese (centred on the old 1960s-era New World supermarket, which became the Little Saigon market in the 1990s, but burned down in late 2016). Further north-west, the Nicholson Street mall and the old Hub Arcade that used to connect the mall with the Target department store on Albert Street is increasingly referred to as Africa Town or Little Khartoum, while a further 2 kilometres or so west, Barkly Street in West Footscray is now home to more than

20 Indian restaurants, bars, food stores and clothing shops, servicing a local community of more than 600 Indian-born residents.

Again, though, Footscray is the exception rather than the rule in the inner city. For the most part, in both Sydney and Melbourne, the major shops, restaurants and businesses to be found in inner city streets and neighbourhoods reflect the tastes and interests of their now wealthy local-born residents rather those of the poor or of recent immigrants. Ethnic shopping and food streets are, like the immigrants themselves, increasingly located in middle and outer suburban shopping districts rather than in inner city ones. In Melbourne the major centre of Greek social and business life is now in middle-suburban Oakleigh, where more than 10 per cent of the local population claim Greek ancestry and where the Eaton Mall is lined with Greek restaurants, cafes and *tavernas*, rather than the rapidly shrinking Greek Precinct in Lonsdale Street in the CBD or indeed in Richmond. Members of these older ethnic communities are thus conforming to the concentric city model by drawing on their economic success to follow the Australian Dream of the acquisition of a house in the suburbs.

Suburbs apart

But what about more recent arrivals who, as we saw in the introduction to this chapter, increasingly begin their new lives in Australia in the suburbs rather than the inner city? As with the census material we used to show how quickly some suburban neighbourhoods changed demographically in the 1970s and 1980s, so too can an examination of municipal rate books give us a sense of just how quickly certain ethnic groups made their mark on local shopping and commercial strips at this time. In Melbourne's Springvale, for instance, rate books from 1984, at the height of debates about the rapid rise in the numbers of Asian immigrants in the country, show that the suburb already had a strong Vietnamese flavour, with the main shopping centre based on and around Springvale Road featuring numerous Vietnamese shops, restaurants and businesses. But none of the people who were registered as the ratepayers on these premises, and who were therefore either the owners of the business or the freehold property, were of Vietnamese or Asian origin. Many of the owners were earlier migrants from continental Europe, a number of whom remained local residents, but others had addresses from across the metropolitan area. Again, some of these may have been former residents of Springvale who had since moved on, or had decided to sell their business and residential property in the area but retain their business property as an investment. In other words, what Springvale was undergoing was a process of succession, something that was to accelerate over the next decade. A survey of the same addresses in 1991 (the latest available for public use) shows that by then, of the 61 shops in the main commercial strip of Springvale Road whose owners are named as individuals rather than companies, 22 were Asian, mostly Vietnamese, with one local person of Vietnamese origin controlling four of the 17 shops within the Springvale Centre arcade at number 258, where 14 shops were controlled by Asian interests. Seven years earlier, a single company registered in well-to-do Toorak had owned the entire arcade.

In Lakemba in western Sydney, similar trends are evident in the rate books from the 1980s but there the shopkeepers in the suburb's main business strip, Haldon Street, most of whom were of Lebanese origin, remained renters rather than owners well into the 1980s and 1990s. But even so, we again see evidence of ethnic transition and economic success, with Greeks, Italians and people from the former Yugoslavia becoming the dominant property-owning group in the suburb's main shopping district in the 1980s, taking over from the Anglos who had until then owned most of the shops. That said, there is some evidence that the Lebanese, or least people and groups with Muslim names, did begin to become owners as well as occupiers in the 1990s, owning at least ten shops in the street by the early 2000s, the last date to which, for privacy reasons, I have access to the records. At the same time, a new development of eight shops and upstairs offices and apartments was under construction by two businessmen with Middle Eastern names on the site of a former Amoco service station at the western end of the street. Nearby, the Lakemba mosque, owned by the Lebanese Muslim Association, became a local landmark when it opened in 1977, while the Muslim Community Cooperative, which provides services for the 'financial, banking and investment needs of the Australian Muslim community by offering Islamic finance products', has been a presence on Haldon Street since the late 1990s. Today it and various other Muslim-owned businesses, Islamic associations, bookshops and support groups are highly visible symbols of a street and a suburb which is perhaps the most important site of both Lebanese and Muslim culture in Australia.

For many Australians from rural or regional areas visiting or moving to Sydney or Melbourne in the period since the 1980s, the city has increasingly presented something of a cultural shock. Footscray, Springvale, Cabramatta and Lakemba no longer look 'Australian' and neither do they sound or smell like it. In an interview conducted for the National Library of Australia's *Australian Generations* oral history project in 2013, one young women who moved to Footscray from a rural town in Victoria in the early 2000s recalled that the suburb:

> was like a cultural and sensory overload, like, there was all
> these weird smells and all these strange sounds and um, yeah,
> it was such an eye-opener. It was amazing though, it was
> amazing eye-opener because, you know, before I came to the
> city all I'd eaten is pizza and Chinese, and, you know, the
> usual takeaway that you can get in the country and growing
> up at primary school, the only kids I'd gone to primary school

with were Koori kids, I'd never seen any other cultures, any
other nationality and here I was in Footscray, which was
literally this melting pot of every single culture, cultural group
you could imagine and it was, just, was overwhelming.

While for this young woman Footscray was a pleasant experience
and its diversity something to be celebrated, for many other Australians places like it can be a potentially frightening introduction
to a city that has changed beyond recognition in barely more than a
generation.

In the early years of rapid Asian immigration, that process of
change was confronting even for locals in suburbs like Springvale
and Cabramatta, which over the years had already witnessed several
waves of migration. In his odd 1984 book arguing against Asian
immigration, Melbourne historian Geoffrey Blainey quoted one
local resident of another rapidly changing suburb, Campsie in inner
western in Sydney, who complained of the cooking smells emanat-
ing from her neighbours' houses and flats, and of the downstairs
Vietnamese family 'drying noodles on the clothesline in the back-
yard'. So too, language difficulties in shops and other businesses
caused anxiety to old residents and new arrivals alike in the rapidly
changing suburbs of Australia's big cities in the 1980s, 1990s and
2000s. Shop signs written in Arabic or Chinese characters became
something of an issue in some of these neighbourhoods at that time,
with municipal councils imposing local by-laws enforcing the use
of English-language signs in shop windows, supposedly as a way
of making streets and neighbourhoods seem more inclusive to all
communities, but more likely in response to complaints from anti-
immigrant groups about feeling excluded from their own areas.

While such sentiments might seem rather absurd and old-
fashioned to people who have grown up with multiculturalism
and diversity as the norm, to dismiss them out of hand as racist or
backward ignores the fact that rapid demographic change, like

the economic change discussed in the first three chapters, affected different people and communities in different ways. Many of the people who were most frightened and confronted by demographic change were also those who were hardest hit by economic restructuring, whether through the decline of manufacturing in the cities or by the collapse of commodity prices and government jobs in rural and regional areas. And nor should we forget that some of these newer ethnic neighbourhoods and their communities have faced and continue to face some real social issues. Along with Springvale, Richmond, Footscray and Cabramatta emerged as major sites of drug distribution, dealing and use in the 1990s. Vietnamese-led drug syndicates and local gang culture had a huge impact on these communities at this time and became a staple of tabloid reporting as cheap heroin flooded the country, mostly from Afghanistan when it was under the control of the Taliban. So too the emergence of radical Islam in recent decades and the involvement of high-profile members of what are often called 'people of Middle Eastern appearance' in organised crime gangs in Sydney have given Lakemba a reputation for lawlessness.

Straddling the divide between reaching out to the new immigrant entrepreneurial class transforming the business profile of these neighbourhoods and their long-standing supporters in 'old' Australia became a real issue for many urban-based politicians, especially conservative ones, from the 1980s onward. In 1988 then Liberal leader John Howard came under strong criticism when he suggested that the rate of Asian immigration should be slowed in the interests of maintaining social cohesion. These remarks saw him driven from his position as Opposition Leader and arguably cost him the immigrant vote for a generation. But in office as Prime Minister from 1996 he presided over a massive rise in Asian immigration, including into his own seat of Bennelong in Sydney's north. Elected to the seat in 1974 when it was solidly 'old' Australian, by the time he lost it in 2007 it had become a quintessential example of the ethnic transformation of Sydney, with 45 per cent of its population born overseas, nearly 15 000 of them in China and Hong Kong alone. Another 4000 were from South Korea, while 7000 were listed as 'other'. While the two largest ancestry groups in Bennelong in 2007 remained the Australians and the English, the latter was rapidly being overtaken by the Chinese, whose numbers had increased by more than 6000 in five years. The suburb of Epping to the north of the seat had become distinctly Chinese, with more than 14 per cent of its residents born in Hong Kong or the mainland, and with more local people claiming Chinese than English ancestry. Howard was famously only the second Australian sitting prime minister to lose his seat, perhaps because to many Sydneysiders, new and old, he seemed to represent the city's past rather than its present and future.

Conclusion

These suburban and outer suburban ethnic pockets are the new heartland of contemporary immigrant Sydney and Melbourne, which in turn form the locus of multiculturalism in Australia. But for many influential cultural commentators these are places that remain out of sight and out of mind. For many, the only knowledge of these suburbs and their residents is through highly sensationalised reports of crime or drug use, or vaguely understood ideas that the best place to get good Middle Eastern food in Sydney is Lakemba or that the best *pho* in the city is to be found in Cabramatta rather than Darlinghurst. In Melbourne, Chinese-run businesses and long-term residents are more likely to be found in eastern suburban Box Hill or Glen Waverley than in Little Bourke Street in the CBD, while further south-east Thomas Street in Dandenong is now known as the Afghan Bazaar Precinct and sits alongside Little India, where 'approximately 30 shops ... featuring speciality goods from India,

Pakistan, Fiji, Sri Lanka and Bangladesh, serv[e] an Indian catchment of some 85,000 people within 20 kilometres'.

As with their predecessors who transformed the streets and neighbourhoods of inner Sydney and Melbourne in the 1950s and 1960s, and then Cabramatta, Springvale and Lakemba in the 1970s and 1980s, these newer migrant communities are often intensely ambitious and entrepreneurial. After all, it takes real initiative to decide to leave your home and family and travel across the world to begin a new life in a new country. For those whose decision to leave was made for political rather than economic reasons the imperative to succeed is perhaps even more the case. Having nothing but personal ambition is a great driver for success, as we have seen with multiple waves of immigrants since the Second World War, not least Blacktown's Frank Lowy, perhaps Australia's greatest migrant entrepreneurial success story. Which is why it has always been a puzzle as to why the Liberals – the political party that portrays itself as the supporter of small business – has long had such an ambivalent relationship with the immigrant business people who should be their natural constituency. Perhaps it is because the party also seeks to represent an older version of Australia that is now more likely to be found outside of Melbourne and Sydney.

It is not only politicians and residents of non-urban Australia who have a narrow sense of what contemporary Australia looks like, however. So too do many of those who live in the gentrified inner cities of Sydney and Melbourne which, while still home to many overseas-born residents, have an increasingly narrow ethnic and social profile, distorted by the presence of thousands of international students studying at local campuses of the nation's major tertiary education institutions and a plethora of smaller private training institutions and colleges. While inner city Melbourne retains a strong (although declining) public housing base, which means it still has large numbers of recently arrived refugee and other poorer and immigrant communities, large segments of its overseas-born population are now international students rather than permanent settlers. Inner Sydney too has similar numbers of international students but not the recent refugees. In the next chapter we chart the emergence of the international student market and the impact it has had on the economy and demography of the inner city in recent decades. An industry that simply did not exist until the 1980s, international education has since emerged as possibly the single largest driver of employment and economic growth in the inner city. It is certainly the largest single generator of export income in the region, and in Victoria's case the largest in the state. But for the presence of these students, and in Melbourne's case the public housing towers, not only might our universities be broke but so too might the inner cities be in danger of becoming even more monocultural than they already are.

6

Studentification:
From trendies to PBSAs

As part of its response to Australia's worsening economic situation and growing international trade imbalances in the mid-1980s, the Hawke government decided that along with manufacturing, tourism and finance, the higher education sector should be part of a multi-faceted solution to what it portrayed as a 'national economic crisis'. As such, several months after its re-election for a third term in mid-1987, it released a discussion paper on the future of tertiary education into the 1990s and beyond. *Higher Education: A policy discussion paper*, or the Green Paper as it was more informally known, canvassed a range of options for the sector, all of which involved a more market-driven approach to the provision of education, a stronger managerial approach to governance, major expansion in enrolments, and a closer alignment between education and research and the economic needs of the nation. The follow-up White Paper, *Higher Education: A policy statement*, released in mid-1988, essentially enshrined these ideas into public policy, which became law under the *Higher Education Funding Act 1988*. Colloquially known as the 'Dawkins Reforms' (sometimes the 'Dawkins Revolution') after the minister who drove the changes, and mostly remembered for the reintroduction of tertiary fees in the form of HECS and HELP, the policies included in these documents were to have profound impacts on students who have since had to pay ever-higher fees, the academics whose work practices were changed beyond recognition, and of course the institutions of higher learning themselves, which were consolidated, merged and dramatically expanded.

In the 30 years since the Dawkins Revolution, while the number of Australian higher education institutions has declined by half, mostly because of institutional mergers, the numbers of students enrolled has more than trebled, from under 400 000 to more than 1.25 million. Of more profound impact on the universities and more so on the demography and morphology of the cities, however, was a change in policy quietly introduced in 1985 that phased down government-funded scholarships for mostly Asian students administered as part of the overseas aid budget and the Colombo Plan and their replacement with a policy that not only allowed, but actively encouraged, universities to charge full fees to international students who wished to come to Australia to study. Mostly aimed at the sons and daughters of the rapidly growing middle class in Asia, this policy, like the reintroduction of fees for domestic students, turned higher education from a public good to a profit-driven industry, but in this case an export oriented rather than a domestically focused one. The market for higher education has been a huge success and is now the third largest export industry in the country, with Australia usually counted as either the third or fourth largest provider of international education in the world, behind the USA and the UK, and alternating with France. Like other aspects of the new economy, provision of higher education to international students has been overwhelmingly an urban phenomenon, with Sydney and more so Melbourne clear leaders in the field, and both cities now regularly listed as being among the top international student cities in the world. The development of this industry has also tracked changes in the global economy, with the first waves of students in the 1990s coming from the then 'Asian Tiger' economies of Singapore, Malaysia, Taiwan and Hong Kong to today when the overwhelming bulk come from mainland China, with India rapidly catching up.

From a small group of just 17 000 (only 1000 of whom were fee-paying) in 1987, the numbers of international students in Australia had by mid-2017 grown to nearly 600 000, almost all of whom were fee-paying. Seventy per cent were based in NSW and Victoria, mostly in Melbourne and Sydney, with large numbers highly concentrated in areas in or near the CBDs. If counted as one group, international students would today rank as the third largest overseas-born cohort in the country after the English and the New Zealanders. More than one in every 50 people in Australia is now an overseas student, a percentage which is obviously far higher in the major cities, largely because that is where most of the big public tertiary institutions are based, and where a large number of smaller private training and language providers have set up in recent years. But it is not just demographically that the growth of this market and this group of residents has changed our cities. Educating them, housing them, feeding them and catering to their needs have all become important urban economic activities. A 2015 report by consultants Deloitte Access Economics for the federal government export body Austrade put the sector's 'measured export earnings at $18.8 billion' but also suggested that this was likely an under-estimate. International education is now Australia's largest service sector export and the third largest export by value overall.

This is an industry that simply did not exist at the beginning of our study period but which, like the factories of the Fordist era and the growth of the tourism industry in the 1980s and beyond, has massively altered the built form of our cities, and most especially the inner areas of Sydney and Melbourne. But unlike the tourism industry, it has also changed the residential structure of the cities as students stay for three years or more rather than the three or four nights common with tourists. The story of these students and the growth of what is now called the 'education export industry' is the subject of this chapter, which examines how the growth of international student numbers has helped to not only revive the economic fortunes of the inner city but also become one of its major industries. I tell this story by documenting the rapid growth of this market from nothing to a huge component of urban life in less than 30 years. I then move on to examine how the growth of international student numbers has changed not only the universities but also local demographics, especially in the CBD and inner areas of the two major capitals. Finally I look at how, in doing so, the provision of international education has helped to make parts of the inner city unaffordable for many locals, thus adding to the sense that these regions are now mostly places for the rich, whether young, old, local or foreign. First off, however, I journey back a decade or so before the Dawkins Revolution to look at how Australia's inner cities developed a student 'feel' in the 1960s and 1970s, and how the changes that this early group of gentrifiers brought to the inner city presaged what was to come in the post-industrial period.

Studentification and gentrification

As elsewhere in the world, universities and students have long been important components of Australia's inner city residential and commercial districts. Students from non-metropolitan areas, and a few who have sought the college experience, have traditionally spent at least some of their undergraduate years in the mostly religious based university residential colleges of older universities in the major capitals or the newer postwar suburban universities which tended to mix religious colleges with secular, sometimes mixed-gender ones. While Australia has never had much experience of university or college towns – other than in Armidale in northern NSW, where the University of New England (UNE) was established in 1938 as a college of the University of Sydney – in the way that is common in other parts of the world, since at least the 1960s and arguably earlier, the inner areas of the capital cities adjacent to the major universities and college campuses have had a student feel. This presence of large numbers of university and college students and their teachers is in part responsible for gentrification, which British urban scholar Darren Smith has argued should rightly be called 'studentification', as it was often students or recent graduates who were the first wave of gentrifiers. Australian urban historian Graeme Davison has also recently drawn a link between the numbers of students who moved to Australia's inner cities to study in the 1960s and the subsequent 'trendification' of these neighbourhoods.

Melbourne's Carlton, home of the city's oldest university, became famous as a centre of student life in Australia in the 1960s and subsequently a major centre of alternative lifestyles and the rise of a movement that supposedly created a distinctly Australian voice in literature and the arts in the 1970s and beyond. The glory days of the suburb and its main drag Lygon Street as a student-led alternative zone were immortalised in local band Skyhooks' song 'Carlton', otherwise known as 'Lygon Street Limbo', released in 1974, and a 1973 book by photographer Les Gray simply called *Carlton*. The song warned of the dangers of Carlton's bohemianism for the uninitiated, while the book featured numerous images of local street life, portraits of local characters and pictures of rundown and recently refurbished local landmarks. An introductory essay by journalist Garrie Hutchinson suggested that Carlton was Melbourne's answer to New York's Greenwich Village. Both were adjacent to major university campuses and in both a diverse range of individuals and groups co-existed in relative harmony – workers and students, immigrants and the local-born, the old and the young, the rich and the poor, and the conventional and the not so conventional – who all lived side-by-side in cramped cottages and grand terraces that had seen better days. Saturday morning would see the locals shopping at Lygon Street's King and Godfree Italian grocer before gathering together next door at Jimmy Watson's wine bar for a drink and chat. At night they could eat exotic Caribbean-inspired food at the then up-and-coming chef Stephanie Alexander's first restaurant, Jamaica House, located at the city end of Lygon Street.

More than 40 years on, Hutchinson's essay and Gray's photos offer us a fascinating time capsule of the optimism and possible naiveté of the student and hippie generation who, alongside the Italian immigrants, made Carlton nationally famous. Theirs was a compelling story of an urban village that, as both Graeme Davison and Tanja Luckins have recently argued, was particularly appealing to a well-educated generation seeking a more cosmopolitan ambience than that on offer in Robert Menzies' Australia. But for all protestations to the contrary, 1970s Carlton was an uncomfortable mix of often mutually uncomprehending old Australia, postwar Italian immigrants, students, and the new residents who were rapidly gentrifying the suburb. Artistic and student Carlton was represented by academics, painters, sculptors and filmmakers, while at La Mama and the Pram Factory a new Australian theatre was born. So too was a new literature, including Helen Garner's 1977 novel *Monkey Grip*, which documented inner Melbourne's inner northern alternative youth and student scene, where her characters drank coffee, found love and scored drugs in Lygon Street, and debated national, personal and sexual politics in smoky pubs in Carlton and Fitzroy. While Carlton's various groups tolerated each other, in reality most had little understanding of each other's lives. The students and the trendies admired the way the immigrants lived their social lives in public, but the latter could not for the life of them understand why anyone would trade a spacious new home in the suburbs for a cramped and damp terrace house in the inner city. Most saw an opportunity too good to be true, and when offered what then seemed like huge amounts of money for a dark hovel, took the cash and built a *palazzo* in suburban Bulleen or Doncaster.

It is Gray's photographs rather than Hutchinson's essay that really evoke a time and place that has gone. While Ti Amo, the Universata cafe and Jimmy Watson's remain, physically and socially Lygon Street – and Carlton more generally – has seen profound change. As the young and the creative began to disappear from the suburb in the 1980s and 1990s so too did its cultural edge. Commercially, Lygon Street retains its Italian flavour but the suburb around it is now more notable for the wealth of its residents than for their Italian ethnicity. Some locals may still occasionally eat and drink in Lygon Street but mostly it caters for tourists and students from the nearby universities who now give the area a cosmopolitan Asian flavour rather than an Italian one. More than 70 per cent of Carlton's current population is overseas-born, with nearly 25 per cent from mainland China. Unlike their shaggy-haired predecessors from the 1970s, however, these students are more likely to live in the thousands of student accommodation blocks that have been constructed in recent years than in a crumbling terrace house that has seen better days. We will come back to these blocks, known as 'purpose-built student accommodation' facilities (PBSAs) later.

Expanding and internationalising the universities

While the number of people who live in the inner Melbourne region has grown numerically since the 1990s as the region has been repopulated, the overseas-born percentage of the area has barely changed since the early 1970s and remains at about 50 per cent. What is most striking, however, is how much geographic settlement patterns, age profile and ethnicity have altered across that time period. Geographically the biggest change is that large numbers of people now live in the CBD, which until the 1990s had almost no permanent residents. Today it has more than 37 000 and is growing rapidly. More importantly, almost all of these are overseas-born (86 per cent), with more than 25 per cent from mainland China alone. In the broader City of Melbourne area, more than 66 per cent of the population is overseas-born, with more than 15 per cent of these from the Chinese mainland. Along with those from Hong Kong, Malaysia, India and Indonesia, these groups constitute more than one-quarter of the municipal population. And they are young: 62 per cent of the Chinese-born are aged 15–24, while a further 30 per cent are in the 25–44 age bracket. These people are overwhelmingly international students.

With just under 215 000 residents, the ABS's Sydney Inner City Statistical Region has a smaller population than does inner Melbourne but, reflecting the city's traditionally much greater residential densities, it also covers a much smaller geographical area that only stretches from Circular Quay in the north, east to Elizabeth Bay and south through Darlinghurst, Redfern and Alexandria to Rosebery. It then arcs west to include Enmore, Camperdown, Glebe, Ultimo and Pyrmont and back through the CBD and Barangaroo to Circular Quay. Sixty per cent of the population of this statistical region is overseas-born and, as in Melbourne, large numbers of these are international students, studying at the University of Sydney and the University of Technology (UTS), both of which have major campuses in or adjacent to the area. The area also borders the University of New South Wales' (UNSW) main campus in Kensington and therefore likely includes a number of international students who study there but live across the statistical border. Nearly 10 per cent of the population is Chinese-born and 30 per cent are aged between 20 and 30, compared with 15 per cent for Greater Sydney. At a more micro-level, in Ultimo, right beside UTS, more than 50 per cent of the population is aged between 20 and 30 and another 20 per cent are under 40. Fully 30 per cent are Chinese-born, with 35 per cent claiming Chinese ancestry. While this area does include Sydney's Chinatown, these figures suggest temporary student visitors more than immigrants and long-term residents. And while an important and highly visible local ethnic group, its Chinese-born people represent less than 10 per cent of the wider Sydney Chinese community.

The growth in these international student numbers from next to nothing 30 years ago is extraordinary. After a slow start in the early 1990s the numbers took off later in the decade, largely in response to cuts in federal funding for higher education, the emergence of aggressive private providers under the Howard government in the late 1990s, and then the rise of China as an economic power, all of which saw the numbers reaching just under 275 000 by 2002. Sixty per cent of these students were based in NSW or Victoria (read Sydney or Melbourne). By that time China was already the largest source country but at just under 50 000 its numbers were low compared with today. More than half of the Chinese were based in NSW, with Victoria the next favoured destination with just over 12 000. Indian students were becoming a presence too, but at that stage ranked behind a number of other Asian countries, including Japan whose 17 000 students were evenly split between the states, but with NSW and Queensland sharing the bulk.

Compared with today these international student numbers are tiny; in mid-2017 the total number of international students was 582 000 nationally, with the Chinese alone numbering more than 170 000. NSW is today home to over 64 000 Chinese students and Victoria to 60 000. The two biggest states are also very popular with Indians, with 29 000 studying in Victoria and 16 000 in NSW. The other states share the remaining 19 000. Alongside these two major source countries, Vietnam has emerged as an important market in the new century, up from just over 4000 in 2002 to 23 000 today, with nearly half of these students based in Victoria. Japanese numbers have dwindled to 11 000, although Australia remains popular with neighbouring South Korea, whose numbers have risen from 18 000 to 22 000 in 15 years. Brazil has also become an important source country, with 23 500 studying here, more than half in NSW, up from just over 4000 15 years ago.

The growth in international student numbers has been matched by the growth in enrolments in tertiary institutions more generally. This has been a national phenomenon, but given that most of the universities are in the capital cities and the larger regional ones, it has by definition had an urban impact. As we saw in chapter 3, the major urban universities are now among the largest employers in the country, and are the largest single employers in many urban and suburban regions, having replaced the factories of MacRobertson's, Holden and Ford in this role. But they are also major residential, commercial and transport nodes too. My own university, Monash, now has more than 72 000 students spread across multiple campuses in south-eastern Melbourne, the CBD and inner urban Parkville, as well as one just outside Kuala Lumpur in Malaysia, another on the fringes of Johannesburg in South Africa, and a teaching and research centre in Prato, Italy. We also have partner campuses with universities in Suzhou in China and Mumbai in India.

Monash is extraordinarily multicultural, with nearly 40 per cent of students internationals and 54 per cent born overseas. Of the 60 per cent who have Australian citizenship, 30 per cent speak a language other than English at home, while the more than 28 000 internationals have a range of citizenships, with the biggest single group being Chinese. Nearly 60 per cent of the internationals have a residential address in Victoria during the semester, and while many live in the CBD and the inner southern suburbs Monash is also a major contributor to the ongoing process of the suburbanisation of multiculturalism discussed in the last chapter. Large concentrations of Monash's international student cohort can be found in the suburbs around the major campuses in Caulfield and Clayton in Melbourne's south-east. In the 10 kilometre suburban belt that straddles Dandenong Road and connects the two campuses live nearly 15 000 Chinese, as well as nearly 2000 from Hong Kong,

2300 from Malaysia and more than 9000 from India. Again, the age profile of all these communities suggests that large numbers are likely students attracted to the area perhaps not only because it is close to the university but also because of its increasingly multicultural permanent residential population and hence feeling of familiarity and safety.

While Monash is big – it is the largest university in the country – its size and the percentage of international students it enrols is no longer unusual, especially in Sydney, Melbourne and Brisbane. Its putative local rival, the University of Melbourne, has just under 50 000 full-time equivalent students (EFTSL in the jargon of education bureaucrats), 17 500 of whom are internationals; while the other big Melbourne institution, Royal Melbourne Institute of Technology (RMIT), has 64 000 students in its tertiary sector and another 14 500 in its TAFE division. Almost 20 per cent of its Melbourne-based students are internationals, and as with Monash it has also has offshore campuses, including two in Vietnam where more than 16 500 students are enrolled. But even the smallest of the Melbourne-based universities such as Swinburne have enrolments in the tens of thousands, with large percentages internationals, whether based in the city or at overseas campuses. Similar numbers are to be found in Sydney, where the University of Sydney has more than 50 000 students, 22.5 per cent of whom are international; UNSW which has just over 53 000 students, 25 per cent international; and UTS with 37 600 students, nearly 27 per cent of whom are internationals. Brisbane's universities are growing too, with the University of Queensland now having 51 000 full- and part-time students, about one-quarter of them internationals. Its inner city neighbour, Queensland University of Technology (QUT), has just under 50 000, but only 7850 internationals, less than 16 per cent.

What is most extraordinary about these numbers is not just how many international students there are, but also how rapid has been the growth in higher education and how important it has become to post-industrial urban economics and demography. In the mid-1970s, at the beginning of our study period, there were fewer than 300 000 higher education students in the whole of Australia, only 171 400 of whom were full time. Large numbers were part-timers, taking diplomas or degrees at night school while working or raising families. In the wake of the abolition of tuition fees in 1973, many of these were mature-age women who were an important part of university and college life in the 1970s and 1980s as can be seen by the growth in part-timers across this period, when they rose to over 120 000 (or 46 per cent of the total) in 1982. A further 41 000 were what were then called distance students, undertaking their diplomas and degrees by correspondence. Again, many of these were women, or people who for various reasons could not attend city-based classes. The then new and regional universities and colleges such as the University of New England based in Armidale, Deakin University in Geelong, and the Gippsland Institute of Advanced Education in the La Trobe Valley specialised in these programs.

Growth really took off when the Dawkins reforms kicked in after 1990. Again, Monash, whose then vice chancellor, geographer Mal Logan, was a key intellectual driver of Dawkins' ideas, shows just how rapid and profound were these changes. From one campus in Clayton in Melbourne's southeastern suburbs with less than 12 500 students in 1988, by 1990 – after having merged with the Chisholm Institute of Technology and the Gippsland Institute, as well as the College of Pharmacy in Parkville – Monash had four suburban campuses as well as a regional one. By the end of the 1990s it had added another campus in outer suburban Berwick as well as its first international partnership campus in Sunway, Kuala Lumpur, Malaysia, which launched in 1998. The South African campus opened in 2001, the same year as the Prato centre in Italy. Today the Faculty of Business and Economics alone, with nearly 17 000 full-time students (and 2000 part-timers), is more than 25 per cent larger than was the entire university in 1988. And while Monash had a long history of enrolling international students, having been an early and enthusiastic supporter of the Colombo Plan from its foundation in the early 1960s, few of the students enrolled in 1988 were international fee payers. Today, the international fee-paying student cohort is more than twice the size of the total enrolment of the entire university before the rapid expansion began. Monash also now has far more postgraduates (22 000) than it had total students in 1988, but what is extraordinary about these is that nearly half of them are internationals, most of whom are studying at the Caulfield campus which specialises in business and commerce and now derives more than 54 per cent of its enrolments from international students. At the larger Clayton campus that figure is under 23 per cent.

Monash's nearest equivalent in Sydney is UNSW. Both were founded in the postwar period, originally as technical universities designed to provide 'practical' educations, and both were built in suburban locations, although, for various reasons to do with gaining access to a suitable site, Monash was established further out of town than was UNSW whose Kensington site is now essentially inner city. The two universities quickly moved away from the technical focus and became fully-fledged comprehensives, although for many years both saw themselves as more democratic and inclusive than their cross-town and more established predecessors. Their respective student mixes seemed to exemplify this, attracting enrolments from the rising middle, working and immigrant classes of their cities. Perhaps not surprisingly both were enthusiastic supporters of the Dawkins reforms, with the vice chancellor of UNSW Michael Birt, like his counterpart at Monash, keen to take advantage of the proposed changes in order to expand his university's size and public profile. Historians Julia Horne and Stephen Garton argue that Birt hoped to use UNSW as a base to create 'a truly statewide university' with multiple campuses, modelled on the University of California system. Logan too had been inspired by the American state system model, although in his case it was Wisconsin (where he had undertaken postgraduate research in the 1970s) that acted as his model.

While the planned multi-campus model did not eventuate, like Monash, UNSW has grown enormously since the 1980s. From under 15 500 students in 1988, by 2015 it had nearly 53 500, with more than 13 500 of these internationals. And whereas Monash spread its wings geographically, UNSW has stayed put, turning its main campus in Kensington into what it calls 'a "city within a city" offering 21st century research and teaching facilities, student accommodation, recreation spaces and retail outlets. UNSW now offers students close to 4500 beds on campus – more than any other NSW university'. Birthplace and ancestry figures for the campus and its immediate bordering areas bear out the success of this strategy. Of the nearly 15 000 people who live there, less than 50 per cent are Australian-born, with only 38 per cent claiming Australian, English, Irish or Scottish ancestry. Nearly 17 per cent were born in China or Hong Kong and 60 per cent are the children of two overseas-born parents. Less than one-quarter have two Australian-born parents and nearly half come from households where a language other than English is spoken at home, the most common being Mandarin and Cantonese which between them accounted for more than 20 per cent of household languages. Given this, it is no surprise that Chinese was the largest ancestry group in the region, accounting for over 20 per cent of responses. The Chinese-born have grown from only 300 in 2001 to more than 2000 in 2016 as the boom in international education has accelerated. Similarly, with 65 per cent of the local population reporting that they have at least some sort of a tertiary education, we can see that in the new millennium Kensington has emerged as a university suburb.

Building the spectacular university

Notwithstanding the rise of the internet and the replacement of the correspondence-course distance education models that UNE and Deakin among others specialised in in the 1970s and 1980s with online teaching, the expansion of enrolments, both domestic and international, since the 1990s has necessitated the physical growth of campuses and facilities. For those of us who work in universities, putting up with the noise and inconvenience of building works has seemingly become a way of life over the last two decades or more. For universities with suburban or regional campuses or the ability to start afresh on a greenfield site, this has not been such an issue as there always seems to be a spare space in which to cram another building. Not so with the older city centre and city fringe-based ones, where space is not only at a premium but also comes with a premium price. One solution to this problem, developed in an earlier period of expansion in the 1960s, was to extend the campus into adjoining residential and commercial regions and simply demolish older housing and replace it with high-rise teaching, research and administrative facilities. Back then, along with other government arms of the Fordist city such as various road building and planning bodies and public housing providers, universities were often far more high-handed in their attitude to existing local residents than were even the most aggressive private developers. In Darlington in Sydney and Carlton in Melbourne expansion by the major universities in the late 1960s and early 1970s did as much damage to old neighbourhoods as did the Department of Main Roads and the Housing Commission. In both cities, in pursuing their expansion plans the universities' administrators as frequently went to war with their own staff, who often led or at least advised local resistance movements, as they did with long-term local residents.

As these areas gentrified, and when being held responsible for the wholesale demolition of heritage buildings became untenable, inner city universities found themselves increasingly stuck for space.

Fortuitously the abolition of tariffs and the associated collapse of manufacturing, and most especially of the inner city-based textile, clothing and footwear industries in the 1980s and 1990s, offered a potential solution. As these industries declined, their former business premises became, by definition, economically redundant, their previous value as productive spaces non-existent. So, in accordance with economic theories that dictate that the uses of land and space should reflect their 'highest and best use', what better solution than to re-use the former factories for academic purposes, or to demolish them and start again? All city-based universities followed this trend to a greater or lesser extent, but perhaps the most aggressive in the early years of higher education as an industry was the University of Melbourne which, under the leadership of Vice Chancellor Alan Gilbert in the 1990s, embarked on a massive building program in South Carlton, the former home of the TCF and printing industries. As an avowedly entrepreneurial VC, Gilbert oversaw a scheme to develop a series of buildings of up to ten levels on sites that had until recently housed factories and storage facilities under and around one of South Carlton's original nineteenth century residential squares, University Square, which like others dotted throughout the suburb was modelled on those found in London's Bloomsbury. The original plan was to bulldoze a number of Victorian-era terrace houses surrounding the square but local protests saw most of these retained and eventually incorporated into the design of the new buildings. Not so lucky was the long-standing lawn bowls club which was demolished to make way for an entrance to an underground car park.

Designed to emulate the success of the privately funded Melbourne Business School which had been built on the southern side of University Square in the late 1980s, Gilbert's scheme, rather unimaginatively called Melbourne University Private, was intended to create what was essentially a private fee-paying university alongside the main public campus. Designed by rising local architecture

142

firm Metier 3 and developed in conjunction with Equiset, a company associated with the Grollo Brothers, who had developed many of Australia's largest buildings in the 1980s and 1990s, Melbourne University Private was to provide new facilities for the faculties and disciplines that most appealed to fee-paying international and postgraduate students: business, law and journalism (which in those early days of the internet still looked like a profession with a future). But, as with a number of such schemes, it was a financial disaster and was eventually closed down in 2005 having cost the university at least $20 million, with some estimates putting the figure as high as $150 million. Whatever the actual cost, the university got a number of new buildings in an expanded footprint and is now a major economic presence in formerly industrial South Carlton.

In an age of marketing, brand consciousness and entrepreneurial vice chancellors such as Gilbert, universities have increasingly sought to use their new and refurbished buildings as a means of advertising themselves to potential students (especially fee-paying international ones), and as a means of attracting potential philanthropic donations from local and international funding sources. If the new signature or statement building were to be designed by a nationally or internationally known starchitect who could bring kudos to the university as a creative and innovative place, all the better. RMIT in Melbourne arguably started this trend with its Building 8, designed by Peter Corrigan and Maggie Edmundson, which was opened by then Prime Minister Paul Keating in 1995. Sitting above a long wall of very ugly 1970s-era Brutalist buildings facing Swanston Street in Melbourne's CBD, Building 8 is a riot of colours, shapes and materials. Describing it as 'a bold and challenging building which serves as an outstanding educational resource and statement about the direction of Australian culture', Keating's opening speech noted that it was 'conceivable that some people might hate it' but it did in his opinion suit its environment and 'definitely suits its educational and cultural purposes. It's slightly mad, but so are the city baths up the road'. In a telling statement about the emerging role of education and the national economy he went on to say that it represented an

> image of optimism and change; an image of Australia in
> the 21st century. And I gather that already it is effectively
> conveying that message in Asia and Europe. We have seen an
> outdated building transformed into a significant contribution
> to Australian architecture and education. Old facilities have
> been improved and modernised to include state of the art
> educational technology.

In the 1990s and through to today RMIT has continued to use its buildings and architecture as a means of showcasing itself to locals and to the world. When I worked there in the late 1990s my department was housed in a converted sewing machine factory on the corner of Swanston and La Trobe streets, which was later gutted and capped with a green plastic 'brain' by Melbourne-based ARM Architects, who had earlier designed the flamboyant refurbishment and extension of the adjacent 1887 Storey Hall which, despite many criticisms, won its designers a Victorian Architecture Medal in 1996. RMIT's most recent major development, the Swanston Street Academic Building, by another Melbourne-based architectural firm, Lyons, has similarly won numerous awards including the 2013 National Public Architecture Award; while the nearby Design Hub Building by Sean Godsell Architects, although having a troubled history with parts of its high-tech environmental heating and cooling systems not working and having to be replaced, is internationally recognised for its green credentials.

As these examples demonstrate, RMIT has looked to local architects for its iconic buildings. Not so its nearest Sydney-based rival, UTS, which snared the internationally renowned Frank Gehry for its new School of Business building which opened in early

2015. Designed to resemble a crushed paper bag and part-funded by Chinese-born developer and philanthropist Chau Chak Wing, after whom it is named, the building has become a tourist attraction as well as an educational facility. Billed as 'a flagship project of UTS's billion-dollar-plus City Campus Master Plan [and] a landmark along the "cultural ribbon" that extends from the Sydney Opera House down to UTS, taking in Darling Harbour and the Goods Line development', the building is, like those at RMIT, alleged to be 'a manifestation of the creative thinking that underpins the teaching and research undertaken by the Business School' and, more broadly, the university.

International studentification

Buildings that showcase the university to potential funding sources and that might or might not provide functional teaching and learning spaces are important to the new education-led economy, but so too is providing places for all the new students to live and sleep. Just as did their long-haired, local-born predecessors in the 1970s and 1980s, international students have made their mark on inner city and suburban neighbourhoods in all sorts of ways. One obvious way is in the businesses and services their presence brings to shopping districts and commercial strips. So too do they underpin the market for inner city and suburban apartment developments which, as we shall see in the final three chapters, have become a key component of the post-industrial inner urban economy since the 1990s. At a more direct level, the emergence of the international student market has led to the repopulation of formerly rundown and in some cases largely abandoned districts such as South Carlton and Ultimo. But rather than live in these areas' old and decaying houses as did their predecessors 40 years ago, many of these students now live in purpose-built student accommodation facilities

(PBSAs) which, like the flagship university buildings, are increasingly being constructed on the sites of former clothing, textile, footwear and other manufacturing establishments in these areas. Just as the universities have become key components of post-industrial society and their new buildings signature motifs of the new urban economy, so too has the development of these accommodation buildings been a direct response to the emergence of the international student market since the late 1980s. Providing this accommodation has not only become a lucrative industry segment for local and international developers, it has also underpinned the construction industry – one of the few sources of employment for blue-collar workers left in the contemporary inner city.

Unlike the flamboyant designs and aesthetic statements that are a feature of many of the newer university buildings, most student accommodation buildings tend towards the basic and utilitarian end of the architectural spectrum. Early examples often involved the conversion of interwar or postwar office buildings which, because of changing beliefs about the role of government or technological redundancy, had become obsolete by the 1990s and were thus ripe for re-purposing. In Melbourne one of the earliest facilities was the old IOOF (later Jensen) building on Swanston Street opposite the State Library of Victoria, designed by architect Marcus Barlow in the 1940s and occupied by the Victorian Department of Education in the 1980s and 1990s. Converted to student apartments in 1997, it was originally known as Melbourne Campus Apartments but is now part of the Brisbane-based national Unilodge chain. Another early conversion was the old Art Deco-era headquarters of the State Electricity Commission of Victoria in Flinders Street, which became a Unilodge in the late 1990s, while the old Modernist-era headquarters of Vicroads, the state government instrumentality in charge of licensing drivers and registering their cars, became College Square, Carlton in 1998. It too is now part of the Unilodge group, which now claims to manage more than 14000 student 'beds' in 63 properties across Australia and New Zealand.

Providing these beds is a big business that is increasingly attracting international institutional investors who build, own and maintain increasingly larger complexes, unlike the older model pioneered by Unilodge which sold off individual strata titled units to mum and dad investors looking for a secure income stream from their PBSA investment. A recent report by property agents and consultants Jones Lang La Salle into the PBSA sector notes that while 'historically the supply of student beds in Australia was dominated by university owned or affiliated providers', the recent increase has been 'largely driven by commercial providers, resulting in commercially operated beds now accounting for the majority of total stock'. It also noted that much of this increase is coming from international institutional investors such as the London-based Global Student Accommodation (GSA), which is seeking to have more than 25 000 beds in the Asia-Pacific region by 2025. Scape, another London-based company, backed by the Dutch pension fund APG, is currently building a 46-storey facility opposite RMIT in Swanston Street and is planning one of 60 storeys around the corner in Franklin Street which when finished will be the world's tallest student accommodation tower. Other recent entrants are Blue Sky, an international private equity firm backed by global merchant bank Goldman Sachs, and Iglu, a local developer backed by Macquarie Capital and the Singapore government's sovereign wealth fund GIC, which has four properties in and around Ultimo in central Sydney as well as one in suburban Chatswood, two in inner Brisbane and another under construction in central Melbourne.

Conclusion

In building in Chatswood, Iglu is not alone in seeking to expand its presence to the suburbs as well as the inner city. While PBSAs are an increasingly prominent aspect of inner city life, they are no longer only found there. They can now be found throughout the suburbs, with many of the newest literally built on the grounds of suburban universities. Some of these are former university-owned colleges and accommodation facilities that have been sold off to private companies in a bid by cash-strapped university managements to raise money that can allegedly be better spent on other things, while others are newly built, developed by poorly located and inaccessible institutions in an attempt to create a European or American-style campus living experience for their increasingly demanding student 'customers'. Distance from transport infrastructure and lack of accessibility to social and entertainment facilities are seen as a competitive disadvantage in the international student marketplace and have become major issues for suburban and regional universities, most of which were located where they are during the Fordist years, partly because they were developed when the car was king, but also for social justice reasons. In an era of big government and a concern with social welfare, the postwar- and 1970s-era universities were seen as a means of bringing education and opportunity closer to the people, especially for women and other disadvantaged groups who needed to remain close to home in order to combine study with family responsibilities.

In the post-Fordist era this sort of idealism runs a very distant second to the needs of the marketplace. For inner city–based universities, what was once their competitive disadvantage – their distance from local student populations, lack of car parking facilities and their inability to expand beyond their cramped grounds – has, in the post-industrial era, become their great advantage. In the new era, in which the marketplace values leisure, pleasure and spectacle over security and stability, the suburban and regional universities are at a distinct disadvantage. As in the 1960s and 1970s when domestic students began the process of gentrifying the inner city, today's students, whether local or international, as young people are looking for a good time as well as a good education while they are at university. In the 1960s and 1970s that good time was associated with the inner city for a small group of early gentrifiers, while the majority looked to the suburban shopping mall and the pub, drive-in or the sports club for their idea of fun. Work, too, was suburban in a big postwar factory or perhaps in the rapidly growing office parks of the 1970s and 1980s. For most people, the inner city was associated with slums and poverty, or perhaps with crime and urban decay.

Not so today when the inner city has become not only the wealthiest part of the metropolis but also where there has been the greatest investment in new sporting, cultural and education facilities, where the major concern is luring international visitors, tourists and students – as much as, if not more so, providing much needed community and other facilities for locals. In the next three chapters we move on to look at the re-emergence of the inner cities from their dark days of decay and restructuring in the 1970s and early 1980s to their current role as the drivers of the national economy. But rather than doing so by revisiting statistics about jobs, exports and new industries, these final three chapters explore how having a good time became a competitive advantage for cities in the post-industrial era, at how the zone of transition has become a lifestyle precinct.

7

Lifestyle destinations:
Building the new inner city

In May 1983 Victorian Premier John Cain announced plans for a major urban renewal development in Chapel Street in the Forest Hill precinct of inner Melbourne's South Yarra. The South Yarra Project as it was then known was the brainchild of Singaporean businessman Jack Chia and was to feature office towers, a hotel, multiple high-rise residential apartment buildings, upmarket retail outlets and a series of canals and waterways linking the massive site to the adjacent Yarra River. The development was to replace a number of industrial buildings, including the former factories of both the Hecla and Electrolux companies, manufacturers of domestic appliances that had long been household names across Australia. From the 1920s to the mid-1970s this had been a location of jobs for working-class men and women and a symbol of Melbourne's strength in manufacturing and secondary industry, but in its new form it was to be an expensive residential address, host to numerous recreational facilities and a site of white-collar employment. It was thus a symbol of the emerging post-industrial and services economy that was already transforming inner urban landscapes across the globe and was to become a major feature of city life in the 1980s and beyond.

Cain presented the South Yarra Project as a vote of confidence in the then economically depressed Victorian economy, and a political triumph for his recently elected Labor government – Victoria's first since 1955. As we saw in chapter 3, this touting of major urban development as a driver of economic growth was to become a key theme in Cain's political strategy throughout the 1980s. In looking to boost Melbourne's construction and development industry, Cain was also seeking to enhance the city's emerging status as a post-industrial city where consumption was overtaking production as the main driver of the economy. In doing so, he was to a certain extent modelling himself on his NSW Labor colleague Neville Wran who, after his first election in 1976, staked his continuing claim on the premiership on the economic record of his government, especially the increasing success of Sydney as a business and financial centre and its growing reputation as the nation's pre-eminent city.

Notwithstanding a series of financial and other problems, as well as numerous reconfigurations of the site in the 35 years since 1983, Como, as the South Yarra development is now known, is one component of the much larger Forest Hill urban renewal area that since the 1980s has seen a former industrial zone – bordered by the railway station in the west, a former quarry at the base of the Yarra River escarpment to the east, and the river to the north – transformed into a high-density, high-rise apartment and upmarket residential, recreational and retail zone. What was once an area that produced manufactured goods and foodstuffs is now dominated by apartment and office towers, the latest a currently under construction 50-storey residential building atop an arcade of international designer-label retail outlets. Along with Southbank, the Docklands, and similar sites in Melbourne, as well as Darling Harbour, Pyrmont and more recently Barangaroo in Sydney, and numerous other urban renewal sites across the nation, Como and its neighbours in Forest Hill are an architectural expression of the impacts post-industrialism has had on the physical fabric of the Australian city since the end of the Fordist era in the 1970s.

As with the South Yarra project, each of these major developments feature high-end, mostly high-rise residences, office buildings
and often, but not always, a retail or leisure-based component. Each
has also been built on centrally located but economically redundant
industrial sites or on land that had previously been used for freight,
shipping, storage or other 'dirty' uses. They were also former sites of
mostly male, mostly blue-collar jobs that had been the major casu-
alties of the restructuring processes that we saw in the first three
chapters of this book. While constructing these new developments
has become a major source of jobs in the new inner city, and one of
the few employment options still provided there for working-class
men, most of them create few if any long-term, secure jobs equivalent to those of the old Fordist era.

As we have seen, the 1970s was not a good time for cities, with
the second half of the decade particularly tough as the first stages
of globalisation destroyed older industries, especially those in the
low-value-added manufacturing sector. First the factories closed
and then whole industries began to disappear, and finally, especially in the English-speaking world, new ideas about the role of
the state and the public sector – what we now call neoliberalism
– meant that governments were increasingly unwilling or unable
to fund not only the completion of the more grandiose modernist
schemes dreamt up in the good times, but in some cases did not
even have enough funds to pay for essential services. This was true
for the smaller industrial cities of what became known as the rust
belt, but it was also true for major cities such as London and New
York. As these cities have emerged as economic powerhouses in the
contemporary global era, we should not forget that in the mid-1970s
both faced major economic and social crises and were pockmarked
with abandoned redundant economic zones, especially former dock
areas and around major railway stations, whose centrally located
goods yards were no longer needed as trains struggled to compete
against the road freight industry. As with New York, the London

of the late 1970s is scarcely comprehensible to those who know it today, having in recent decades been remade by global corporations, governments and philanthropists who have poured billions into revitalisation schemes and the construction of urban landmarks such as new museums, galleries, and other tourist and lifestyle infrastructure. Gentrification has had a major role in these transformations but so too has the move to creativity, spectacle and the economics of culture which, like contemporary immigration policy, has a distinctly urban focus.

While the crisis of the city was an international phenomenon in Australia, deindustrialisation was, as we have seen, much more of a problem for the older south-eastern capitals and smaller manufacturing cities than it was for the newer sun belt ones of the west and the north. Sydney was affected but it was spared to a certain extent by its emerging role as the country's international tourism, financial and immigration gateway. While Melbourne had traditionally been the nation's commercial capital, its major strength was in domestically focused manufacturing rather than finance and the emerging industries of tourism and the media which were increasingly concentrating in Sydney. So, as with many other manufacturing cities internationally, the second half of the 1970s were not kind to Melbourne, especially its inner areas where most of the older industries were based. While parts of the inner city were beginning to gentrify, much of the inner ring was looking shabby, with many of its high streets characterised by boarded-up shops and abandoned business premises. A 1977 report by the MMBW, at that time the city's metropolitan planning authority, warned that although the inner area of the city 'contains a wider range of socio-economic groups, the general picture is an area in which the incidence of relative poverty and unemployment and a large range of social problems is considerably higher than that generally found in the rest of the metropolitan area'.

Projects like Como, Southbank and the reinvention of the Docklands were part of a deliberate policy to revitalise and repopulate inner Melbourne and to help it try to keep up with the rapidly globalising Sydney. And to a large extent it has worked. Melbourne's population, like that of Sydney, is now growing at a rate not seen in over 100 years, and both cities have some of the most expensive real estate in the world. Each has a vital urban economy based on business and personal services, hi-tech industries, and – as we saw in the last chapter – major strengths in education and research. And since the 1990s each has seen a massive build-up of new apartment developments, mostly but not always constructed on land formerly occupied by factories and other industrial uses. However, as with many of the other urban issues discussed in this book, the effects of these changes and the associated benefits and costs have not been evenly spread socially or geographically. As we saw in the first three chapters, many of the major job losses associated with the decline of manufacturing in the 1970s and 1980s hit first and hardest in the inner city areas before later becoming a much bigger problem in the outer areas and the regions, and in the cases of Broadmeadows, Liverpool and Elizabeth remains a problem today.

So too immigration and ethnic diversity was a major feature of the old inner areas before the 1970s, but much more so of the outer suburbs from the 1980s onwards. As immigration moved outwards so too did genuine ethnic diversity, but oddly as the inner city gentrified and became much more about culture and creativity than immigrants and their cultures, the now more homogenous residents of these areas and their various representatives in politics, the media and elsewhere increasingly began to talk about their cosmopolitanism and diversity and the many lifestyle options they offered. Most of these terms were euphemisms, code words for wealthy, educated, highly cultured and internationally focused, but also often young, female, hedonistic and, in some neighbourhoods, gay. As old jobs and old industrial structures disappeared from the inner city, they were replaced not only by the new jobs that we saw in chapter 3 but also by new buildings catering to the dwelling and other needs of the new residents, as well as their increasingly expensive wants and desires. Whether international tourists or students or young people looking for a big night out, from the 1970s whole areas of the inner regions of the major cities were remade to cater for the emerging post-industrial economy based on leisure, pleasure and what was to become known as the creative economy.

In these last three chapters we look at the effects of this new economy on the physical fabric of the contemporary Australian city, the reworked, rebuilt and revitalised places such as Como, which were extensions of and sought to leverage the economic and social cachet of existing suburbs. We also explore the creation of completely new suburbs such as Southbank and Barangaroo which simply did not exist before the 1980s and were deliberately created as artificial places devoted to post-industrial economic and social pursuits. In doing so, we explore first the new and re-imagined built form of the inner city before moving on to look at how consumption has become, like education and finance, a major component of the restructured inner city economy. Finally, we look at how culture and fun, broadly defined, has not only become a feature of the day- and night-time economy of these regions but also too often a victim of the tensions between people looking for a good time and those new residents who want fun when it suits them and peace and quiet when it does not.

Old neighbourhoods, new uses

Melbourne's South Yarra Project was part of a deliberate strategy devised by John Cain's new government to revitalise the urban landscape of inner Melbourne as a means of reviving and reori- enting the Victorian economy away from its over-dependence on manufacturing which, even before the onset of the Hawke gov- ernment's restructuring processes in the mid-1980s, was clearly in trouble. Whitlam's 1973 cuts to tariffs had had a major impact on long-established Melbourne-based manufacturers such as Hecla while, notwithstanding ever-higher tariffs on TCF products in the later 1970s, the increasing industrialisation of Asia was having a devastating effect on employment in those fields, again large percentages of which were based in Melbourne, and especially inner Melbourne. Recessions in 1975 and then again in 1982 did not help things, leaving many areas of the inner city looking rundown, shabby and increasingly bleak. A follow-up report to the MMBW's 1977 study of Melbourne's inner area by Urban Economic Consultants warned of a looming economic and social crisis and suggested that if 'the overseas pattern of the rundown of larger cities were repeated in Melbourne then the consequences for the inner areas would be very grave indeed'. These consequences might include 'unemployment rates of 15–20 per cent … with more than double that for certain groups such as the young, who are forced to remain in the inner city'. The report went on to intimate that if these trends were left unchecked, there existed the real possibility of the emergence in inner Melbourne of British- or American-style urban decay and social disorder.

So in the 1970s inner Melbourne was not a place of excitement or spectacle. There were pockets of gentrification and a growing appreciation of the importance of the city's Victorian-era heritage but for the most part the inner city was looking shabby and way past its best. A recently digitised collection of photos taken by architectural historian Graeme Butler in the late 1970s and early 1980s confirms this sense of decay. What were once grand Victorian-era mansions in East Melbourne were now semi-derelict rooming and share houses, while former neighbourhood shopping strips such as Brunswick and Gertrude streets in Fitzroy were mostly closed and boarded up, their owners having followed their immigrant customers to the suburbs. Indeed, much of inner Melbourne seemed to be facing real economic crisis and stagnation, with a developing sense that the city's days of economic and social pre-eminence might be coming to an end.

Former Victorian Treasurer Rob Jolly has confirmed this sense of decay and despair, one outcome of which might have been the election of the first Labor government in Victoria in 27 years in April 1982. He recalls real concerns about Melbourne's future prosperity and a strong sense among his colleagues that the city and Victoria more generally were particularly vulnerable to economic restructuring and a changing international economic order. Jolly recalls inner Melbourne as being in decline, its economy 'moribund' and lacking 'long term growth opportunities' in new industries beyond its traditional reliance on manufacturing. There was also a sense of decay, with evidence of the rapid collapse of traditional industries visible across the inner city. While individual factories and in some cases whole industries had closed down in the wake of the 1975 and 1982 recessions, the collapse of the early 1970s property boom had left the CBD pockmarked with any number of 'bombsites', still being used as 'temporary' open air car parks nearly ten years later. Across the river, Southbank, which should have been the ceremonial gateway to the CBD from the south was instead, other than the then under construction Victorian Arts Centre, essentially 'derelict', a 'slum area' of abandoned factories, car yards and rusting remnants of its former maritime past.

The number of manufacturing jobs in inner Melbourne declined by a third in the decade 1971–81, with a further third lost during and after the recession of 1982. Many of the factories that closed down at this time were, like Hecla in South Yarra, long-established businesses in prominent locations, their highly visible loss seemingly adding to the sense of economic crisis. The 1970s also saw a number of major retailers, including high-profile department stores, close their doors or be absorbed into the then emerging national retail chains. As with manufacturing, inner city retail employment declined rapidly in Melbourne in the 1970s, with almost 7000 jobs –

one-quarter – disappearing between the censuses of 1971 and 1981. Again, given that many of the businesses that closed were large enterprises housed in multistorey retail emporiums in the CBD and major urban thoroughfares, the sense of decline was palpable. In both the CBD and in secondary shopping destinations such as Chapel Street, Prahran and Smith Street, Collingwood, a number of Edwardian-era department stores closed in this period, unable to compete with the newly emerging car-based shopping malls of the suburbs. While some of these buildings were readapted for use as office space, supermarkets and arcades, others were abandoned or had their upper floors closed off and boarded up. In some cases they remain that way today, nearly 40 years later.

While Sydney was also undergoing restructuring, it did not have the same sense of gloom and doom as its southern rival. In part this was because it was gaining strength in the new sunrise industries of finance, tourism and the media, but also because of its increasing role as Australia's gateway city. As international travel (and immigration) moved from a reliance on the ocean liner to the aeroplane, Sydney's Kingsford Smith Airport, rather than Port Melbourne's Station Pier, became the nation's front door. Having the nation's new symbol, the Sydney Opera House, right at the heart of the city was, in the dawning age of image and city branding, also something of a bonus. Sydney's better weather and nearby surf beaches were also becoming increasingly important advantages in the competition for international investment. But not everything was rosy. While the areas surrounding Circular Quay were looking fine, especially in comparison to Melbourne's Yarra River precinct, to the immediate west of the CBD and then along the Parramatta River, deindustrialisation and restructuring were having a devastating effect on blue-collar jobs and formerly working-class communities. So too was the decline of the retail sector, with department stores in particular trouble. Long-standing retailers like Grace Brothers, Anthony Horden's and Mark Foys in the CBD, and others in the major inner suburban shopping strips, collapsed or were taken over at this time, leaving great empty spaces in their wake. More prominently, the containerisation of international shipping in the 1970s meant that, as in London and elsewhere, inner Sydney lost thousands of jobs on its docks as these migrated from Darling Harbour and its surrounds to Port Botany, which became the city's major port when it opened in 1979.

Repopulating the inner city

It should come as no surprise then that in both Sydney and Melbourne the areas that were the first to be subjected to major urban renewal were former sites of industrial production, shipping and warehousing, in Melbourne's case South Yarra (Como), Southbank and the Docklands, and in Sydney Darling Harbour and Pyrmont. We will come back to the consumption and spectacle elements of each of these projects and their successors in the next chapter, but for now I want to look at the residential components of these new developments, which were an important element in not only repopulating the inner city after the declines in the 1970s but were part of a deliberate strategy to rebrand these neighbourhoods as high-value residential districts rather than declining industrial working-class ones. Unlike other formerly working-class and immigrant inner city neighbourhoods, which were the first to be gentrified in the 1960s and 1970s, these places did not feature large numbers of rundown nineteenth century dwellings whose cultural and heritage value could be leveraged for economic gain, but were rather non-residential brownfield sites which needed to have their past associations with industry and dirt re-imagined for a better future. Some sites and some buildings were able to be reused and adapted for new purposes, their former uses as warehouses and factories adding to their prestige value in a rapidly deindustrialising society in which the industrial era and its heritage was beginning to take on a patina of nostalgia; but for some of the largest, their vast, minimalist architectural forms were difficult if not impossible to recast as industrial chic as opposed to simply industrial.

In seeking to reuse these buildings as offices, residences and creative spaces, Australian cities followed a global trend first seen in New York's Lower Manhattan, where, as documented by urban sociologist Sharon Zukin, from the 1970s firstly artists and then more well-to-do people and then property developers had turned the area's abandoned workshops into lofts, where working and living spaces were combined to create new neighbourhoods with exotic sounding names such as SoHO (South of Houston Street) TriBeCa (Triangle below Canal Street) and NoHO (North of Houston Street). As geographer Julie Podmore has argued, since the 1980s what she calls the 'SoHo syndrome' of loft conversions and the revalorisation of industrial spaces as high-end residences has gone global and become one of the key symbols and signifiers of contemporary global urbanism. Cities across the world have re-invented former industrial areas and buildings as loft or warehouse districts, sometimes drawing on the names invented in Manhattan in the 1970s and 1980s as monikers for either individual developments or whole districts. Renaming and rebranding redundant and derelict or semi-derelict neighbourhoods as chic or edgy was one way to revive them, but another was to reconstitute ways of understanding the inner city and its history through language. Areas that had once been written off as slums, or zones of transition, became 'cosmopolitan' and 'diverse', even as they lost their foreign-born residents, before in the 1980s becoming lifestyle destinations, attractive because of their access to the new jobs and opportunities of the CBD, but perhaps more importantly because they were near the new and expanding social and leisure opportunities of the re-emergent inner city.

The term 'lifestyle' is, of course, essentially meaningless, but it became ubiquitous in much of the western world from the 1980s onwards. It was particularly important in real estate parlance as a way of rebranding areas that had an unsavoury past, especially neighbourhoods that had previously had a reputation for crime, poverty and pollution. For this reason, it was especially useful as a means of re-inscribing industrial and formerly non-residential areas as desirable addresses. In the Australian context it was also a useful counterpoint to the term 'Australian way of life' which, as historian Richard White has demonstrated, was a term used by conservatives in the postwar period to signal suburban stability and rectitude, often in contrast to the ideas and attitudes of people with 'foreign' backgrounds or ideas. Lifestyle was thus a politically neutral, but highly value-laden label that denoted urban sophistication without the elitist cultural connotations of that word, cosmopolitanism without the sometimes fraught ethnic or racial associations of that term, youthfulness without age prescriptions, and wealthy and expensive without the class and income aspects of that social category.

As governments and the private sector set about repopulating the Australian inner city in the 1980s and 1990s then, the term lifestyle became ubiquitous in advertising new or re-imagined neighbourhoods. As a close observer of both the deindustrialisation of the Australian inner city and its post-industrial renaissance, I became a regular visitor to the apartment display suites which became a common feature of bleak, often cold and windswept former industrial sites of Melbourne at this time. These display suites were the post-Fordist version of the old suburban display homes pioneered by mass builders such as AV Jennings from the 1930s and which became a fixture of family Sundays in the postwar years. In common with those suburban display homes, the newer apartment display suites showcased their ultra-modern appliances and conveniences but, in contrast to the suburban dream of private front and backyards, they were about access to the CBD and its jobs and social opportunities, and in-house facilities such as gyms and swimming pools. The display suites would also invariably feature mocked-up model apartments, often encased in photo-shopped images of the views potential buyers would experience from their high-rise eyries. In short, they were all about lifestyle.

When visiting these display suites I began to collect the sales brochures on offer and quickly became aware just how ubiquitous was this term in the marketing of these places. In the early 1990s most of the new developments in former industrial areas of inner city Melbourne and Sydney were low-rise blocks of apartments on sites within or adjacent already gentrified areas such as Colling-wood, Fitzroy, Pyrmont and Surry Hills. Some were built on the sites of former service stations, or were conversions of large former factories and warehouses such as the old Goldsborough Mort Wool Store in Pyrmont which was restored and extended to become apart-ments and a hotel in 1995, the old Mark Foys warehouse building in Surry Hills which was converted to apartments in the late 1990s, and in Melbourne a number of the former Foy and Gibson and MacRobertson's buildings in Collingwood and Fitzroy which were converted to apartments in stages throughout the 1990s. Across the inner areas of both cities the conversion of former clothing, textile and footwear factories, as well as Edwardian and interwar-era food and drink production facilities into residences became common in the 1990s.

The largest and most conspicuous sector of the 1990s apart-ment boom, however, was the conversion of city centre and city fringe office buildings for residential and hotel purposes, and the construction of new high-rise residential buildings in the CBD and adjacent formerly industrial areas. Like the renovated terrace houses and cottages of the inner suburbs, older industrial buildings and architecturally ornate interwar office buildings could be mar-keted not only for their locational advantages, but also because their age meant that they exuded a certain old world solidity and charm, and as such could stake a claim to heritage and scarcity value. Not so a number of redundant 1960s-era Modernist office buildings which were similarly converted to residential use in the 1990s. While most of these were only 20 or 30 years old, like the old factories of Fitzroy, Surry Hills and Redfern these too were victims of globalisation; in this case both the neoliberal fashion for small government and the technology and communications revolutions, with the former meaning they were deemed surplus to the requirements of a shrinking state and the latter because their low ceilings and small floor plates could not cope with the wires and cables needed in the contemporary, globally connected office building.

While the average 3 metre-plus floor–ceiling height typical of this era quickly became too small for commercial use, it was generous for residential purposes. Stripped down to their cores and waiting to be recycled as either luxury apartment complexes, or as we saw in the last chapter, purpose-built student accommodation complexes, hollowed-out 1960s-era office buildings, many of which had for decades been the headquarters of major companies or of downsized or privatised government and semi-government departments, became a common sight in the inner cities of Sydney and Melbourne in the late 1990s. In Sydney the conversion of the old Caltex office building on Kent Street in the CBD to the Stamford on Kent hotel and apartment complex was advertised by former model and style icon Maggie Tabberer in the *Sydney Morning Herald* as somewhere that 'would suit me to a T'. In Melbourne's Carlton, the former Australia Post headquarters building in Rathdowne Street became the Panorama on Rathdowne Apartments, a mock version of a tapered Art Deco New York building combining the best of 'grand metropolitan living' with 'unlimited views' and an 'unlimited lifestyle' in 1995. Two years later the old 28-storey Department of Defence Building in South Melbourne became the St James Apartments, 'the most stunning address on St Kilda Road', offering 'an unending smorgasbord of recreational, entertainment, sports and other lifestyle options'.

The most fundamental change to Australia's inner city residential landscape and dwelling culture to emerge out of the post-1980s building boom, however, was the development of new purpose-built residential high-rise towers in the CBD and formerly industrial and commercial areas directly adjacent to it, such as South Yarra's Forest Hill, Southbank and the Docklands in Melbourne, and Pyrmont, Ultimo and Alexandria in Sydney. Whereas before 1990 there were less than ten high-rise residential buildings in Melbourne's CBD and very few in Sydney, most of which were built in a mini city-living boom in both cities in the early 1970s and a second short-lived one in Sydney in the early 1980s, today there are literally dozens in both cities, most of which have been built since the mid-1990s. A number of these developments combine residential dwellings with hotels and serviced apartments, and offer residents access to facilities normally associated with hotels. Often constructed by Asian-based developers and marketed to Asian buyers, including the parents of international students, these buildings are modelled on the integrated resort-style complexes that were a feature of the rapidly growing cities of South-East Asia in the 1980s and 1990s and China in the 2000s. As we have seen, Caltex Australia's former headquarters in Sydney combined a Stamford Hotel with residential apartments when it was converted by the Singapore-based Stamford Land Corporation in the late 1990s, while nearby the never-built Harrington Grande apartments in The Rocks were marketed to potential buyers as the 'right concept', combining location, views, 'rare freehold title' and '5-star hotel facilities including heated indoor pool, spa, gym, sauna, concierge, and high level security parking and intercom systems'.

While neither Sydney nor Melbourne's CBDs were traditional residential addresses, they did at least have the advantage of being well known as sites of business, leisure and culture. And while neither was at that stage well served with retailers selling groceries and other household items, they did have the basic infrastructure and services necessary to create a viable residential community. This was not the case in former industrial locations such as Melbourne's

Southbank and Sydney's Pyrmont, both of which were developed as market-driven residential and commercial zones on mostly abandoned industrial land virtually from scratch in the 1990s and 2000s. Originally conceived as an arts and leisure precinct with some small provision for residential development by the Cain Labor government in the 1980s, Melbourne's Southbank really only came in to its own in the 1990s after its centrepiece, the Southgate retail and office complex, opened in 1990. The massive Crown Casino hotel complex was to follow in 1997. Residences began to appear from the early 1990s, at first mostly in low-rise buildings adjacent to the new ABC radio centre opened in 1992, but by the late 1990s Southbank was to become dominated by tall and then very tall high-rise residential complexes. As with South Yarra's Como and Sydney's Pyrmont, parts of which were rebranded as 'Jacksons Landing' by developer Lend Lease when it redeveloped the CSR sugar refinery site in the late 1990s, the lifestyle on offer and on display in Southbank was essentially placeless and could be found in any redeveloped post-industrial urban landscape anywhere in the world.

Lifestyle developers

Just as the manufacturing economy gave rise to individuals and companies that went on to become local and national household names in the postwar Fordist years, so too has the post-industrial era seen some such names arise, as retailers and service providers became icons of new ways of living. In recent years some of the most prominent of these have been the developers who have transformed our city skylines with new offices, hotels and apartment blocks. Some of these are well-known, high-profile figures, such as Harry Triguboff and his Meriton company in Sydney, which claims to have 'designed, developed and built more than 75,000 apartments across the east coast of Australia' since its establishment in 1963.

Triguboff believes he and his company 'spearheaded the apartment revolution [in Australia] with sophisticated, high-quality apartments', which, while debatable, does contain elements of truth in that Meriton is probably the most high-profile of the development companies that have ridden the post-industrial apartment wave that really got underway in Sydney in the 1980s and spread in the 1990s and beyond. In recent years the company has been especially prolific in redeveloping former industrial locations such as Alexandria and Pyrmont into high-density residential zones. Other developers are less well known, such as Dick Dusseldorp, who founded what was to become Lend Lease in Sydney in 1958 before taking it global in the 1970s and 1980s. It is now one of the largest construction and development companies in the world, responsible for, among other things, major development projects such as the redevelopment of the Elephant and Castle district in London. It was also the developer of the 2012 London Olympics athletes' village.

In Melbourne the post-1990s apartment boom gave rise to what is sometimes called Melbourne's Meriton, Central Equity, a company founded by two school teachers and an accountant in the early 1970s, which since the early 1990s has developed more than 70 projects, mostly apartment blocks on former industrial sites in the inner city but also some middle-ring infill suburban estates and more recently outer suburban fringe developments. After humble beginnings renovating and on-selling old, rundown houses in the 1970s and then getting burnt in the commercial property crash of the late 1980s, the three moved into the inner city apartment market with a number of small, low-rise developments in Carlton and Fitzroy in the early 1990s, before becoming the leading players in Southbank, responsible for at least 30 of the high-rise projects that have become the dominant feature of that area since it was opened up for development in the 1980s. Their most recent towers in Southbank and the CBD rise to 50 storeys plus. As with the integrated complexes described above, most of the company's projects are specifically targeted at Asian buyers and feature on-site gyms, pools and tennis courts, as well as full-time concierges and grounds staff.

Like Jack Chia, the man behind the original South Yarra Project, many of these developers are either immigrants or the children of immigrants. Significant numbers of the first wave were Jewish, often people who had arrived as refugees from European pogroms and later Nazism in the 1920s and 1930s, or as Holocaust Survivors in the late 1940s and early 1950s. Some achieved financial success in the TCF industries in the postwar years before either investing their excess profits into property in the 1960s and 1970s, or, as things began to sour in those industries in the 1980s and 1990s, turning to property development as a means of diversifying their interests. Still others invested in property as a means of providing a secure retirement income for themselves or their families as the once vital bodies of young immigrants began to age.

Others, such as Melbourne's Grollo and Pellicano families, were poor immigrants from Italy who had little in the way of formal education but great business sense and the ability to recognise an opportunity when they saw it. For some, that meant supplying goods and services to their fellow immigrants or the wider Australian community, like Frank Lowy and Westfield or the Vietnamese and Lebanese business people we saw in chapter 5, and then parlaying those profits into property, while for others it was in seeing that manufacturing was dying and getting out and diversifying before the bust. For others still, property development, beginning small and gradually expanding by re-investing profits into the business, has been the basis of their success. In recent years I have set out to document the stories of numerous immigrants who arrived in Australia with quite literally nothing (in the case of stateless persons not even a passport), who have gone on to achieve personal and financial success through property development, most of whom, unlike Meriton's Triguboff, have quietly gone about amassing fortunes in what is now one of the few industries left in Australia that produces a tangible physical product rather than an invisible service-based one.

Property development is in many ways an exemplar of the post-industrial economy in that it is more about image than substance and more about making short-term profits from selling consumption goods (in this case apartments) rather than building productive long-term businesses. It also provides the highest rewards to those who gamble their (or others') capital rather than to the people who actually do the work of construction. These workers are often employed on short-term contracts and paid per job rather than as full-time, continuing employees as were the factory workers of the Fordist era. Oddly enough though, apartment development, like its close relative the provision of international education, has emerged in recent years as a major export industry. Like Central Equity, from the 1990s onwards, Australia's major apartment developers began to market their wares to Asian investors, mostly the parents of international students studying at the city-based universities but also to the rapidly growing middle classes of South-East Asia and China who were seeking a safe haven abroad for their new wealth. Changes in foreign investment rules in the 1990s meant that overseas owners could buy residential property in Australia, whereas until then they had been limited to commercial, farming and tourist assets. They were, however, restricted to new properties and until 2008 could only buy up to 50 per cent of the dwellings in any one development. That rule was relaxed in the wake of the Global Financial Crisis, when it was extended to 100 per cent, a policy only reversed in 2017.

Needless to say, this has been a bonanza for developers, who have sold literally thousands of apartments to overseas purchasers in recent years, with one Reserve Bank of Australia report from 2014 suggesting 'that the value of approved foreign investment in residential property in Australia has increased, rising from around $6 billion annually in the 1990s to more than $17 billion in 2012/13'. It went on to note that this is mostly an east coast phenomenon, with

foreign investment in new dwellings ... concentrated in New
South Wales and Victoria [read Sydney and Melbourne].
In 2012/13, investment in new dwellings in these two states
accounted for almost four-fifths of the total value of foreign
residential investment approvals, much larger than the
three-fifths share that these states have in the overall stock of
housing in Australia.

And while many of those purchases are of apartments developed
by Australian companies such as Meriton and Central Equity, both
of which maintain sales offices in major Asian and Chinese cities,
others are increasingly being developed by offshore companies,
especially Singaporean, Malaysian and more recently Chinese-based
ones. The most recent towers are also of a size and magnitude way
beyond anything envisaged in the early stages of the urban renewal
era of the early 1980s. In Southbank, the north end of Melbourne's
CBD, Sydney city and Alexandria and Green Park, and even in
suburban Parramatta, towers now rise to 50, 70 and 80 storeys and
beyond. In Bathurst Street, Sydney, Chinese state-backed developer
Greenland is currently building a 66-level 235 metre tower of more
than 475 apartments, while Hengyi, 'a subsidiary of Shandong HYI
Group, a powerful player in China's Shandong province', currently
has more than 1700 apartments under construction in one 69- and
another 72-storey tower in central Melbourne, the latter on part of
the site of the old Carlton Brewery. Each of these towers, like most
of those under construction in Melbourne and Sydney at present,
was majority sold to foreign buyers. Fundamentally, they are an
export commodity, earning Australia foreign currency on a product
that can never be taken home.

Conclusion: New cities, new spaces

Designing and selling these giant towers has created thousands of post-industrial service sector jobs since the 1980s, while building them has similarly created thousands of more traditional blue-collar ones. Opening up the residential development market to 100 per cent international ownership was possibly a masterstroke of the Rudd government in its efforts to get Australia through the Global Financial Crisis, possibly saving thousands of jobs at that time and creating many more in the building boom that has followed. But it will likely be a long-term economic and social disaster. While foreign capital has had a long history in Australian urban development, it is only in recent years that we have allowed foreigners to own the majority, let alone all, of the individual units in multistorey residential blocks. Managing these blocks, especially as they inevitably age and require substantial renovation and repair, will likely become a major problem for Australian cities in the twenty-first century. Locating the dozens or sometimes hundreds of individual foreign owners of aging apartments and seeking to compel them to pay for costly repairs on investments that they have never seen, let alone lived in, will almost undoubtedly become a policy headache for city and state governments into the future. Recent fires and reports of substandard finishes on many of these buildings suggest this may already be becoming an issue, even before the boom has run out of steam. We are not alone in this of course as it is a feature of residential development in a number of post-industrial cities worldwide, many of which have similarly looked to property development as a means of reviving their cities in the post-Fordist era. But other than possibly Vancouver, Toronto and London, Sydney and Melbourne have probably gone further down this path than any other major cities in any democracy in the world.

Rezoning redundant industrial land for residential and commercial re-use has radically altered Australian cities, especially the inner regions of Sydney and Melbourne, with the latter today barely resembling its decaying, crumbling early 1980s self. Property development, and especially the emergence of the high-rise residential sector, has revitalised older neighbourhoods and created new ones virtually from scratch. The new residents who have populated these districts and filled the towers have brought life, wealth and a certain vitality to what were sometimes bleak, dying neighbourhoods which in the 1970s were losing their economic strength as well as their residents. As with the international students whose presence has changed the social and cultural profile of former student districts, so too have these new residents changed the commercial profile of formerly working-class or industrial neighbourhoods. In the next chapters, we move on from the residential structure of the new inner city to see how changing economic imperatives, including mass tourism and the commodification of culture, have altered both its morphology and demographics.

8

Business, leisure and pleasure:
Reinventing the inner city

Like millions of other visitors from around the globe, one of my favourite things to do when in Sydney is to walk the harbour foreshore from the McElhone Stairs in Potts Point, past the redeveloped Finger Wharf in Woolloomooloo, around past Mrs Macquarie's Chair, the Botanical Gardens and on to the Opera House and the Harbour Bridge. If I am feeling particularly energetic I keep going through The Rocks, around past Walsh Bay, Millers Point, Barangaroo and on to Darling Harbour. Essentially traversing the city's front and back yards, there are few urban walks anywhere in the world that more readily evoke a sense of the way a city understands itself, nor of the way it is understood internationally. In this foreshore walk of barely 10 kilometres we have the story of Indigenous possession, dispossession and resistance, convictism, trade, wealth and poverty, industrialisation and deindustrialisation, and most recently Sydney's emergence as a post-industrial, finance- and leisure-oriented city reaching to out the world. We also see the good sides and the bad of a city that might be too fond of the power of the dollar. However, what we also see in this part of Sydney is the city at its best, a place where, while many of the newer projects are semi-privatised spaces, the harbour foreshore is mostly public land accessible to the many rather than closed off for the few.

While most of the new offices, hotels and apartments that have so altered the fabric of Sydney and the rest of our cities in the last few decades were built by private developers, the ideas that led to the reinvention of the inner city as a site of post-industrial activity and leisure-oriented spaces often came from governments and the public and community sector. In the 1970s and early 1980s it was local community activists who first recognised the appeal of the built heritage of the nineteenth century inner city and led the charge to retain it. Similarly it was local ethnic business leaders who were behind moves to celebrate diversity and immigrant shopping and dining strips. State and local government bodies were also important drivers of these changes. Whereas today many celebrate the entrepreneurial city and think the appropriate role for governments is to simply declare cities 'open for business' by deregulating everything in sight and then getting out of the way, much of the most innovative thinking about reusing the redundant spaces of the inner city for new purposes has come from government and semi-government organisations.

As we saw in chapter 1, until the 1970s, across much of the western world there was general agreement that governments had a key role to play in ensuring the smooth functioning of the city. Government and semi-government organisations that went by an alphabet soup of acronyms were a key feature of city life in the Fordist-era city and were responsible for the upkeep of urban arteries, including roads, bridges, public transport, water, sewerage, electricity, gas and much else besides. Never exactly popular, these organisations and their often sclerotic, bureaucratic ways were for the most part tolerated so long as their ambitions were kept in check. Thus, the Housing Commission of Victoria (HCV) maintained reasonable support among the populace until it decided to raze whole sections of the inner city in the late 1960s, while Melbourne's MMBW only really lost its way when it decided that building freeways through these same areas was a good idea. So too

New South Wales' Department of Main Roads (DMR) overstepped the mark when it decided that an elevated freeway through Darling Harbour, Pyrmont and on into Glebe was the transport system of the future.

While, as historians Graeme Davison, Renate Howe and David Nichols have recently shown in the their book *Trendyville*, in the 1970s opposition to these organisations and their plans usually came from the Left, by the 1980s and 1990s their worst enemies were on the Right. Whereas the Left had derided them as bureaucratic monoliths doing the bidding of (and sometimes being paid by) big business, the neoliberal Right saw them as featherbedded government monopolies beholden to their employees and the unions rather than the taxpayers and residents who paid their wages. To a certain extent, both critiques had merit. These were overly bureaucratic organisations, stuffy, turgid, dull, blokey and often arrogantly dismissive of residents and their needs. Some were also hugely overstaffed, acting as employers of last resort for socially and politically connected individuals and families. But at their best these bodies were fine organisations, devoted to providing the best solutions to the myriad problems of the increasingly complex twentieth century city, to providing dispassionate and disinterested advice to governments and serving the public as opposed to private interests.

For all sorts of historical and technological reasons, these organisations often owned or controlled large acreages of urban land, much of it in the heart of the city. By definition, maritime and port authorities controlled the docks and wharves as well as harbours and river foreshores that were often directly adjacent to the CBDs of most of the major cities, while railway departments and other semi-government authorities were responsible for the vast swathes of land and infrastructure that surrounded major railway stations, wharves and other freight hubs, as well as the wholesale and retail markets that were, again, often at the very centre of the cities. Similarly, public transport authorities often found themselves with excess facilities, such as tram depots when these were replaced by buses in most Australian cities (including the old tram sheds at Sydney's Bennelong Point which were replaced by the Opera House); while many power utilities, especially the gas suppliers who owned the land on which they used to make and store gas derived from burning coal, found themselves with huge amounts of well-located, if polluted, land when Australian cities switched to natural gas in the late 1960s and early 1970s. For these reasons, many of these government and semi-government organisations and utilities were at the centre of initiatives to transform these redundant urban spaces from industrial to post-industrial uses in the 1970s and 1980s.

In this chapter we continue our journey through the physical, social and cultural landscapes of the revitalised post-industrial Australian city. We begin by looking at the importance of branding for cities in the early post-industrial era before moving on to look at some of the decision-making processes that recognised that the old economic and social order was dead and that therefore the old urban landscapes and physical structures of the industrial city were redundant and should be replaced. *With what* and *for whom* were important aspects of these questions, and ones that have not fully been resolved to this day. Finally, we discuss that, while the inner city and some key suburban nodes have been revitalised with new or updated sporting and cultural facilities in recent decades, whether the beneficiaries of much of this largesse have been those who need it least – wealthy locals and international visitors – rather than those who have found themselves on the wrong side of restructuring and globalisation.

City branding

Conceived at the height of the postwar Fordist economy in 1956, the Sydney Opera House became something of a national joke in the

175

1960s. Plagued by construction delays, cost overruns and a series of ugly spats between its Danish-born architect Jørn Utzon and various ministers and arms of the NSW government, for many Australians the Opera House seemed to be a folly. That its name and purpose was linked too closely in many people's minds with high culture and what satirist Barry Humphries used to call 'the Yartz', rather than more practical things such as roads and bridges, did not help matters. In an era of rapid population growth and fairly basic public services, it was seen as something of an indulgence, an attempt by a long-standing right-wing Labor government to bring some cultural heft to a city better known for its beaches and sunshine than for artistic endeavour. In seeking to bolster its cultural infrastructure, the Cahill government was following an example that cities on the make have pursued for centuries, if not millennia. It is no accident that the great cultural institutions of the world are found in the capitals or principal commercial cities of empires or great trading nations, nor that, in seeking to establish their credibility on the world stage, new or rising cities have long sought to steal or buy the cultural artefacts traditionally associated with civilisation. They also asserted their might by plundering the cultural artefacts of cultures they deemed inferior to their own, a process Indigenous Australians among others have been seeking, with some success, to reverse in recent decades through the repatriation of artefacts and the remains of their ancestors that were taken to Europe and elsewhere in the nineteenth centuries and beyond.

As financial power moved across the Atlantic in the late nineteenth and early twentieth centuries, the social and financial elites of cities such as New York, Philadelphia, Boston and Chicago sought to bolster their cultural credentials by buying up European cultural artefacts (including whole castles and grand houses) and transporting them across the ocean to be lodged in either a grandiose private house or a public building suitably designed in the neoclassical style deemed most appropriate to these things. Australian cities were not immune to these processes, and in a colonial setting where there has long been what historian Graeme Davison has recently referred to as a fear among intellectuals and the broader settler population that perhaps Europeans and other non-Indigenous people do not 'belong' here, these markers of European civilisation were used in some of the earliest public buildings. The University of Sydney, Australia's oldest, was founded in 1850; while in Melbourne the university, National Museum, Gallery and Public Library were all established in the early 1850s, almost immediately after separation from NSW. As in the USA, it is no accident that all of these buildings were designed in the neoclassical style, meant to demonstrate antiquity and solidity.

For years an embarrassment, in hindsight the delays in finishing the Opera House were a godsend for Sydney, as its much postponed opening coincided not only with the downturn in the local and international economy and the beginnings of the movement away from manufacturing towards services, but also and relatedly an international move towards the use of a city's cultural facilities for economic purposes. This is a phenomenon that we usually associate with the period since the 1980s, which was when, as urban sociologist Sharon Zukin has argued, 'the disappearance of local manufacturing industries and periodic crises in government and finance, culture [became] more and more the business of cities [and] the basis of their tourist attractions and their unique, competitive edge'. She is right on this, and in the 1980s and more especially the 1990s and beyond, city governments across the world have increasingly sought to capitalise on and monetise their culture and cultural infrastructure as part of their post-industrial economic strategies, but there is an argument that the modern form of these processes began in the 1970s or even earlier, rather than the 1980s.

One means of capitalising on culture was to build an iconic structure, explicitly designed to become the international pictorial symbol of a city. This became very common in the late 1960s and

early 1970s when cities worldwide began to seek to not only capitalise on the emergence of the mass tourism market but also the
telecommunications revolution then getting underway by building
huge towers that could serve multiple purposes – usually both a
tourist icon with inbuilt viewing platform facilities combined with
a giant antenna to beam television and satellite signals. Together,
these structures acted as a means of both advertising a city to tourists
while also demonstrating its technological prowess and its role as a
place of the future rather than one of the past. The 1960s and 1970s
was thus the era of the urban megastructure, some of which have
indeed gone on to become the global symbols of their city: Tokyo
Tower from 1958, Seattle's Space Needle, which dates from 1962,
and Toronto's CN Tower from 1976, among many others. While
these examples all come from democracies, these kinds of structures
seemed to hold particular appeal to authoritarian and communist
governments, with East Berlin's Fernsehturm (TV Tower) from
1969 probably the best known (and possibly the ugliest).

Sydney got one when the Sydney Tower (informally known as
Centrepoint) opened in 1981. Arguably, however, Sydney Tower
was already passé by the time it opened, partly because if every city
has such a structure then the term 'iconic' loses its meaning and currency but also because, by that time, the Opera House had already
taken on that role. As we saw in the introduction to this book,
almost as soon as it opened in late 1973, the Opera House and the
adjacent Harbour Bridge became not only the default international
images of Sydney as a city, but also of Australia as a nation. Lacking
an urban icon could be a major impediment to economic success
in the post-industrial era, so arguably the Opera House heralded
a new international phenomenon: the use by emerging cities of
architecturally adventurous cultural buildings as a marker of their
urban sophistication and arrival on the international stage. In an
era of city branding, architectural commentator and critic Deyan
Sudjic has suggested that the iconic cultural facility has, along with

the postmodern or statement office building, become an integral component of the global city ranking race and a must-have for emerging cities, whether in the US south and west, the Middle East or Asia. As reported in the *Guardian* in 2017, Chinese cities, especially those in the booming Pearl River Delta, but also increasingly in the industrialising western regions, are now at the forefront of these processes.

That these buildings should be designed by either a globally recognised starchitect, or in China's case a western-educated Chinese one, was a given. Bilbao's Guggenheim Museum, designed by Frank Gehry, became the international standard for how a declining former industrial city might reinvent itself as a cultural destination in the post-industrial era when it opened in 1997; but, as suggested by Zukin, in the post-industrial era it is not only former industrial cities or cities on the make that have pursued this strategy. From Paris's Centre Georges Pompidou, designed by Renzo Piano and Richard Rodger and opened in 1977, to London's Tate Modern (Herzog and de Meuron 2000) and the redesigned Museum of Modern Art, New York (Yoshio Taniguchi and Kohn, Pederson, Fox 2004), major global cities have also joined this race, acutely aware of the economic benefits to be derived from the cultural institutions.

Urban renewal

The walk around Sydney that began this chapter is emblematic of the importance that culture and 'buzz' have to the new inner city. So too, history and heritage are increasingly important elements of a successful urban story, vital in providing the city with a sense of longevity and permanence and thus ensuring that it does not develop a reputation as Disneyfied or worse, inauthentic, like Dubai or some of the instant cities of the Gulf. My Sydney walk has all these authentic features and more. As I walk Sydney's foreshore I am often struck by the thought that if this area did not exist in reality you'd be hard-pressed to invent a more iconic post-industrial tourist landscape. That last word is important, as this is a landscape and a highly curated one at that. The western half of the area, beyond the Bridge, is the result of a series of interventions since the 1970s that has seen the community, governments and the private sector debate, sometimes vigorously, and too often (in the case of government and business) rather cosily remake these areas for new uses. As Shirley Fitzgerald and Hilary Golder argue in their 1994 history of Darling Harbour, Ultimo and Pyrmont, 'from the late 1970s, the various levels of government and private developers would produce an apparently endless stream of plans and discussion papers' about what do with these areas as they deindustrialised and became ever more rundown.

Sometimes these plans saw governments and semi-government organisations bowing to community pressure to keep these places human in scale and for any changes to respect their history and heritage, or to include sizeable affordable housing components in new developments, as seen in the abandonment of plans to demolish and rebuild The Rocks and Woolloomooloo in the early 1970s and the curtailment of the freeway program through Darling Harbour, Ultimo and Pyrmont a few years later. Too often, however, the plans simply involved riding roughshod over local sensibilities. Competing visions of what post-industrial Sydney could be played out in various new proposals put forward for these areas in the 1970s, 1980s, 1990s and beyond. While in 1974 the Maritime Services Board of NSW was still making major investments in dock and freight facilities at Darling Harbour, including the 'commissioning of Australia's largest wharf shed, No. 5 Berth Darling Harbour', less than five years later the Wran Labor government was seeking to close the area to shipping and wharf-related activities and reinvent it as the major site of celebrations for the 1988 national Bicentenary.

Thwarted in an attempt to base a proposed international Expo there (that went to Brisbane instead), in 1984 the Wran government decided that it would redevelop Darling Harbour as a bicentennial gift to the nation. An avowedly tourism-related venture, and the 'greatest urban redevelopment in Australia's history', the new Darling Harbour was designed to provide 'all the facilities essential for an international city'. Whereas once upon a time these facilities would have included factories and port infrastructure, in the 1980s they had morphed into a convention and exhibition centre, a 12 000 seat entertainment arena and 'Australia's foremost casino and one of the nation's largest and most luxurious hotels'. Also included was an aquarium, a national maritime museum and 'the largest Science and Technology Museum in the world, the Powerhouse Museum'.

The mechanism for achieving this vision in time for the Bicentenary was the *Darling Harbour Authority Act*, introduced in 1984, which according to planners Maurice Daly and Patrick Malone granted powers to the Authority that 'superseded those of the City Council, the National Trust, and the State Planning Department', and made it 'accountable only to the Premier and his designated Minister Laurie Brereton'. The intention was to explicitly 'circumvent established planning procedures and to stifle opposition'. The language and style of brochures put out by the government and semi-government authorities responsible for Darling Harbour in the 1970s and 1980s provide important insights into the contrasting demands and styles of urban stakeholders in the Fordist and post-Fordist eras. Whereas in 1974 the Country Party Minister responsible for the Maritime Services Board's Darling Harbour redevelopment, Leon Punch, could extol the importance of new berths and sheds for the improvement of the city's hard infrastructure and capacity to handle shipping in a rather grim black-and-white brochure simply entitled 'Darling Harbour Redevelopment', a glossy 1986 colour brochure entitled 'Sydney's New Dimension: Darling Harbour' put out by his successor, the Labor

Party's Laurie Brereton, looked forward to the area becoming 'Sydney's western gateway of business, leisure and pleasure'. While the former was about the importance of trade in goods, the latter was about 'intangibles' and Sydney's new role as 'a financial, commercial residential and tourist city of world standing'.

In many ways Darling Harbour, and later the redevelopment of the wider Ultimo, Pyrmont, Cockle Bay and East Darling Harbour (Barangaroo) area, became an exemplar of the desire to re-create Sydney, good and bad. By incorporating aspects of the area's industrial and maritime heritage in the Powerhouse and Maritime museums, the retention of the swing bridge and later the reinstatement of a version of the pre-European foreshore at Barangaroo, the area's multiple and contested histories are embedded in the landscape. But as with many of these reinvented former maritime sites globally, much of it is also essentially generic, a placeless landscape of concrete, glass, bars, restaurants, hotels and apartments that could be in Baltimore, Liverpool, Hamburg or London, or the redeveloped dockside of any other former port city anywhere in the world.

Melbourne did not have a ready-made urban icon to rival Sydney's shiny new Opera House, nor did it have a sparkling blue harbour or indeed much of a waterfront at all, further entrenching its growing sense of second-city inferiority. This was not so important when the major banks and other national businesses were still based there but it became a real issue as the drift of economic, political and cultural power that had begun in the 1960s began to accelerate in the late 1970s and into the 1980s. Like every other major Australian city, Melbourne had followed Sydney's lead in the 1960s by embarking on new cultural projects, with the new National Gallery of Victoria (1968) on St Kilda Road the first stage of a new cultural precinct that eventually lined the southern entrance to the CBD. Much like a contemporary Modernist-era business headquarters, however, the design of the NGV by local architect Roy Grounds was not conducive to iconic status, resembling as it did more an inward-looking bluestone fortress than an inviting, welcoming public building. So too, the follow-up theatres and performance spaces of the Arts Centre did little to open up the south bank of the Yarra River as Melbourne's front door. That the river was polluted, neglected and cut off from the CBD by Flinders Street Station and the butt-ugly high-Modernist Gas and Fuel Corporation towers on the opposite side of St Kilda Road did not help matters. What to do about this lack of a pictorial symbol became a Melbourne obsession for the next 25 years and was arguably only finally resolved with the opening of Federation Square (Lab Architecture and Bates Smart) in 2002.

The city's search for a post-industrial future was at times comical – a 1978 international design competition to come up with an icon for the city included such gems as a huge sculpture in the shape of an 'M' and another which resembled a giant pair of breasts – but especially after the election of the Cain government, a senior member of which was architect Evan Walker, urban revitalisation became an example of public policy at its very best. While a campaign to 'Give the Yarra a Go' had been prosecuted by the *Age* newspaper since 1980, it was Walker working with his cabinet colleagues, and especially Treasurer Rob Jolly, who was responsible for turning the Yarra River waterfront from what was essentially an embarrassing joke into a leisure, cultural and tourism showcase. Jolly recalls that while in cabinet discussions he would draw on his training as an economist to set out ideas for how Melbourne might use its cultural assets for economic purposes in the post-industrial era, Walker would use his training as an architect to translate these into sketches of how the city might look in the future if these ideas were enacted.

A 1984 statement on the future directions of the Victorian economy, developed under Labor, drew on these ideas and skills, as well as emerging international ideas about the importance of culture, tourism and leisure to urban economic success and as a means of

183

remaking Melbourne as a post-industrial city. As that statement
noted, the 'national role of Melbourne as a major trading, cultural
and sporting centre', was one of Victoria's 'competitive strengths'
that could and should 'be harnessed for economic purposes'. For
this reason, the government promised to make public and privately
owned redundant inner city land available 'to build up strategi-
cally important sectors of Victoria's economy including tourism,
research, [and] the media industry'. The most obvious place to
begin this process was Southbank, some of which was owned by the
government, but much of which was in private hands and would
thus need to be compulsorily acquired. Southbank was declared an
'action area' suitable for 'intensive redevelopment as a tourism and
cultural precinct' with potential for comprehensive redevelopment
for 'arts, tourism, housing and commerce' related activities. Unlike
the Wran government in NSW, Victoria's Cain government was
drawing more on the language and ideas of big government and
Keynesian economics than neoliberalism to drive its urban renewal
agenda. But the outcomes were much the same, with Southbank
having many of the same features of redeveloped former industrial
and maritime areas across the globe: hotels, apartment towers, exhibition and cultural facilities, multiple restaurants and bars, and a
smattering of heritage sites, often marooned among the glass and
glitz of what is now a major party zone.

Cain's successor as premier, Jeff Kennett, drew on a more
overtly free-market approach to urban renewal when his government embarked on the city's next big waterfront project, the Docklands. A massive site of more than 200 hectares just west of the CBD
with more than 7 kilometres of land directly on the waterfront,
Melbourne's docklands had been controlled for many decades by
the Melbourne Harbour Trust and then from 1978 by the Port of
Melbourne Authority. Like similar port areas internationally, Melbourne's docks were a world unto themselves. Since tides and thus
ships don't follow normal working hours, by definition, ports and

docks operate 24 hours a day, seven days a week, with shift work being the norm rather than the exception. These areas therefore have their own rhythms and traditions, with early-opening pubs and cafes just some of these. They were also traditionally tough, male-dominated places where management and unions were almost constantly at war with each other. Crime, ranging from petty theft to extortion and drug dealing, was also a common feature of these places, with murder a reasonably regular occurrence, especially in Melbourne in the 1970s when the Painters and Dockers Union was essentially a front for organised crime.

Unlike Sydney and most other major ports around the world, however, Melbourne's dock workers were not residentially segregated from the wider metropolis. In part this was because the main deep-water freight port was situated next to the CBD, which until recently has never had a residential population, but also because good public transport links meant that even when dock workers were hired by the shift rather than permanently, most could access the employment hubs from the suburbs without too much difficulty. And while the inner suburbs of Port Melbourne, West Melbourne and to a lesser extent Kensington, all had dock workers and sailor residents, the city never really had port or maritime suburbs like, say, The Rocks, Millers Point and Woolloomooloo, or indeed Fremantle or Port Adelaide. What that meant was that the docks, although located right at the heart of the city, were one of Melbourne's many hidden urban secrets. And because the city is topographically flat, unlike, say Sydney or San Francisco, in order to see ships docking and loading and unloading in Melbourne, ship-spotters had to climb buildings or high fences to get their maritime thrills.

For those who preferred secrecy to carry out their nefarious deeds, or wanted to keep strangers out to avoid thefts, this was a good thing. But when Melbourne's docks became redundant, selling a vision of what might become of this land became a real issue for governments. Whereas Sydneysiders might never have visited

Darling Harbour, they could not help but know that their city was surrounded by water and that shipping was a vital part of the city's history and economy. Having been sealed off from the city centre for decades by high fences, railway lines and a major freight truck route, Melbourne's Docklands were virtually unknown to most locals. Following another initiative of the Cain Labor government, which had hoped to use it as an athletes' village for a failed 1996 Olympic Games bid, the precinct was relaunched as a private-sector-driven project by the free-market Kennett government after it came to power in 1992. Modelled explicitly on the British Thatcher government's 1980s Docklands Enterprise Zone, the Kennett government's thinking was that this would be a market-led development that would reflect the wants and desires of the marketplace rather than meddling bureaucrats and planners. Divided into seven zones and put out to public tender, Docklands' subsequent architecture and built form is a microcosm of global-era urbanism. As such, it is, like nearly all similar former dockside renewal projects across the world, essentially generic, mostly conforming to a rather bland global format.

Marketing the seven Docklands zones became another task for the creatives and marketing professionals of Melbourne's new post-industrial economy. Just as what had once been Forest Hill became Como, and Pyrmont became Jacksons Landing, so too the mostly nameless zones of the former docklands had to be reinvented for the post-industrial era. Just to the west of the CBD, what had once been a hill but which had long since been flattened in order to accommodate the movement of trains was renamed Batman's Hill after one of Melbourne's founders, John Batman, who had once lived there, while the southern end of the unimaginatively named Flinders Street Extension became Yarra Waters (later Yarra's Edge) when developed by Sydney developer Mirvac. Similarly, the south side of Victoria Dock became Victoria Harbour when it came under the control of Lend Lease, while its north side became

New Quay when sold to local developer MAB. Further north, the area where the big ferris wheel now stands became Waterfront City (it has recently been renamed The District), under the control of Dutch financial giant ING. In renaming the area, the developers sought to link the appeal of this rather windswept and soulless forecourt to a local sense of history and heritage, while closer to the CBD, Digital Harbour was presumably an attempt to tap in to the late 1990s dot-com zeitgeist.

Sport and events

While fancy new apartments, offices and exhibition and convention centres, along with new or updated cultural facilities, have been central to the revitalisation of Australian cities, arguably the biggest and most successful investments have been in sports-related infrastructure. Locally, Melbourne took the lead in this process but in doing so was following trends that had been developing internationally since the 1950s when, in the USA especially, football, baseball and basketball teams essentially auctioned themselves off to whichever city would offer them the most money and best facilities. The Brooklyn Dodgers started this trend when they moved to Los Angeles in 1957, but it became endemic in the 1970s and 1980s and beyond. Australian sports teams were not so mercenary, although the then VFL's (Victorian Football League's) South Melbourne team's decision to move their base to Sydney in 1982 was deemed heretical to some diehard Swans fans, who sought to block it. But the Swans' decision to move north made sense and reflected the problems faced by geographically based and defined sports clubs internationally in the post-industrial era. A by-product of the industrial era, organised and professional sport emerged in the nineteenth century, with teams – sustained by passionate local supporters – often linked to a region or neighbourhood through industry or local employer ties. Team names or logos often reflected these links – for example, North Melbourne, formerly known as the 'Shin Boners' because of the team's base near Melbourne's stock yards and cattle markets; while Port Adelaide might have been officially known as the Magpies but was colloquially known as the 'Wharfies' for obvious reasons.

As Australia followed the USA's lead and suburbanised in the postwar years, so too did loyalty to historic sporting teams and grounds begin to break up. One solution to declining attendances and revenues was for sporting administrators to move spectatorship to television, while another was to attempt to follow the fans to the suburbs, or as in the case of South Melbourne to look further afield for an untapped market. The ultimate act of suburbanisation in the Australian football code was the creation of purpose-built suburban stadiums, such as VFL Park developed in outer suburban Waverley and opened in 1970, and Football Park developed by the South Australian National Football League (SANFL) at West Lakes which opened in 1974. While both were state-of-the-art (albeit unfinished) facilities, like the suburban universities we saw in chapter 6, their geographic locations reflected the ideas and attitudes of the Fordist era, in that they were located in suburban areas and thus near where the fans lived, but were largely inaccessible except by car. Their suburban locations also meant that their target market was families with children rather than corporate types and tourists. Like the decision to place universities in the suburbs, this local (or less kindly, parochial) outlook and attitude made a lot of sense in the inward-looking Fordist 1960s and early 1970s; it was to become a major problem in the more outward-focused post-industrial 1980s and beyond.

Relocation to the suburbs coincided with the first waves of inner city factory closures, which meant that the departure of sporting clubs and facilities fed the growing sense of inner city crisis. In Melbourne the Cain government sought to deal with these combined problems almost as soon as it came to office in 1982. Made aware that the VFL was planning to move its showpiece Grand Final from the inner city Melbourne Cricket Ground (MCG) to its Waverley headquarters, the new government declared the match 'a major sporting event' of state significance and passed legislation to ensure that it would always be played at the MCG. Further, as part of its 1984 'future directions' statement, the government sought to recognise the importance of sport to Melbourne's culture and to harness this and its broader benefits for economic purposes:

> Melbourne is widely regarded as the sporting capital of
> Australia. Apart from the obvious publicity and tourist
> activity generated by events like the Melbourne Cup, the
> Australian Rules Grand Final and the Australian Open
> Tennis Tournament, sport is important in employment
> and decision-making. … Other indirect links exist too: for
> example the association between the Melbourne Cup and
> Melbourne's leadership in the Australian fashion industry.

The government therefore decided to spend taxpayer dollars on building new or refurbished sporting facilities, including installing lights at the MCG, thus heralding the arrival of what soon became a Melbourne winter tradition which, following the national expansion of the VFL/AFL (Australian Football League) in the 1980s and 1990s, spread to the rest of the nation: night-time football.

The Labor government's sports-led economic recovery strategy was further enhanced when in 1988 the Australian Open tennis tournament was moved from suburban Kooyong to the new National Tennis Centre (now Melbourne Park) on the CBD fringe. What was essentially an historical anomaly meant that Melbourne was one of only four cities worldwide that owned the rights to hold a Grand Slam tournament, the other being global giants London, Paris and New York. But as traditionally the last one in the yearly calendar, the Australian leg was in danger of becoming an afterthought. The poor facilities at Kooyong and often wet conditions in December did not help. The solution was to move the tournament to January (thus making it the first on the annual calendar and hence a must-win if a player was to take the 'slam'), and the development of a purpose-built, all-weather facility on the eastern edge of the CBD. The retractable roof of the tennis centre meant that it was also useable for concerts and other indoor events, and thus, like the adjacent MCG, was to be a year-round facility, a drawcard for tourists, and a reason for people to come back to the city. Similar logic was used in the late 1990s when, under the Kennett government, the AFL agreed to abandon its increasingly dilapidated Waverley headquarters for a new stadium to be built by the private sector as a drawcard and anchor for the Docklands development. It too has a retractable roof and is thus a multi-purpose facility able to host multiple events, most notably rock concerts.

With its long history of mass attendance at sporting events, Melbourne led the Australian field in using sport as a driver of the new economy but it was not alone in doing so. Across the world, new and refurbished sporting facilities are now a feature of inner city areas, especially formerly industrial zones that have been repurposed for leisure and pleasure purposes. So too, most major cities in Australia, and increasingly smaller regional ones as well, now have designated sports precincts, usually on the fringe of the CBD. The SANFL's decision to abandon its West Lakes stadium and move AFL matches to the rebuilt Adelaide Oval is the latest example of the power of sport to revitalise the city. What were sometimes embarrassingly poorly attended football matches at windswept and inaccessible West Lakes are now regularly sold out, with 50 000 spectators, many of whom get a pre-game meal or drink at the numerous bars and restaurants that now line the route from the CBD to the stadium. In recent years, regional Geelong has similarly refurbished its stadium and turned it into a tourist drawcard, host to day and night football matches as well as international cricket, while in Perth the new 60 000-seat multipurpose stadium adjacent to the casino at Burswood, 4 kilometres east of the CBD, hosted its first cricket and AFL games in 2018.

For much of the period from the mid-1980s through to the recent past, the ultimate prize in seeking to use sport to revitalise the city was to get the Olympics, which Sydney achieved in 2000. While some Olympic events were held in the repurposed Darling Harbour area and the redeveloped inner city sports precinct at Moore Park, the main athletics stadium and most of the swimming and other events were held at the purpose-built Sydney Olympic Park, 16 kilometres west of the CBD, which, while not inner city, did share many of the other features of such developments in that it was abandoned former industrial land that has been reinvented for post-industrial purposes. While, like the 1988 Bicentennial, the Olympics sped up that process, as with Darling Harbour it was already underway, with many of the older industries and factories having closed down in the 1980s, and especially as a result of the early 1990s recession. Once a rubbish dump, Sydney Olympic Park is now home to both the Olympic Stadium and a smaller venue that hosts Greater Western Sydney AFL matches, an indoor basketball and concert arena, tennis centre, aquatic centre, hockey centre and the Sydney Showgrounds among other facilities. It also boasts four hotels as well as thousands of houses and apartments, mostly in the adjacent suburb of Newington, developed by property developer Mirvac as the original athletes' village.

Conclusion: The divided city

Hosting major events, such as the Olympics, Commonwealth Games, Expos, and regular sporting contests, is now one of the key industries of the post-Fordist city. As older industries left the cities, such events filled the physical and economic voids left behind and are now key components of revitalised post-industrial urban economics. So too the regular artistic and cultural festivals or one-off blockbuster shows that are now so much a feature of the urban calendar, and the new and refurbished cultural institutions and venues that host them. These are now key economic assets, central to success in the contemporary global economic race. Just as the factories of the Fordist era were a physical expression of the importance of production to that economy, so too the convention centres, arenas, stadiums and cultural facilities of our times demonstrate that consumption, leisure and spectacle are the driving forces of ours.

Although now dramatically modified from their original visions, Melbourne's Southbank and Docklands are, like Sydney's Darling Harbour, Ultimo and Pyrmont, testament to the success of the idea of drawing on well-located but economically redundant industrial land to help to create a new urban economy in place of the one that was rapidly passing into history. In recent years Brisbane, Perth and Hobart, as well as regional cities such as Newcastle and Geelong and others, have similarly sought to embrace the waterfronts on which for years they had turned their backs. As port regions, these are places that once looked outwards to the world, entrepots in the jargon of urbanism and economics, but notwithstanding the invariable presence of a festival marketplace and the waterside dining features of such developments, too often the fortress-like buildings and the ubiquitous presence of casinos – which by definition have a business model based on keeping people and their money inside rather than encouraging them to enjoy the unique history and opportunities of the contemporary city – give these places a sense of exclusion and alienation rather than welcome. That many, especially in Sydney and Melbourne, are anchored by the corporate headquarters of major financial institutions, feeds this sense of exclusion over inclusion, of 'us' rather than 'you'.

While even in the Fordist period many of these locations were closed off to the public for safety and security reasons, there was a sense that, like the beaches, Australia's urban waterfronts, and indeed its artistic and cultural facilities, should be public resources available to all, not just the fortunate few. So too, the role of government and semi-government organisations was to provide facilities for all members of the public, not just those who could afford the entry price. There was also an egalitarian spirit about many of our public spaces and especially the rather dilapidated sporting facilities of the pre-1990s period that encouraged social mixing rather than segregation. Before sport was a business the corporate box seemed to many of us an extravagant if not slightly ridiculous place rather than somewhere to which an invitation was something to be aspired to. So too in those days of greater equality, governments and civic bodies strived to place community sporting and cultural facilities in locations where they would be most accessible to locals rather than tourists, to the suburban majority rather than the increasingly wealthy inner city minority. Like the new suburban universities, these facilities were part of the postwar social contract, a by-product of the growing prosperity of the Fordist years that many thought should be used for the benefit of the many rather than the few.

Sporting and cultural events mostly leave us with memories to cherish rather than physical objects to hold, but for all that they are no less important economically, providing jobs and livelihoods not only for the players and the performers involved but also for thousands of others who work in hospitality, retail, catering, logistics and event management among other occupations, many of which barely existed in their current form a generation ago. So too the thousands of hotel rooms and new bars and restaurants that have sprung up to cater for the crowds that now throng the city streets after a big game, a big concert or a major festival event. As we shall see in the next chapter, however, it might be that our cities are now too successful, too safe and too wealthy to be afforded by the young people who make them lively and vibrant. In the contemporary post-industrial period there is an international debate that says that while many of the spaces of the 1970s-era industrial city had outgrown their original purposes, they did allow room for a generation of writers, performers and artists to make their mark and to create the ideas, the songs and the art that were to become a vital component of the emergence of the post-industrial economy in the 1980s and beyond.

On the town: Popular culture and the new Australian city

A day or a night out at a sporting or cultural event or indeed a weekend away with family or friends centred on a match, a concert, a show or a blockbuster exhibition is now a standard part of life for many Australians. Whole sections of our cities have been refurbished and rebuilt to accommodate these crowds and to part them from their money. Often formally designated as arts and leisure precincts, or entertainment quarters the major activity (and industry) of these places is the pursuit of pleasure. That many are former docks or sites of manufacturing tells us much about what drives the contemporary post-industrial economy. A generation of Melburnians has now grown up equating Southbank with a casino rather than the old Allen's Sweets sign that used to sit atop its factory there, while for young Sydneysiders and the millions who have arrived there from the country, interstate and overseas since the 1980s, Pyrmont is a place you go to make a bet or to avoid the lockout laws rather than to earn a living doing backbreaking work in CSR's local sugar refinery. As with similar former industrial but now post-industrial regions across the globe, the sounds and smells of these former working-class districts have changed radically within a generation. While Pyrmont once resounded to the noise of freight trains moving goods along the old metropolitan goods line, today that has been replaced by the clank of the bells of the trams of the Light

Rail line, and in Southbank the factory whistle has been replaced by the whoosh of flames from the casino's hourly 'Gas Brigades'. And while Allen's and CSR disgorged a sweet but somewhat nauseating smell of burning sugar across their neighbourhoods, today the most common smell of these places is food cooking in the dozens of restaurants that line their waterfronts, or possibly later at night the smell of fresh vomit on the footpath.

It would be a mistake, though, to think that remaking the city as a place of fun is something that is unique to the present. City centres have long had this role and have traditionally been a magnet for those, especially the young, on the lookout for a good time. In part because of their importance as sites of economic and social interaction, cities are often also at the forefront of cultural change. Just as city centres were places where governments and powerful individuals and organisations sought to show off their greatness and strength through major buildings and cultural institutions, so too have they long been places where we find the highest concentration of venues associated with more popular forms of culture, including shopping, pubs and hotels, music and dance halls, nightclubs, movie and live theatres, and other forms of street life. For this reason, they are often the places where new forms of popular culture and new forms of entertainment are pioneered. Cities have also traditionally been places of social and sexual interaction and experimentation, where large crowds come together for official and unofficial gatherings. As historian Judith Walkowitz and others have shown, these aspects of city life have long been a cause of tension along class, gender and generational lines, with politicians and commentators from a variety of political viewpoints lamenting behaviours they deem deviant or anti-social.

Entertainment has thus always been a feature of cities and a central component of the urban economy, albeit often associated with the black economy and rather shady characters than with respectable society. Whereas in the past these things were a component of the urban economy, now they are often the main drivers of it. As historian Michelle Arrow reminds us in her study of popular culture in Australia, for many young people 'Friday has been the gateway to most people's weekends, the start of a two-day window when their time becomes their own'. The Easybeats' song 'Friday on my Mind' captured the importance of the weekend for a generation of teenagers and young people who couldn't wait to get to the city to dance, drink or otherwise obliterate the reality of their boring and mundane jobs in the factory or the office, or to get away from the social and moral strictures of their parents. In the 1960s and well into the 1970s the 'five day drag' did mean that the time for partying was limited to the weekend, as the desk and the lathe were always waiting to call you back.

In the post-industrial economy, however, fun *is* the economy and the bars and clubs of the city are open seven days a week, often 24 hours a day. In many places they have replaced the factories and many of the offices that once employed these young people, and are now large-scale (if badly paying) employers in their own right. The other major difference from a generation ago is that these entertainment zones are no longer cheap places to visit or in which to live. As with the zone of transition we discussed in chapters 4 and 5, for most of the twentieth century inner city regions were often associated with detached young men and recent immigrants to the city, places in which people were trapped because of discriminatory residential practices rather than places in which the wealthy aspired to live. The success of major city centres in reinventing themselves as sites of business, leisure and pleasure has reversed this and today, other than the tens of thousands of international students we met in chapter 6, they are increasingly residentially exclusive, more likely populated with a well-to-do and aging, gentrifying demographic than with young people looking for cheap accommodation near the bars, pubs and clubs of the inner city.

In this chapter we finish our journey across the new landscape of the contemporary Australian city by exploring another side of urban rejuvenation: the role of popular and youth culture in bringing life and buzz back to what in the 1970s were often derelict, moribund places. In doing so we mostly explore what is increasingly called the 'night-time' economy of the city: the bars, restaurants, pubs, clubs and casinos that are now such a feature of inner city life. We also look at the role that shopping plays in the economy of the city, and how from the 1980s onwards, city centre department stores and arcades, as well as inner urban shopping strips and suburban malls, were reinvented as lifestyle destinations, places to see and be seen as well as to buy things. Before we get to the new city, however, we journey back again to the decaying one of the 1970s to see that all was not bad back then, and that in fact the genesis of the success of the city and especially the refurbished inner city actually has its origins in what many now call the crisis years, but which those of us of a certain age fondly recall as the best years of our lives.

Music and the restructuring city

In Melbourne and Sydney, as with many cities across the world, the macro story of the 1970s-era crisis and the suffering caused by deindustrialisation and restructuring masks another story of how new forms of art, culture and especially music were enabled by the free time, reasonably high unemployment benefits and student allowances, and access to cheap accommodation made possible by economic decline and depopulation. Sharon Zukin's recent study of New York's reinvention, *Naked City*, documents some of this story, one outcome of which was the emergence of punk rock sometime in the mid-1970s. The origins of punk are disputed and variously traced back to the clubs of New York's Lower East Side and the Bowery in the mid-1970s or West London's Ladbroke Grove slightly later. The story of punk in New York, alongside the emergence of the hip hop and rap scene in the South Bronx, is well told in the 2007 documentary *NY77: The coolest year in hell*, while across the Atlantic the emergence of the London punk scene from the squats and abandoned houses of West London is the subject of documentary maker Julien Temple's *Filth and the Fury*, which charts the rise and fall of the Sex Pistols, and Don Letts' *Westway to the World*, also from 2000, about The Clash.

It was not just in the big international cultural centres that such music and counter-cultural scenes emerged at this time, however. Purists argue that punk rock can be traced back to the late 1960s Detroit of Iggy and the Stooges but similar scenes were a common feature of decaying cities around the world in the 1970s and early 1980s. In Australia the small but vibrant punk scenes in all the capitals and a few of the smaller regional cities have left a legacy that is still with us today, especially in Melbourne. Mostly based in the restructuring inner city, like those of the Lower East Side and West London, these scenes are increasingly becoming the stuff of legend, admittedly more in the minds of the cognoscenti than the general public. The music and the musicians of this period were first chronicled in journalist Clinton Walker's 1982 *Inner City Sound* and have continued to be a theme of numerous other books and articles he has published since. The Melbourne scene has also been portrayed in the feature film *Dogs in Space* (1986), set in a Richmond share house in 1978, a follow-up documentary on the film and its protagonists, *We're Living on Dog Food*, made in 2009, and an ABC radio *Hindsight* documentary, 'Do That Dance', from 2012. The era is also the subject of an episode of the 2001 *Long Way to the Top* ABC television series about the history of Australian rock and pop music, and a growing number of biographies and memoirs – mostly of those who made a name for themselves in later bands or in the fashion or creative industries.

Most of these studies focus on the key artists of the period and their musical influences and legacies rather than the environments in which the music they created evolved. Unlike the stories of the emergence of punk in New York and London, in Australia (other than Melbourne's St Kilda, which is always presented as a semi-gothic rundown former pleasure zone rife with junkies, gangsters and prostitutes), the decaying inner city neighbourhoods that housed the musicians rarely feature. In these accounts, the young musicians – overwhelmingly male – who made these scenes were all on the dole, drank too much and took lots of drugs, while living in rundown houses and flats which were invariably squalid, but rarely do they ever mention the social and economic difficulties facing inner city neighbourhoods at this time, and thus why living there was so cheap. Unlike the accounts of punk in New York and London of the mid-1970s, or indeed of Manchester, Coventry and Birmingham at the same time, in most of these accounts inner Melbourne and Sydney act as mere backdrops to the story of the music and the musicians, so the crisis of the city and the inner urban economy rarely get a mention. Instead, these neighbourhoods and their older residents are always secondary to the musicians and their creative genius.

There were a number of punk scenes across Australia at this time and while in many ways they were all derivative of what was happening overseas, each also had its own distinctive and local inflection. The largest scenes were based in the two big cities, which meant that they also became magnets for aspiring musicians from elsewhere. The main players often consciously presented themselves in opposition to the mainstream Australian music industry and what they still call the 'suburban beer barn' culture of Oz Rock, although some, such as the band Hunters and Collectors, saw themselves as having a distinctly Australian outlook and attitude, albeit with a punk style. In Melbourne, the St Kilda scene – featuring Nick Cave, Rowland Howard and others – is perhaps the best known of these groupings and was probably the most British or European in outlook. Centred on the (at that stage) very seedy Fitzroy Street and the Upper and Lower Esplanades, a series of formerly grand but now faded pubs and rotting entertainment venues, such as the George Hotel, the Prince of Wales (POW), the Esplanade Hotel (the Espy) and Bananas, facilitated musical experimentation as they could be easily remodelled to provide performance space for live music in what had previously been dining rooms, ornate hotel ballrooms or large early twentieth century dance halls. Strip clubs that were popular with bucks' groups and other men on weekends, and which were closed or under-utilised during the week, could also be easily adapted to become experimental music venues on mid-week nights. In Sydney the Trade Union Club and the Strawberry Hills Hotel in Surry Hills performed a similar role (although without the strippers).

St Kilda had multiple music venues but it was also an attractive place to live for young people because it had a plentiful supply of flats to rent, some of which were built in the 1930s, but most of which were rapidly thrown up six-pack blocks built as investments in the 1960s and 1970s. These places were mostly built without creature comfort in mind and designed to be inhabited for a good time rather than a long time. Their sheer numbers (about 75 per cent of all dwellings) and cheap rents meant that St Kilda's population densities were some of the highest in the metropolitan area. While, as we have seen, many of the rest of the inner neighbourhoods of Melbourne lost population in the 1960s and 1970s, St Kilda's increased, largely because of this growth in flats. Many of the young renters worked in white-collar jobs in the CBD or attended art colleges in nearby Prahran and Caulfield. A review of asking prices for one-bedroom flats in St Kilda advertised in the *Age* in August 1977 shows they cost about $30 per week. Two-bedroom flats typically went for $35–$45. This at a time when entry-level wages for 18-year-old clerical workers were about $70 per week after tax, student allowances about $50 per week and unemployment benefits $52.50 for those over 18. In the 1970s St Kilda was also home to a large number of rundown former mansions which could be let by the room, or by groups of people: 'share houses' in the Australian vernacular. Such sharing made renting even cheaper, with three-, four- and five-bedroom houses costing less than $20 per week per person. Late 1970s St Kilda thus combined a large group of experimental musicians, a ready audience, and cheap and abundant accommodation and venues: just the right mix for a new scene to emerge.

Across the river in the inner north and east of Melbourne, the formerly working-class and ethnic and manufacturing neighbourhoods of Carlton, Fitzroy, Collingwood and Richmond featured a variety of housing types, ranging from small rundown cottages to large terrace houses and dilapidated Victorian-era mansions. These too became share houses as their former residents, often immigrants from Italy and Greece, departed for big houses in the suburbs. This phenomenon is well documented in Helen Garner's semi-autobiographical novel *Monkey Grip* (1977) set in Fitzroy and Carlton in the mid-1970s, Leonie Stevens' novel *Nature Strip* (1994) set in the same neighbourhoods a few years later and in Richard Lowenstein's film *Dogs in Space* (1986), which was quite literally filmed in the house he and others had shared in Richmond in the late 1970s. In those days, inner city rents were cheap, with three-bedroom houses in Carlton costing $65–$75 per week in August 1977 and neighbouring Fitzroy even cheaper at $55–$65 per week. In Sydney share houses in similar neighbourhoods also typically cost about $20 per room, with even a 'deluxe' three-bedroom terrace in Surry Hills advertised in the *Sydney Morning Herald* for only $80 all up in August 1977. For a young student or unemployed person in inner Melbourne or Sydney in the late-1970s, then, rent accounted for only about one-third of their living costs. The rest could go on food, clothes and entertainment.

As nineteenth century working-class suburbs, these areas were also home to numerous small corner pubs which sometimes had unused dining or upstairs function rooms which could be readily adapted as music venues. As we have seen, the Strawberry Hills Hotel in Sydney's Surry Hills served this function, as did various other pubs in Darlinghurst, the CBD, Glebe and elsewhere. In Melbourne the upstairs room of Fitzroy's Champion Hotel became an important punk music venue in 1978, while the back dining and basement areas of both the Kingston and Royal Oak hotels in Richmond were adapted to host band nights at around the same time. Musician Paul Kelly has described the Kingston's band room as 'a dim square cavern', crowded on weekends and other nights, while the Royal Oak's Tiger Room (later Tiger Lounge) has near iconic status in Melbourne's punk history. Population density was not as high in these neighbourhoods as it was in St Kilda but the inner north was the location of a number of Melbourne's major tertiary institutions and it had a substantial student population. One of those institutions, RMIT, was the home of the independent Triple-R radio station, launched in 1976, which acted as both a conduit for new music from overseas to locals and an outlet for local music to gain a wider audience at home. In Sydney, the ABC's youth station Double J, then based in seedy William Street, Darlinghurst, played the same role.

Although membership of the various punk scenes overlapped somewhat, there were some distinct differences. The St Kilda scene was very art-school oriented, with fashion and 'the look' perhaps more important than the music. It was also militantly apolitical. The guiding lights were private school–educated boys, who, according to one of their major protagonists, the Primitive Calculators' Stuart Grant, affected an upper-class, English-accented world-weariness, bored with the world and the tedium of everyday life. The Boys Next Door's 1979 song 'Shivers', with its opening lines 'I've been contemplating /suicide /But it really doesn't suit my style /so I think I'll just act bored instead /to contain the blood I could have shed', perhaps best captures this attitude. Although songwriter Rowland

Howard insisted the song was a satire of teenage angst, it became and in many ways remains the anthem of the St Kilda scene. Melbourne's inner north sound was, on the other hand, more political and angry. Most groups shunned paid work, but for the Fitzroy scene this was because work was destructive of the soul rather than something someone else (e.g. parents) should do. While all groups revelled in the squalor and vice of late-1970s St Kilda and Darlinghurst and the grittiness of rundown Fitzroy and Newtown, the more political groups were at least aware of the fact that the cheap houses they rented and the empty shopfronts and factories they practised in were the by-products of a flatlining economy.

Festivals

As industry declined in the 1970s and 1980s, the buzz of artistic endeavour and cultural production increasingly became one of the defining features and economic strengths of the post-industrial city. One important aspect of this was the emergence of the now almost weekly round of events – community, sporting, cultural, musical and ethnic – some of which are genuinely long-standing and grassroots, but most of which are products of the post-1970s era: 'invented traditions', to borrow and slightly misuse an idea first enunciated by British historian Eric Hobsbawm. As with the ethnic street festivals discussed in chapter 5, most of these were instigated at the behest of local traders looking for a way to promote and differentiate their shopping precinct in the face of competition from the growing popularity of major suburban shopping malls, but state and local councils were also significant drivers of these policies. In going down this path, however, politicians and business leaders had to be very careful. Promoting and celebrating ethnic diversity and community harmony is one thing, but being seen to hand over tax- and rate-payers' money, resources and support to hippies, punks, political radicals, and the gender- and sexually-fluid is another, and very susceptible to the sort of moral outrage that attracts radio listeners and television viewers, not to mention sells newspapers.

While in Sydney, state and local governments – both Labor and Liberal – kept something of a distance from these new social movements in the 1970s and 1980s, in Melbourne the Cain government, likely out of desperation to do something, anything, to revive the urban economy, embraced them. Soon after coming to power in 1982 the new government appointed flamboyant former South Australian premier Don Dunstan as a member of the Victorian Economic Development Corporation, charged with finding new economic opportunities for Melbourne and Victoria. He was later chairman of the Victorian Tourism Commission, whose brief included finding ways to enliven Melbourne in order to attract more tourists. One of his recommendations was to follow the lead of his hometown of Adelaide in promoting a festival culture, hence one of the initiatives included in the government's 1984 economic initiatives statement was a campaign to promote 'Melbourne as a Festival City'. This idea and this policy thus explains why the beginnings of so many of the city's festivals can be traced to the mid- to late 1980s: Spoleto (now Melbourne International Arts Festival; MIAF), first held in 1986; a Writers Festival also first held that year; and the Melbourne International Comedy Festival, first held in 1987. This calendar has grown markedly in the years since, with the Melbourne City Council's website now promoting 59 'fantastic festivals or major events … that are on throughout the year' ranging from White Night Melbourne in February, though to the Melbourne International Jazz Festival in June, Melbourne Fashion Week in September and Melbourne Music Week in November.

While MIAF and the Writers Festival and possibly Fashion Week are about high art and culture, the others are emblematic of a conscious decision by the Cain government, and to varying degrees its successors since, to harness Melbourne's strength in alternative art, culture, music and comedy as a key facet of the restructured urban economy. As an urban-centred government with a distinct strength and level of support within the inner city arts community, the Cain government was able to both draw on and support these alternative art forms and hence the new government's events strategy actively tapped into this emerging scene and made money and other government resources available for young artists to develop and sell their ideas. Some of this money came through employment programs initiated by the federal ALP government elected in March 1983, but much was also done at state level, including the Fringe arts festival launched in 1983, and in the same year 'with a grant from the Victorian Ministry for the Arts', 'an organisation dedicated to promoting and supporting new and innovative Australian fashion, the Fashion Design Council (FDC)' whose 'annual fashion parades, held at St Kilda venues such as the now lost Earl's Court, Seaview Ballroom and The Venue, were the alternative fashion industry events of the year'. Perhaps the most successful of these initiatives, however, was the annual Comedy Festival, managed in its first year by ALP fixer and future author Shane Maloney, which now claims to be 'one of the three largest comedy festivals in the world, alongside Edinburgh Festival Fringe and Montreal's Just for Laughs Festival'.

The Fringe and the Comedy festivals were (and are) odd beasts. As with its progenitors in Edinburgh and Adelaide, the Fringe is an arm of the main acts festival but also its supposed antithesis. In theory, created in opposition to the mainstream art and culture focus of the main festival, with content designed to shock more traditional audiences, as a partly government-funded event it is by definition a component of Melbourne's cultural calendar and thus semi-official. The Comedy Festival has a similar problem. Formally instigated as part of the policy of revitalising the city, the festival was based on the recognition that since at least the 1970s Melbourne's inner city had increasingly come to be seen as the centre of Australia's emerging comedy scene. Venues such as the Flying Trapeze in Fitzroy and the Last Laugh in Collingwood gave a voice and a microphone to a range of young stand-up and cabaret artists who would go on to form the basis of the golden age of Australian comedy in the 1980s and beyond. The Comedy Festival tapped into this culture, but also extended and formalised it and, in doing so mainstreamed it.

Similar processes occurred with other oppositional movements, many of which, like alternative music, theatre and comedy, had a distinct geographic focus. While real estate spruikers increasingly talked of lifestyle locations and latte land, perhaps the most important urban district to emerge in recent decades is the gay ghetto, usually a residential and commercial district in the inner city, often but not exclusively linked to gentrification. While neighbourhoods with high concentrations of gay men and women have long been a feature of major cities internationally, these distinct 'ghettos' only became an overt feature of urban landscapes in the more tolerant, post-sexual revolution and liberation era. And while historians such as Garry Wotherspoon have shown these places were common, if furtive, in most of the major Australian cities before the 1970s, it was only in the post-industrial era that they became recognised and celebrated as a culturally and economically important component of the urban landscape.

By far the most important of these in Australia is Sydney's Oxford Street, Darlinghurst, which, as historians Clive Faro and Garry Wotherspoon note, became not only the undisputed centre of gay life in Sydney and Australia in the 1970s but was also increasingly recognised as the nation's only genuine 'queer street'. In the 1980s this reputation was to go international as Sydney emerged alongside New York, San Francisco and Amsterdam as one of the world's great gay metropolises. Faro and Wotherspoon masterfully evoke the hedonistic spirit of late 1970s Sydney:

Just to imagine a walk along lower Oxford Street at night
in the late 1970s is to feel the energy of a whole new kind of
Sydney: spilling onto the pavement are the punk drag queens
of Patchs disco, the pallor of their make-up offset by their
hair in spikes of green, purple, magenta ... Meanwhile across
the road some single figures in tight jeans, white t-shirts and
handle-bar moustaches idle past, make their way toward the
sandstone wall of what had once been the gaol: the early session
of that dance of desire, 'cruising the Wall', has just begun ...

As this passage admirably demonstrates, as with its stunning topography and important architectural and historical legacies, Sydney was almost made for the post-industrial revolution: its density, sun, humidity, and laissez-faire attitude to squalor, vice and inequality was a perfect fit for an economy and society built on leisure and pleasure.

Sydney's Gay and Lesbian Mardi Gras, which today is one of the nation's largest public festivals and street parades, grew out of this period. Beginning as a celebration of gay pride and a protest march against discrimination and police brutality against gay men and lesbians in June 1978, as it wound its way up Oxford Street, Darlinghurst from Taylor Square towards Hyde Park, the first Mardi Gras parade was broken up by police who 'arrested 53 men and women, many of whom were beaten in cells'. Thus, Mardi Gras began as a revolt but as it grew in popularity and importance as a political and social event over the next decade (especially as it became a symbol of defiance and survival in the face of the AIDS epidemic), it also became increasingly important economically and thus something for the new economy to exploit. From the late 1980s and then especially in the early 1990s it became one of the key dates on the Sydney events calendar. It also began to attract local and state government support as well as private funding as a major generator of economic activity. According to the Mardi Gras website:

The event began to enjoy extensive media coverage from the
mid-80s onwards and the crowds continued to swell, from
200,000 in 1989 to over 500,000 in 1993. Large numbers of
interstate and international travellers had started flying in for
the event as well, generating an estimated $38 million for the
NSW economy.

Its most recent annual report states that '37 per cent of our
attendees come from interstate or overseas. Mardi Gras is a key
tourist destination as the largest LBGQTI festival of its kind in the
world.'

On the streets

Oxford Street's transformation into Australia's most important gay
strip in the 1970s and 1980s reflects another of the stories of change
that have affected cities in the post-industrial period. Like other traditional high streets across the country in the middle third of the
twentieth century, in the 1960s and early 1970s Oxford Street was
rundown and dowdy, increasingly seen as a place to pass through,
'lost in a blur of speed and motion under the overriding incentive
to reach a destination which lay at either end of its extremities',
according to Faro and Wotherspoon. Once an important local and
regional shopping destination, by the 1960s Oxford Street, like its
near neighbour King Street in Newtown, was facing the challenge
of suburbia and the car. As the population of Sydney's inner suburbs
declined and as people and jobs spread to the suburbs, so too did
the need and desire to shop local. Similar problems affected Smith
Street, Collingwood and Chapel Street, Prahran in Melbourne, as
well as Brunswick Street, Fortitude Valley in Brisbane. What had
once been the great strengths of these locations, their proximity
to dense residential populations and good public transport links,

became their biggest handicaps. As shoppers moved away and the car became the dominant mode of urban transport, these streets lost their locational advantage and became ever more unpleasant environments: congested, polluted and more and more rundown.

As we saw in chapter 5, the influx of immigrants to these suburbs and neighbourhoods in the postwar period revived the fortunes of some of these streets as they began to cater for the needs of locally dominant ethnic groups, but this was more true of the smaller family-run stores than the large multistorey department stores that had been a feature of these more important inner urban strips. Like the big multistorey factories of the early industrial era that dominated the back streets of these neighbourhoods, the old department stores were by the 1970s economically redundant, increasingly superseded by the suburban shopping malls then being pioneered by entrepreneurs, like Frank Lowy's Westfield. So too the local grocery stores, owned by the likes of Moran and Cato, were increasingly challenged by the one-stop and car-friendly supermarket. Then, as immigrants began to move to the suburbs and as jobs began to be lost in traditional inner city industries, these streets began to look increasingly 'old and fusty, a dated relic of a bygone era'.

What to do with these streets was an issue that taxed the minds of local and state politicians, planners, and local business and property owners in the 1960s and 1970s. One common solution was to demolish houses and factories in adjacent back streets so as to create car parking spaces for shoppers, and thus adapt a nineteenth century urban landscape to the needs of the later twentieth. Another was to demolish a row of shops and replace them with a new-build supermarket, usually complemented by basement car parking. The supermarket would be accessed via the car park or through an arcade to the street, which might or might not retain its original facade. In more recent times, the car park and shops are sometimes complemented with cafes and cinemas, and capped with multiple levels of offices and apartments. The problems faced by these streets in adapting to the post-industrial era have thus mostly been resolved by market forces and gentrification rather than intervention. As the localities in which they are based have become more attractive and desirable places to live, so too has the land on which they sit become more valuable and has thus found higher and better uses.

As with former industrial spaces that were reinvented as sites of culture, leisure and pleasure, so too these rundown strips were reimagined as something else, beginning in the 1960s and in various waves since. As we saw in chapter 6, one powerful source of this reimagining was studentification, where places like Melbourne's Lygon Street and Sydney's Glebe Point Road became increasingly attractive to the burgeoning numbers of students and staff who were at that stage enlarging the universities. Another, exemplified by Oxford Street, was to become associated with a particular cultural or subcultural group. A third was to become a commercialised and commodified leisure, pleasure and vice zone such as Darlinghurst Road in Kings Cross or to a lesser extent Fitzroy Street, St Kilda and King Street, Melbourne; Brunswick Street, Fortitude Valley in Brisbane; Hindley Street in Adelaide; and James Street, North-bridge in Perth. In the 1970s and beyond, these places also emerged as nightclub zones, with older venues such as pubs, live theatres and restaurants refurbished into live music venues or discos, sometimes, as in Melbourne's King Street, turning what was once an essentially abandoned area and a ghost town after dark and at weekends into a thriving entertainment destination, albeit one now increasingly dominated by strip clubs.

Another option was the reinvention of the street as somewhere associated with the growing market for antiques, second-hand and recycled goods. In some places, such as Queen Street in Sydney's Woollahra and High Street in Melbourne's Armadale, such businesses have become the mainstay of the local economy as these increasingly upmarket and expensive pursuits have moved from the fringe to the mainstream. Another option was to become associated with either designer clothes boutiques or, more commonly, those associated with street wear and youth fashion, overtly copying the model pioneered in Kings Road, Chelsea and Carnaby Street in London in the 1960s. In Australia, Melbourne's Chapel Street is arguably the most successful example of this. Food and the increasing fetishisation of cuisine since the 1980s has been another factor in the reinvention of these strips, many of which are now known as eat streets or foodie destinations. More recently, the relaxation of restrictions on gambling and the sale of alcohol has changed the ambience of entertainment zones, the former arguably for the worse and the latter for the better. Off-course gambling was legalised in most states in the 1960s through the creation of government-owned Totalisator Agency Boards (TABs), which became a fixture of high streets in the 1960s and 1970s and in some states pubs in the 1980s. They have since been privatised and, like many of the thousands of poker machines that have spread outwards to all states bar Western Australia since the 1990s, are mostly owned or controlled by private companies, some local offshoots of international companies and others associated with major Australian supermarket chains.

So too casinos, which after first being legalised in Hobart in 1974 are now a feature of all the state capitals and some regional centres. In some places they rival universities, hospitals and prisons as major local employers, far exceeding manufacturing. Similarly, the relaxation of liquor licensing laws, pioneered in Victoria under the Cain government, has to a certain extent broken the monopoly of hotels on the on-premises sale of liquor, and allowed the creation of small, European-style bars that combine the sale of alcohol with food, and the provision of entertainment has seen the burgeoning of what is increasingly called a small bar culture. Many of these bars are located not on the traditional high streets but in smaller back streets and laneways. Another idea developed by the Cain government in Melbourne in the 1980s, unused lanes and alleyways in the CBD and inner suburbs have been reactivated as sites of consumption and leisure, rather than production and distribution, as a way of bringing life back to the city.

The 'night-time' and 'sharing' economies

Pubs did not go away of course, but like the localities and streets in which they are based, they have had to adapt to changing times and demographics. This is not a new phenomenon. Historians of the Australian pub, Diane Kirkby, Tanja Luckins and Chris McConville, have demonstrated that the Australian pub has long been one of the nation's more adaptable institutions, morphing from rough tents and shacks though to grand edifices, and on to sterile swill houses and then to suburban beer-barns in the 1960s. In the 1970s and 1980s many converted their former dining rooms into band venues, while from the 1990s onwards the legalisation and spread of poker machines has seen many become suburban quasi-casinos, or sports bars as they are sometimes euphemistically called. But while many remain important parts of the physical, social and cultural fabric of the cities, rising real estate prices mean that many old inner city pubs now sit on prime sites, more valuable as development opportunities than as businesses whose primary function is the serving of alcohol or the promotion of new or avant-garde forms of culture and music. The same forces that saw the closure of dozens of CBD hotels in the 1960s as their valuable sites gave way to office developments is now being repeated in inner city neighbourhoods across the country, as their corner locations (which for various historical reasons were where pubs stood) are redeveloped as apartment blocks.

Those rapidly proliferating apartment blocks provide solid profits to developers and bring new residents to the inner city but in doing so they also potentially kill off one of the key strengths of the new urban economy: fun and pleasure. This is the dilemma at the heart of gentrification and urban revitalisation. Streets and neighbourhoods become interesting and sought-after and therefore expensive because they attract the young, the bohemian and those looking for a good time. The new residents tend to be young or transient when they first arrive and don't mind a bit of noise or squalor but as they age or get priced out, things can change. What seemed like colour and excitement can quickly become a noisy nuisance. Wealthier residents, visitors and tourists bring money but they also force up prices, whether for food, drink or groceries.

They also attract a certain type of business, meaning that urban high streets have an unfortunate sameness about them. The first to go are often the local small businesses and shops such as the butchers, greengrocers and ethnic cafes that made them attractive to the new arrivals. These shops are quickly replaced by the visible signs of gentrification: firstly second-hand and vintage shops, then hipster cafes and bars and then more upmarket restaurants. Chain stores also proliferate, meaning that, like the rather generic re-imagined and revitalised post-industrial waterfront landscapes we saw in chapter 8, these streets and neighbourhoods could be just about anywhere in the world. While the chains often operate 24 hours a day, seven days a week, the bars and restaurants cater for what is increasingly called the 'night-time economy' and so do not open during the day, thus giving the streets a dead feel in daylight hours and a sometimes violent reputation at night. Such a reputation, deserved or not, can then lead to a clampdown, such as the lockout laws that some think have killed off Sydney's nightlife since their introduction in 2014.

A related problem is noise, especially from live music venues and nightclubs. In recent years gentrifying inner cities have witnessed numerous battles between developers and residents on the one hand and venues on the other. Complaints about noise and the behaviour of arriving and departing patrons have become a fixture of inner city politics since the 1990s as new residents do battle with new and established venues to stake a claim of ownership on these neighbourhoods. As cultural planner Kate Shaw has shown, many of these new developments are adjacent to existing live music venues, with the latter 'under pressure from [a] raft of issues', such as noise complaints or simply being located on increasingly valuable and developable land. One solution pioneered in Melbourne has been the introduction of 'agent of change' regulations which put the onus on new developments, whether residential or commercial, to ensure their residents will not be affected by noise. Under these regulations, it is not existing venues that are forced to change their practices to accommodate their new neighbours, but rather the new neighbours who are required to pay for the installation of sound-proofing in the venues.

While this is potentially a workable solution to the rising tensions of the new inner city, a more long-term threat lies in the increasing cost of real estate. As the inner city has become more attractive in the post-industrial era, so too have property prices risen faster than inflation. As have rents. The rooms in share houses that cost musicians and their fans $20 a week in 1970s St Kilda, Fitzroy and Darlinghurst now cost around $300 in Melbourne and at least $350 in Sydney. And whereas in the 1970s unemployed young people and students would only need to spend about one-third of their allowance to rent one of these places, today – assuming they were entitled to benefits in what is a now much stricter and heavily-policed system – they would need to spend more than 100 per cent. Or simply leave and seek to recreate some of the ambience of places further out, or in the regional cities such as Newcastle or Castlemaine.

The newer, wealthier residents of the inner city can quickly become rather territorial about 'their' neighbourhood and 'their' community. And while normally the opinions of rate-paying residents count for more than those of renters, who are rightly or wrongly perceived to be more transient, or those of tourists and visitors who are there for a good time not a long time, given that the businesses which cater for these visitors are now often the life-blood of the local economy, politicians increasingly find themselves in a bind about who to support – those who vote or those whose businesses help to keep rates down? The emergence of the 'sharing economy' has exacerbated these tensions. In common with residents of rejuvenated cities internationally, Australian inner city dwellers now find themselves sharing not only their streets and venues with tourists, but increasingly their residential buildings as well. Visitors are attracted to these neighbourhoods for the same reasons that locals were and are – their facilities, ambience and leisure and entertainment facilities. But whereas more long-term residents might be coerced into turning the noise down rather than face public shaming tomorrow or Monday, visitors will by then have gone home or moved on to the next party town. At a more basic level, that $300 per week room might be worth the same per night if let to tourists, meaning that absentee landlords – an increasingly important segment of the rapidly developing inner city apartment market – have an incentive to maximise their returns, whatever the social costs to their neighbours. It may be that the very success of an economic model based on leveraging fun for profit might be the thing that kills it.

Conclusion

In her 1995 book the *Cultures of Cities* Sharon Zukin noted how in the post-industrial era her earlier loft-living artistic protagonists had inadvertently become the saviours of the urban economy in the 1980s and beyond. As popular culture became more and more the focus of urban economics, culture – both established and experimental – increasingly became the driver of economic growth and real estate appreciation. In the late 1980s and beyond, savvy developers and urban politicians kept a close eye on the movement of artists into particular neighbourhoods, knowing that in all likelihood these would soon be the next urban gentrification hotspots. Artist-led gentrification has in recent years become an international cliché, with city governments desperately seeking to use creativity and innovation, broadly defined, to market their city to investors and tourists alike.

Such government- and market-led cultural rejuvenation comes with a political and an artistic price, however. For artists there is the Faustian bargain of becoming safe and official and thus the antithesis of the cultural outlaw. With rock music there is an in-built generational aspect to this; in order to retain its vitality, music needs a never-ending supply of young and angry artists seeking to express themselves in a way that is relevant to their peers. Such new sounds can come from places of economic equality and opportunity but more often than not it is poverty, exclusion or possibly the free time that unemployment brings that drives musical and artistic creativity. Across the globe there is currently a debate about whether interesting new forms of culture can really be forged in the booming, increasingly expensive and unequal urban environments of the contemporary post-industrial city. While politicians and civic leaders might not like to hear it, there is an argument that, as in the 1970s, the best way to generate new forms of art and thus new branches of the cultural economy to exploit into the future might be to either turn a blind eye to minor welfare fraud and social deviance among the young or to actively intervene in the housing market to seek to ensure equality of access to the city and its cultural and residential spaces for those who are poor, whether permanently or temporarily. Or perhaps at the more extreme end, politicians and civic leaders might need to think about engineering or, as in the case of the 1970s, accidentally presiding over an economic downturn in order to drive a new generation of creativity. It may be that the very thing that will save the new urban economy is its collapse.

Conclusion:
Globalisation and the Australian city –
An opportunity wasted?

Even though Australia has long been one of the world's most urbanised societies and has in recent years become one of its most multicultural, there still exists a sense that the 'real' Australia is somewhere 'out there' in the Outback and that the cities are somehow alien and parasitic, places where the true wealth of the nation – created in the Bush or down the mine – is squandered. We see evidence of this in the way that decisions to build regional or mining infrastructure are hailed as nation building, while money spent in the cities – other than on freeways – is somehow wasteful. An example: my commute from my home in Melbourne's inner city to my office at Monash in Clayton is about 25 kilometres. If I take the very expensive private tollway, the journey can take anywhere from 40 minutes to an hour or so. On the toll-free roads it can take anywhere up to two hours on a bad day. On public transport it usually takes about an hour, but that hour involves two trains and, for the last 3 kilometres or so, a connecting bus that links the Fordist-era, car-based campus with the train network. Until recently that bus came every 15–20 minutes but since 2011 a shuttle service has operated every few minutes during semester time. Even so, every morning at Huntingdale station a queue of mostly international students forms, waiting for an inefficient bus that stands in for a train link that was promised 50 years ago and is yet to be delivered. That queue of international students is, like the bulk coal and iron ore carriers and the gas tankers that clog our northern ports from time to time, an export bottleneck and an economic cost to the nation. What is more, it is a cost to an emerging high-value-added industry rather than a declining extractive one.

Had the windfall profits from the mining boom and the economic opportunities that grew out of the industrialisation of China been used to build or rebuild urban infrastructure such as the Monash train line, or invested in genuine skills training and enhanced manufacturing productive capacity, our cities could have become economic powerhouses, gateways to and from the booming nations to our north. While it is true that of the nation's top ten export-earning industries only two – education and financial services – are predominantly urban based, that this is so reflects national policy decisions that were deliberately taken in the late 1990s and early 2000s, rather than some accidental outcome of forces beyond the nation's control. Not only has Australia wasted many of the opportunities afforded by the emergence of Asia in the 1980s and 1990s, but even more wasted were the huge windfalls of the early 2000s mining boom which were given away as tax cuts to the already wealthy or as subsidies to property speculators rather than invested in long-term productive assets. Without being too partisan, future historians are likely to see the Howard Liberal government's 1999 decision to halve capital gains tax as probably the worst economic decision of the globalising era. What that decision, combined with unlimited deductions for losses on residential investment expenses (negative gearing) did, was to effectively declare that in Australia profits from speculative capital gains would be handsomely rewarded, while the risks associated with long-term saving and productive investment in high-value-added research, development and production would be punished. It is no accident that Sydney and Melbourne property prices began to climb rapidly after this policy was implemented. Add in the Rudd government's 2009 decision in the wake of the Global Financial Crisis to allow 100 per cent foreign ownership of new residential property and it is no surprise that our house prices are so high, or that they are so vulnerable to an internal or external economic shock.

More than 40 years on from the beginnings of the process of freeing up the Australian economy, there remains a debate about whether, without a solid manufacturing industry and a genuine high-value services one, Australia can truly remain a First World country into the globalised twenty-first century. Dominated as it still is by exporting unprocessed commodities and selling fixed assets such as real estate to foreigners, Australia's economy retains many of the features of the 'banana republic' Treasurer Keating warned us about in 1986. There is also an ongoing debate about whether the means used since the 1970s and 1980s to attempt to achieve international competitiveness have been worth it. Critics from both the Left and the Right have argued about the speed of the rollout of tariff reductions; the impacts of these on different regions, groups, communities and classes; and whether Australia's decision to undertake unilateral tariff cuts and deindustrialisation have left the country economically isolated and vulnerable to an external shock. There is also an ongoing debate in the major cities about whether mass immigration and rapid population growth continue to be beneficial or whether we have embarked on what is sometimes called a 'population ponzi' whereby economic growth is simply a function of an ever-larger population. As with the seemingly invincible Japanese model of the late 1980s, there is a question about whether our current success is simply a mirage based on inflated property prices and hype rather than solid productive and sustainable foundations. Still others wonder whether endless population and economic growth is environmentally sustainable in a continent with a dry and warming climate.

As an historian, I have more insight into what happened in the past than ability to predict the future, but certainly there is little historical evidence to suggest that the levels of population growth, house prices and the rate of apartment building we are currently seeing in Sydney and Melbourne can go on forever. While in the post-Fordist era cities and nations no longer need to produce tangible goods in order to be economically successful, they do need to produce and trade at least something of intrinsic value, whether it be ideas, financial services, education, research or cultural products. Selling coffee, food and massages to each other, and constructing and trading residential investment properties among ourselves or indeed selling them to overseas investors looking for a safe place to park their money might be a source of short-term jobs and profits but is simply not sustainable in the longer term at the urban level, let alone the national one. Genuinely productive cities and societies invest in industries that produce long-term future dividends rather than short-term speculative profits.

While the current property boom may still have years to run, it could just as easily collapse at any time, leaving individuals and banks with massive debts which, as in Ireland after its property bubble burst in 2008, will likely be transferred to the public sector balance sheet. And, as in the wake of the collapse of the Marvellous Melbourne boom of the 1880s, many individuals who have come late to the property party will be left with debts they will never be able to repay and, unlike in parts of the United States where many of those who got caught up in the subprime crisis were able to simply walk away from their properties and their debts, in Australia, as in Ireland, those debts will remain a burden for years to come. Similarly, those who have looked to property investment to fund their retirement will find that it is yield (that is, rental income) rather than potential capital gains that should be the determinant of a property's worth. They will learn that it is income from rent rather than nominal capital gain that funds a retirement, as it is impossible to live on the latter until the property is sold and the gain realised. They may also find that what until recently looked like a massive windfall gain has become a massive loss, which in turn means that what was planned to be their retirement income has become an expense that will need to be paid from a government pension.

None of this may come to pass of course. And none of it needs to. While in hindsight it is tempting to look back and see the causes of our present economic and social malaise in policies such as opening up the economy to global competition, the elimination of tariffs and the deregulation of the financial sector, there is no reason why these things needed to have led to our current situation. If, instead of chasing short-term speculative profits, Australian individuals, businesses and government had taken advantage of the economic, social and cultural opportunities afforded by the industrialisation and urbanisation of Asia to create a genuinely innovative, high-wage society, then the country could easily have been one of the great success stories of the global era. Similarly, if the benefits and costs of globalisation had been more evenly shared then perhaps we would not have some of the current concerns about high rates of immigration, expensive housing and the growing sense that the gaps between rich and poor, urban and rural, young and old are rising and widening.

Initially highly sceptical of the arguments of free-market economists, like many of my contemporaries at some point in the late 1980s or early 1990s I became a convert to the idea that globalisation did indeed have the capacity to open up all sorts of new economic and social possibilities for a better world. Like others, I came to accept that new information and communications technologies and the urbanisation and industrialisation of Asia meant that it simply made no sense for Australia to continue making things that could be better produced at a fraction of the cost elsewhere. Instead, as did the Jackson Committee, free-market economists and increasing numbers of the social democrat Left, I accepted the argument that those things should be manufactured in less developed countries whose wage and other costs were much lower than ours, and that we should move further up the global supply-chain to a high-value-added manufacturing- and services-based economy.

The opening of Eastern Europe and Russia after the collapse of communism similarly offered new possibilities for what then US

President George Bush called a 'new world order' based on free trade, multilateralism and more open borders. For a short while in the early to mid-1990s there seemed to be a possibility that globalisation might just deliver a world that was better and fairer for all, especially for those in the developing world, and for many groups in the developed world, such as women, immigrants and their children, the LGBQTI community and others outside the mainstream, for whom the economic opportunities of the Fordist era were often more illusory than real. As such, and like many of the politicians, planners and urban thinkers I have discussed in this book, I began to recognise that not only would most of these opportunities be found only in cities, but increasingly in open, multicultural ones like Sydney and Melbourne, where being different was not only acceptable but increasingly the norm. I also began to recognise that such differences and openness to new ideas and ways of thinking were not only attractive features of contemporary city life, but also increasingly important competitive economic advantages.

The terrorist attacks on the World Trade Center in 2001 and the emergence of fundamentalist forms of religion and nationalism helped to put paid to some of these hopes, resulting in the closing of borders in much of the developed world and increasing numbers of wars elsewhere. But so too across much of the English-speaking world, including Australia, did a slavish devotion to ideas about the virtues of the free market and the supposed benefits of liberal economics mean that globalisation increasingly came to be associated in many people's minds with speculation and greed, with the sometimes obscene profits the winners from economic change were amassing from privatisation and the financialisation of the economy and, on the other hand, the unemployment, displacement and misery that seemed to be the lot of the losers from these processes.

While in Australia – as in the USA, the UK and elsewhere – many of the winners from globalisation have been urban dwellers, so too have many of the losers. Add to those the residents of the smaller capitals and regional cities and towns who have seen their manufacturing businesses close, and banking, retail and government jobs cut in the name of efficiency, is it any wonder that we are seeing electoral revolts against what are sometimes called the 'urban elites'? While Sydney has generally profited from its role as the nation's most global city during this period, plenty of its residents, especially those who live in places like Liverpool, which is a long way literally and figuratively from the Opera House and the Harbour Bridge, have missed out on most of these profits. In North Sydney nearly 40 per cent of households earn more than $3000 per week, while in Liverpool only 6 per cent do. Similarly, in Broadmeadows and Elizabeth, few of the locals, and especially formerly blue-collar male workers, have much to show for 40 years of economic 'reform'.

But again, it did not have to be like this. There is an argument that, had political, business and civic leaders played their cards better, Sydney could have become one of the world's great cities in the global era and been seen as an exemplar of urban success in the twenty-first century. After all, not many cities can offer such a mix of natural beauty, instantly recognisable architectural icons, ethnic and cultural diversity, and a prime location in the Asia-Pacific time zone. In the same vein, Melbourne's civic and political leaders could have done more to leverage its frequent designation as a globally 'liveable city' and its extraordinary ethnic and cultural diversity as important economic assets, competitive advantages that are highly valued in the global era, to create one of the world's truly great multicultural cities. So too, Adelaide, Brisbane, Canberra, Darwin, Hobart, Perth and Australia's many regional cities could have drawn on their natural and human strengths to actively develop viable post-industrial, global futures.

While in the wake of the resurgence of nativist and nationalist politicians and political movements across the world in recent years there may be an emerging question about the future direction of global economic policy, it is highly unlikely that the information, communication and transport technologies that have brought the world closer together in recent decades can or will be unwound. Some form of globalisation will likely remain in place for decades to come and, given current economic and technological trends, that globalised future will almost certainly be urban. The cities that will lead that trend will also almost certainly be socially and culturally diverse, multicultural, tolerant and open to new ideas and ways of thinking – the very features that distinguish Australia's biggest cities. As we have seen throughout this book, at various times over the last 40 years Australia's national, state and city leaders have sought to harness these strengths and to use them for the advantage of all, but in recent years a real complacency appears to have set in, with speculative profits taking precedence over long-term planning. Without wanting to end this book on too down a note, I fear that future generations will look back and ask why the urban opportunities of the early global era in Australia were so wasted.

Sources

Introduction: Globalising the Australian city

Figures throughout this book on population change and employment across time are derived from ABS Censuses 1971–2016. Since 2001 these have been available on-line via QuickStats. Contemporary and projected population figures for the City of Melbourne are available through its Research and Statistics portal. On the importance of suburbia and home ownership to Australia's historical sense of itself see Graeme Davison, 'The First Suburban Nation?', *Journal of Urban History* (1995). For an overview on the international historical literature on deindustrialisation since the 1970s see Steven High, 'The Wounds of Class: A historiographical reflection on the study of deindustrialization, 1973–2013', *History Compass* (2013). Also see Steven High, Lachlan MacKinnon and Andrew Perchard (eds), *The Deindustrialized World: Confronting ruination in postindustrial places* (2017). The quote about abandonment in London in the 1970s comes from Joe Kerr's introduction to his and Andrew Gibson's *London: From Punk to Blair* (2003). For a review of the literature on the emergence of 'world' and 'global cities' since the 1970s see Ben Derruder, Anneleen De Vos and Frank Witlox, 'Global City/World City', in Ben Derudder, Michael Hoyler, Peter J Taylor and Frank Wilcox (eds), *International Handbook of Globalization and World Cities* (2012). On the emergence of immigrant gateway cities see among others Audrey Singer, *The Rise of New Immigrant Gateways* (2004), and Marie Price and Lisa Benton-Short,

'Immigrants and World Cities: From the hyper-diverse to the bypassed', *GeoJournal* (2007). On the role of culture and creativity in successful post-industrial cities see Sharon Zukin's *The Cultures of Cities* (1995) and *Naked City: The death and life of authentic urban places* (2010). Charles Landry, Richard Florida and Jan Gehl's ideas can be found at their respective personal websites.

1 Opening up and closing down

The quote about the achievements of the 'duumvirate' come from Jenny Hocking with Clare Land, Natasha Campo and Sarah Tayton, *Gough Whitlam: Guide to Archives of Australia's prime ministers*, National Archives of Australia (2016). On the Whitlam government more generally see Jenny Hocking, *Gough Whitlam: His time* (2012). On Elizabeth and its experiences of growth and decline from the 1950s, the 1990s and beyond see Mark Peel, *Good Times, Hard Times* (1995) and *The Lowest Rung: Voices of Australian poverty* (2003). The figures for the various indices of misery across Australia, the UK and the USA are derived from data generated by the Economic Research Unit of the Federal Reserve of St Louis (FRED). The Crossroads group report, *Australia at the Crossroads: Our choices to the year 2000* was written by Wolfgang Kasper, Richard Blandy, John Freebairn, Douglas Hocking and Robert O'Neill in 1980; the quotes used here can be found on pp. 211–15. John Button's views and policies on tariffs and protection and the Swedish Model come in Frank Bongiorno, *The Eighties: The decade that transformed Australia* (2017), pp. 286 and 53, and John Button, *As It Happened* (1998), pp. 341–61. Andrew Scott's interpretation of *Australia Reconstructed* is contained in his chapter 'Australia Reconstructed' in Andrew Reeves (ed.), *Organise, Educate and Control: The AMWU in Australia, 1852–2012* (2013). The figures for the employment profile in the privatised utilities sector come from the Australia Institute report, *Electricity Costs: Preliminary results showing how privatisation went seriously wrong* (2017).

2 The twilight of the Fordist city

Beyond the sources on deindustrialisation already noted above, on deindustrialisation in Australia see Dennis Glover, *An Economy is Not a Society: Winners and losers in the new Australia* (2015), Erik Eklund, *Steel Town: The making and breaking of Port Kembla* (2002) and Adrian Regan's thesis, 'Re-manufacturing the City: Geelong, 1945–1993', (2013). There were two reports on inner Melbourne published by the MMBW in 1977; the first was produced in-house and is called *Melbourne's Inner Area: A position statement*, while the second, *Socio-economic Implications of Urban Development*, was undertaken for the Board by Urban Economic Consultants; the figures on employment sectors come from the former. *Fitzroy Industrial Land Use and Development Trends* (1978) was produced for the Council's Urban Planning Office by consultant Roz Hansen. This history of Victoria Street is based on Seamus O'Hanlon and Simone Sharpe, 'Becoming post-industrial: Victoria Street, Fitzroy, c.1970 to now', *Urban Policy and Research* (2009). The quote about displaced workers in Broadmeadows in the 1990s comes from Mark Peel's *Lowest Rung*, p. 118, while those from the recently redundant Ford workers come from the *Age*, 7 October 2016. The information on unemployment rates among redundant Mitsubishi workers is from Kathy Armstrong, David Bailey, Alex de Ruyter, Michelle Mahdon and Holli Thomas, 'Auto plant closures, policy responses and labour market outcomes: A comparison of MG Rover in the UK and Mitsubishi in Australia', *Policy Studies* (2008) and an interview with Andrew Beer, SBS News, 17 August 2016.

3 Working and not working in the post-industrial city

Employment figures throughout this chapter are drawn from the 2016 Census, while those for the Japanese stock market and Tokyo land price declines come from FRED. Those for crane counts in the major capital cities come from Rider Levett Bucknall, Oceania Research & Development and Communication's July 2017 'Crane Index'. David Graeber sets out his thesis about the value or otherwise of many modern jobs in *The Utopia of Rules: On technology, stupidity and the secret joys of bureaucracy* (2015) and has recently expanded on it in *Bullshit Jobs: a Theory* (2018).

4 Cosmopolis: Urban multiculturalism

The figures for immigration and settlement in this and the following chapter are derived from the ABS' five-yearly censuses going back to 1947. Tim Colebatch's analysis of the ethnic make-up of contemporary Melbourne and Victoria can be found in 'One census, three stories', *Inside Story*, 5 July 2017. Rachel Stevens and I discuss the urban nature of Australian multiculturalism in 'A nation of immigrants or a nation of immigrant cities? The urban context of Australian multiculturalism, 1947–2011', *Australian Journal of Politics and History* (2017). Much of the material in the first half of this chapter is drawn from that article. The concentric model of the city was first described in Robert Park and Ernest Burgess, *The City: Suggestions for investigation of human behavior in the urban environment* (1925). Frank Lancaster Jones documented the Italians of Carlton in 'Italians in the Carlton area: The growth of an ethnic concentration', *Australian Journal of Politics and History* (1964). The story of Nhill's Karen community can be found in 'The Karen of Nhill: An experiment in regional settlement', *Impact*, 17 February 2014.

5 Global migrations, local impacts

David Harvey's jibe that contemporary Manhattan is now one giant gated community can be found in his *Rebel Cities: From the right to the city to the urban revolution* (2012), p. 23. The description of the 1975 Festival of All Nations comes from the *Melbourne Times*, 5 November 1975. The transcript of Mike Zafiropoulis' 1979 speech is from the Public Records Office Victoria (PROV) file: VPRS11790/P/1/43 'Festival of All Nations'. The information on ownership of shops in Springvale comes from rate records of the former municipality now held by PROV, file nos. VPRS 17780/1/12 and 24. Those for Lakemba come from Canterbury Council's rate records, now held by Canterbury-Bankstown Council. My thanks to Lia Chinnery from the council for granting me access to these. The quote about Footscray's sounds and smells comes from an interview with an anonymous source for the Australian Generations Oral History Project, 20 and 22 June 2013, while the allegation about the food habits of immigrants in Campsie in the early 1980s comes from Geoffrey Blainey, *All For Australia* (1984), p. 132. The issue of non-English-language signs in shopping strips was discussed in the *Sydney Morning Herald*, 12 February 2003, while the descriptions of the variety of foods and products available in contemporary Dandenong are from the City of Dandenong's website.

6 Studentification: From trendies to PBSAs

The figures here for local, international, full-time and part-time students, as well as the number of higher education institutions in the 1970s and 1980s come from the Green Paper. The 'Dawkins revolution' and its ongoing impacts is comprehensively discussed in Stuart Macintyre, André Brett and Gwilym Croucher, *No End of a Lesson: Australia's unified national system of higher education* (2017). The figures for international students, their source countries and the growth of the sector since the early 2000s come from Australian Government, Department of Education, 'International Student Data 2017'. The Deloitte Access Economics Report is *Growth and Opportunities in Australian International Education* (2015). On studentification internationally see Darren Smith, 'Studentification – the gentrification factory', in R Atkinson and G. Bridge (eds), *Gentrification in a Global Context* (2005). On studentification and the gentrification of Carlton see Graeme Davison, 'Carlton and the Campus: The University of Melbourne and the gentrification of inner Melbourne, 1958–1975', *Urban Policy and Research* (2009), and Tanja Luckins, 'Gentrification and cosmopolitan leisure in inner-urban Melbourne, Australia, 1960s–1970s', *Urban Policy and Research* (2009). 'Trendies' and their impact on the Australian inner city are discussed in Renate Howe, David Nichols and Graeme Davison, *Trendyville: The battle for Australia's inner cities* (2014). The figures for enrolments and the origins of students for the various universities are drawn from information available on their websites. The story of Monash and its post-1980s growth is drawn from Graeme Davison and Kate Murphy, *University Unlimited: The Monash story* (2012), while that of UNSW comes from Julia Horne and Stephen Garton, *Preserving the Past: The University of Sydney and the unified national system of higher education, 1987–1996* (2017). The quote about UNSW as 'a city within a city' comes from 'UNSW At a Glance' (2015). The transcript of Keating's speech opening RMIT's Building 8 can be found at Australian Government, Department of Prime Minister and Cabinet, 'PM Transcripts'. The JLL Report on PBSAs is entitled *Australian Student Market Accommodation Review* (2016).

7 Lifestyle destinations: Building the new inner city

For the story of the Como site see Simone Sharpe, 'The Como Project, South Yarra: From factories to apartments', *Green Fields, Brown Fields, New Fields: Proceedings of the 10th Australasian Urban History, Planning History Conference* (2010). Tony Dingle and I interviewed Rob Jolly on 28 April 2008 and Evan Walker (with Victor Sposito) on 7 May 2008. Much of the information on Melbourne in this section draws on my article, 'The Events City: Sport, culture and the transformation of inner Melbourne, 1977–2006', *Urban History Review/Revue d'Histoire urbaine* (2009), while the discussion of lifestyle developments draws on my chapter, 'Selling lifestyle: Post-industrial urbanism and the marketing of inner-city apartments in Melbourne, Australia, 1990–2005', in Steven High, Lachlan Mackinnon and Andrew Perchard (eds), *The Deindustrialized World: Confronting ruination in postindustrial places* (2017). Richard White unpacks the term 'Australian way of life' in *Inventing Australia: Image and identity, 1688–1980* (1981). The quotes about the Stamford and Harrington apartments in Sydney come from the *SMH*, 4 and 11 July 1998, while those about the Panorama and St James come from my brochure collection. The information on the source of international demand for dwellings in Australia comes from Maurice Gauder, Claire Houssard and David Orsmond, 'Foreign investment in residential real estate', *Reserve Bank of Australia Bulletin*, June Quarter (2014), while the quote about Hengyi comes from the *Australian Financial Review*, 21 April 2015.

8 Business, leisure and pleasure: Reinventing the inner city

Graeme Davison discusses the fear of intellectuals and others that non-Indigenous peoples did not belong in Australia in *City*

Dreamers: The urban imagination in Australia (2016), pp. 255–68. The Zukin quote about the economic role of culture in the contemporary city comes from *Cultures of Cities*, p. 2. Deyan Sudjic documents the attempts by governments in the 1980s to use or re-use their cultural assets for branding purposes in *The 100 Mile City* (2002), while attempts to do the same in contemporary China featured in the *Guardian*'s 'Cities' series, 18 March 2017. The history of Pyrmont, Ultimo (and Darling Harbour) and the attempts by the Wran government in the 1980s to reinvent Sydney's waterfront is told in Shirley Fitzgerald and Hilary Golder, *Pyrmont and Ultimo: Under Siege* (1994). Information on the 1974 proposal to develop the No. 5 Goods Shed at Darling Harbour comes from a pamphlet put out by the NSW Maritime Services Board that year simply called 'Darling Harbour Redevelopment', while the quotes about the later plans for the area's comprehensive redevelopment come from The Darling Harbour Authority, *Sydney's New Dimension: Darling Harbour* (1986). The criticisms of the *Darling Harbour Authority Act* come from Maurice Daly and Patrick Malone, 'Sydney: The economic and political roots of Darling Harbour', in Patrick Malone (ed.), *City, Capital and Water* (1996). The Victorian ALP's plans to reorient Melbourne's economy towards services and spectacle were set out in *Victoria: The next step. Economic initiatives and opportunities for the 1980s* (1984). Kim Dovey discusses Southbank and the Docklands in *Fluid City: Transforming Melbourne's urban waterfront* (2005).

9   On the town: Popular culture and the new Australian city

On the history of the city as a place of both fun and danger see Judith Walkowitz, *City of Dreadful Delight: Narratives of sexual danger in late-Victorian London* (1992). The quote about the meanings of Friday comes from Michelle Arrow, *Friday On Our Minds: Popular culture in Australia since 1945* (2009). Stuart Grant recalled Melbourne's 1970s punk scene in an interview with me on 25 May 2017, while Paul Kelly discusses the Kingston Hotel in *How to Make Gravy* (2011). The numbers and descriptions of contemporary Melbourne's various festivals and events comes from the City of Melbourne's website, while the information on the Fashion Design Council is drawn from Julia Powles, 'Rewind: Image codes, art about fashion: The FDC and the "Precocious polemics of fashion"', ACCA (nd). The quotes about the Melbourne Comedy Festival and the Sydney Mardi Gras come from their respective official websites. The information and quotes about Oxford Street come from Clive Faro and Garry Wotherspoon, *Street Seen: A history of Oxford Street* (2000), pp. 205, 206, 238 and 240. Changes in the historical role and character of hotels in Australia are detailed in Diane Kirkby, Tanja Luckins and Chris McConville, *The Australian Pub* (2011), while Kate Shaw sets out the challenges of contemporary gentrification for inner-city music venues in 'Independent creative subcultures and why they matter', *International Journal of Cultural Policy* (2013).

Abbreviations

ABS	Australian Bureau of Statistics
AFL	Australian Football League
ALP	Australian Labor Party
ACTU	Australian Council of Trade Unions
CBD	central business district
DMR	Department of Main Roads (NSW)
GMH	General Motors Holden
HCV	Housing Commission of Victoria
MCG	Melbourne Cricket Ground
MIAF	Melbourne International Arts Festival
MMBW	Melbourne Metropolitan Board of Works
PBSA	purpose-built student accommodation
QUT	Queensland University of Technology
RLB	Rider Levett Bucknall
RMIT	Royal Melbourne Institute of Technology
SANFL	South Australian National Football League
SEMIP	Southeast Melbourne Innovation Precinct
TCF	textiles, clothing and footwear
UNE	University of New England
UNSW	University of New South Wales
UTS	University of Technology Sydney
VFL	Victorian Football League

Acknowledgments

As with all books this one has had a long gestation, dating back to an ARC-funded project (DP0663310) on deindustrialisation and the emergence of the new post-industrial Melbourne I began with my friend and mentor Tony Dingle in 2006. Simone Sharpe and Carla Pascoe worked with us as research assistants on that project while Adrian Regan joined us to undertake a PhD thesis on similar processes in Geelong. Many of the ideas developed here grow out of research by and conversations with all four. So too did discussions on deindustrialisation and urban change at a symposium held with colleagues from Melbourne and London in Prato, Italy in 2009, and conversations and collaborations with Steven High and his colleagues at Concordia University in 2013. The sections on immigration and the city reflect ongoing collaboration with Rachel Stevens and draw in part on materials collected as part of the ARC-funded Australian Generations Linkage project undertaken with colleagues from Monash, La Trobe, the ABC and the National Library of Australia (LP100200270), while some of the ideas in the final chapter are developed from a later ARC project on music and the city (DP160100537) led by Shane Homan with Catherine Strong, John Tebbutt and Sam Whiting.

The more immediate impetus for the book was a conversation with Phillipa McGuinness after a symposium in honour of Graeme Davison's *City Dreamers*, held in Melbourne in late-2016. My thanks to Graeme and Brendan Gleeson for inviting me to take part in that symposium and to all attendees for the feedback on my paper that day. Phillipa's enthusiastic response to my ideas and support for this book since have been truly inspirational. So too the support of her team at NewSouth, especially Paul O'Beirne who guided the book through to publication. Fiona Sim was an excellent copyeditor and a pleasure to work with. Numerous individuals and organisations including the State Library of Victoria, National Archives of Australia and the National Library of Australia have given permission to reproduce the images, maps and words used throughout the book. Special thanks to Peter Milne and Helen Frajman of M33 Gallery for permission to reproduce the image of The Boys Next Door from 1978, Graeme Butler for the photo of Gertrude St Fitzroy in 1979, Rita Romeo of Denton Corker Marshall Architects (DCM) for permission to use the image of the model of the proposed South Yarra Project and to Catherine Strong for the use of her image of Bon Scott in AC/DC Lane. The maps were drawn by Kara Rasmanis, while Ricky Birmingham of Mushroom Music approved the use of the lyrics from 'Shivers'.

I'd also like to thank my students and colleagues at Monash, whose ideas and support over the years have helped to see this to fruition. Special mentions to Reto Hofmann who read and commented on the original proposal and to Michael Hau whose suggestions for changes to the manuscript have improved the outcome no end. At a more personal level this book would not have been possible without the love and support of family and friends, too numerous to mention individually. It is dedicated to my partner Tanja, whose ideas and loving support are essential to everything I do, our son Patrick who makes it all worthwhile and to my lifelong inspiration, my mother Ethel who did not live to see it to print.

Index